HOLLYWOOD MUSICALS,
THE FILM READER

Hollywood Musicals, The Film Reader explores one of the most popular genres in film history. The mainstay of film production throughout the studio era, the musical endures today through animated features, teen dance films, and features such as Evita and Moulin Rouge.

Combining classic and recent articles, each section explores a central issue of the musical, including genre and stardom, gender and spectacle, race and sexuality, and features an editor's introduction setting debates in context. From Gold Diggers of 1933 to Dancin' in the Rain, Hollywood Musicals demonstrates that musicals were always more than simple entertainment, and examines why certain topics, films and stars have become central to studies of the genre. Sections include:

- Generic forms – examines how musicals achieved their cultural currency through their form
- Gendered spectacles – considers the representation of sexual difference in spectacle
- Camp interventions – reads against the grain of the genre's outward appearance of 'wholesome', 'straight' entertainment
- Racial displacements – traces the significance of race and ethnicity in the musical's use of entertainment traditions

Contributors: Rick Altman, Lucie Arbuthnot, Carol J. Clover, Steven Cohan, Richard Dyer, Jane Feuer, Patricia Mellencamp, Linda Mizejewski, Shari Roberts, Pamela Robertson, Michael Rogin, Martin Rubin, Gail Seneca, and Matthew Tinkcom.

Steven Cohan is Professor of English at Syracuse University. He is author of Masked Men: Masculinity and the Movies in the Fifties (1997) and co-editor of Screening the Male (Routledge 1993) and The Road Movie Book (Routledge 1997).

IN FOCUS

In Focus: Routledge Film Readers
Series Editors: Steven Cohan (Syracuse University) and Ina Rae Hark (University of South Carolina)

The In Focus series of readers is a comprehensive resource for students on film and cinema studies courses. The series explores the innovations of film studies while highlighting the vital connection of debates to other academic fields and to studies of other media. The readers bring together key articles on a major topic in film studies, from marketing to Hollywood comedy, identifying the central issues, exploring how and why scholars have approached it in specific ways, and tracing continuities of thought among scholars. Each reader opens with an introductory essays setting the debates in their academic context, explaining the topic's historical and theoretical importance, and surveying and critiquing its development in film studies.

Exhibition, The Film Reader
Edited by Ina Rae Hark

Experimental Cinema, The Film Reader
Edited by Wheeler Winston Dixon and Gwendolyn Audrey Foster

Hollywood Musicals, The Film Reader
Edited by Steven Cohan

Hollywood Comedians, The Film Reader
Edited by Frank Krutnik

Horror, The Film Reader
Edited by Mark Jancovich

Movie Acting, The Film Reader
Edited by Pamela Robertson Wojcik

Movie Music, The Film Reader
Edited by Kay Dickinson

Stars, The Film Reader
Edited by Marcia Landy and Lucy Fischer

Queer Cinema, The Film Reader
Edited by Harry Benshoff and Sean Griffin

Forthcoming Titles:

Color, The Film Reader
Edited by Angela Dalle Vacche and Brian Price

Marketing, The Film Reader
Edited by Justin Wyatt

Reception, The Film Reader
Edited by Barbara Klinger

HOLLYWOOD MUSICALS,
THE FILM READER

Edited by Steven Cohan

Routledge
Taylor & Francis Group

LONDON AND NEW YORK

First published 2002
by Routledge
2 Park Square, Milton Park, Abingdon, Oxon OX14 4RN

Simultaneously published in the USA and Canada
by Routledge
270 Madison Avenue, New York, NY 10016

Reprinted with corrections in 2004
Reprinted 2006

Routledge is an imprint of the Taylor & Francis Group

Designed and typeset in Novarese and Scala Sans by
Keystroke, Jacaranda Lodge, Wolverhampton
Printed and bound in Great Britain by
Biddles Ltd, King's Lynn, Norfolk

British Library Cataloguing in Publication Data
A catalogue record for this book is available
from the British Library

Library of Congress Cataloguing in Publication Data
has been applied for

ISBN 0–415–23559–6 (hbk)
ISBN 0–415–23560–X (pbk)

Contents

PART FOUR: RACIAL DISPLACEMENTS 155

Acknowledgements

1. Richard Dyer, "Entertainment and Utopia" from *Only Entertainment* (London, Routledge, 1992), pp. 17–34. © 1992 Richard Dyer. Reprinted by permission of the publisher.
2. Jane Feuer, "The Self-reflective Musical and the Myth of Entertainment," in *Quarterly Review of Film Studies*, Vol. 2 No. 2 (1977), pp. 313–26. © 1977. Reprinted by permission of Gordon & Breach Publishers.
3. Rick [Charles F.] Altman, "The American Film Musical as Dual-Focus Narrative" from *The American Film Musical* (Bloomington: Indiana University Press, 1987), pp. 16–27. © 1987 Charles F. Altman. Reprinted by permission of Indiana University Press.
4. Martin Rubin, "Busby Berkeley and the Backstage Musical" from *Showstoppers: Busby Berkeley and the Tradition of Spectacle* (New York: Columbia University Press, 1993). © 1993 Columbia University Press. Reprinted by permission of the publisher.
5. Patricia Mellencamp, "Sexual Economics: *Gold Diggers of 1933*" from *A Fine Romance: Five Ages of Film Feminism* (Philadelphia: Temple University Press, 1995), pp. 50–73. Reprinted by permission of Temple University Press. © 1995 Temple University. All rights reserved.
6. Lucie Arbuthnot and Gail Seneca, "Pre-text and Text in *Gentlemen Prefer Blondes*," in *Film Reader*, 1982, pp. 13–23. Reprinted by permission of the publisher, Department of Television/Radio/Film, Northwestern University.
7. Steven Cohan, "'Feminizing' the Song-And-Dance Man: Fred Astaire and the Spectacle of Masculinity, in the Hollywood Musical" from *Screening the Male: Exploring Masculinities in Hollywood Cinema* (London: Routledge, 1993), pp. 46–69. © 1993 Steven Cohan. Reprinted by permission of the publisher.
8. Richard Dyer, "Judy Garland and Camp" from *Heavenly Bodies* (New York: St Martin's Press, and Basingstoke: Macmillan, 1986), pp. 178–86. © Richard Dyer. Reprinted by permission of St Martin's Press, LLC and Palgrave.
9. Matthew Tinkcom, "'Working Like a Homosexual': Camp Visual Codes and the Labor of Gay Subjects in the MGM Freed Unit" from *Cinema Journal* 35, No. 2, Winter 1996, pp. 24–42. © 1996 the University of Texas Press. All rights reserved.
10. Pamela Robertson, "What Trixie and God Know: Feminist Camp in *Gold Diggers of 1933*" from *Guilty Pleasures: Feminist Camp from Mae West to Madonna* (Durham: Duke University Press, 1996), pp. 62–79. © 1996 Duke University Press. All rights reserved. Reprinted with permission.

11. Shari Roberts, "'The Lady in the Tutti-Frutti Hat': Carmen Miranda, a Spectacle of Ethnicity" from *Cinema Journal* 32, No. 3, Spring 1993, pp. 9–23. © 1993 the University of Texas Press. All rights reserved.
12. Carole J. Clover, "Dancin' in the Rain" from *Critical Inquiry* 21, Summer 1995, pp. 722–47. © 1995 University of Chicago. Reprinted by permission of the University of Chicago Press.
13. Michael Rogin, "New Deal Blackface" from *Blackface, White Noise: Jewish Immigrants in the Hollywood Melting Pot* (Berkeley: University of California Press, 1996) pp. 177–91. © 1996 Michael Rogin. Reprinted by permission of University of California Press.
14. Linda Mizejewski, "Beautiful White Bodies" from *Ziegfeld Girl: Image and Icon in Culture and Cinema* (Durham, N.C.: Duke University Press, 1999), pp. 176–90. © 1999 Duke University Press. All rights reserved. Reprinted with permission.

Hollywood Musicals,
The Film Reader

Introduction: Musicals of the Studio Era

This reader brings together scholarship on the Hollywood musical of the studio era, those lavish entertainments produced during the 1930s, 1940s, and 1950s, now remembered primarily for Fred Astaire's graceful footwork, Judy Garland's affecting voice, Carmen Miranda's outrageous costumes, or Busby Berkeley's kaleidoscopic camera work. Once synonymous with Hollywood product as a whole, the movie musical is an outmoded genre by today's standards. To be sure, musicals of the studio era have not disappeared since they are reissued on home video, shown on cable networks, exhibited at museum screenings, and taught in college courses. Many viewers appreciate these old films for their nostalgic value as conservative, wholesome entertainment of a bygone era. When a financially troubled Metro-Goldwyn-Mayer repackaged numbers from its most celebrated musicals in the anthology *That's Entertainment* (1974), the publicity appealed to this audience by exclaiming, "Boy, do we need it now!" This nostalgic gloss invests musicals with new value as a commodity, different from the past when dozens were produced each year. Nostalgia for old musicals measures the historical distance of recent audiences from the genre's once important cultural function as the epitome of mass-produced, mass-consumed entertainment.

There are just as many contemporary viewers, however, particularly younger ones, who do not care about or recognize the genre's nostalgic pleasures. To them musicals are an odd species of entertainment: the plots seem not only escapist but hackneyed, recycled from film to film; the characters lack psychological depth and their passions are corny, chaste beyond belief; the Tin Pan Alley songs are out of synch with contemporary musical styles; the big production numbers are too over-the-top to be taken seriously. Most alienating of all, the convention of a character bursting into song or breaking into dance with inexplicable orchestral accompaniment, the hallmark moments in any movie musical, occasions laughter rather than applause because it breaks with cinematic realism.

Although formal conventions of studio-era musicals have been successfully imported to music videos, which are essentially solo or production numbers without the burden of being fitted into a narrative, today the genre resurfaces only occasionally as a full-length theatrical feature. Audiences have no trouble with animated musicals, such as Disney's *Beauty and the Beast* (1991), presumably due to animation's grounding in fantasy. Otherwise a new musical has great difficulty attracting young adults in large numbers unless it takes the plot of a teen film that incorporates dance into its narrative, as in *Footloose* (1984) and *Dirty Dancing* (1987) (Feuer 1993: 123–38). This incarnation simply updates the comparable teen appeal of the genre in the 1940s—when Mickey Rooney and Judy Garland put on shows in their barn or an unused theater, and swing bands made regular guest appearances to back them up with the music topping the charts— but this modification of the genre, as the opening week grosses in the United States for *Save the Last Dance* (2001) proved yet again, apparently helps to give the inclusion of dance numbers a more realistic plot motivation that today's audiences more willingly accept.

In short, there may be no getting around it: according to contemporary audience tastes and industry economics, the Hollywood musical as it once flourished is now impossible to take seriously except as an artifact of nostalgia. This attitude is not entirely off the mark; even during the studio era the musical was always something of "an impossible genre." Martin Rubin uses that phrase when he characterizes the movie musical as a film containing "a significant proportion" of numbers that are "impossible—that is, impossible from the standpoint of the realistic discourse of the narrative" (Rubin 1993: 37). A number is "impossible" when it is motivated, performed, and/or photographed in spatial, temporal, or logical contradiction to the otherwise realistic fictive world of the movie's plot, its diegesis. In illustration, Rubin mentions the paradoxical impossibility of Fred Astaire and Ginger Rogers flawlessly performing a dance on roller skates in *Shall We Dance* (1936), even though their characters do not know how to skate, or of Judy Garland spontaneously and perfectly singing with a big band orchestra in *Presenting Lily Mars* (1943), even though her character is an unrehearsed amateur who has crashed the party at which the orchestra is playing.

Impossible song and dance numbers such as these two star turns occur in studio-era musicals all the time. As impossible are the spectacular production numbers which became identified with Busby Berkeley, the subject of Rubin's book. A Berkeley show number opens on a perceivable theater stage or nightclub floor but quickly exceeds the spatial confinement of this setting; the editing first matches a camera viewpoint with that of the audience shown watching the number within the film but then unaccountably shifts to perspectives outreaching what that fictive audience could possibly see or hear. This disregard for cinematic realism characterizes the numbers in the many musicals Berkeley did for Warner Bros. and MGM, but it also occurs in musicals made by others with their equally impossible production numbers, such as Esther Williams' water ballet in *Bathing Beauty* (1944) or Betty Grable's nightclub finale in *Pin-Up Girl* (1944).

Hollywood genres resist a perfect definition that applies to each and every case, and the musical is no exception. Some musicals, particularly backstage stories that confine numbers to a theatrical setting strictly located in the diegesis, such as *The Jolson Story* (1945) or *A Star is Born* (1954), appear to keep the genre's potential impossibility firmly within bounds. Rubin's definition is nevertheless a good starting point, for it focuses attention on why a movie musical, even those two just mentioned, does more than add some show numbers to a plot. Rather, the musical needs to be approached as a genre which typically and inevitably sets its impossible numbers in some kind of dialectic relation with narrative, heightening, disrupting, revising, or multiplying the codes of cinematic realism ordinarily determining a film's diegesis. Rubin's definition likewise explains why musicals are perhaps even more "impossible" to accept today if viewed through contemporary audience expectations regarding the realist discourse of commercial narrative film. For it now does seem impossible to watch studio-era musicals with eyes unaccustomed to the conventions shaping filmed numbers in relation to the plot enveloping them. Musicals worked their magic and gave great pleasure in the past because the genre's realistically impossible conventions once spoke more directly and, as each of the essays included here argues, more meaningfully to audiences, albeit toward varying ends.

It is therefore worth restating what is perhaps the most salient fact about the movie musical: well over half a century ago the genre was enormously popular, a staple of film production throughout the studio era. Musicals were the signature genre of Metro-Goldwyn-Mayer, dominating its annual production slate in the 1940s and early 1950s. Although MGM and musicals are now synonymous in people's minds, the other studios regularly produced them too. These often single-handedly made up a company's annual profits, as Betty Grable's musicals did for Twentieth Century-Fox throughout the 1940s, and the Fred Astaire–Ginger Rogers series did for RKO-Radio Pictures throughout the 1930s (Gomery 1986: 96, 136). Not only were they crucial to a studio's earnings, much the way that action films and science-fiction epics contribute to profits today, but like those two genres, musicals were expensive to make, designed to show off technological innovation and special effects, and served as a studio's tentpole product each year, for instance, as holiday attractions and as vehicles for major stars.

Because of its popularity in the past, the studio-era musical has received a great deal of attention in film studies. This collection represents why scholars keep returning to this genre to investigate its formal properties and cultural importance, just as it documents how continuing interest in the musical traces notable changes in focus and method in the analysis of film over the past several decades. To help locate the musical at the intersections of this exciting scholarship and the genre's industrial history as a product of the studio system, the rest of this introduction provides background not explicitly covered by the essays reprinted here but still connected to their concerns.

All talking, all singing, all dancing

The musical is inseparable from the history of the Hollywood studio system as it emerged through the transition from silents to talkies in the late 1920s. Technically speaking, although there were some silent versions of operettas, even scenes of dancing photographed without sound but shown with live orchestral accompaniment, the musical required sound above all else before it could exist on film. When the era of sound conversion is remembered, it now almost goes without saying that the musical was introduced with a bang as the genre that best showed off and surprised then delighted audiences with the new Vitaphone technology (sound played on disc in synchronization with the image) heralded by Al Jolson's breaking into speech and then song in the otherwise silent Warner Bros. film, *The Jazz Singer* (1927): "you ain't heard nothing yet!"

The simultaneous arrival in Hollywood of sound and musicals by now seems axiomatic of the industry's history. MGM's *Singin' in the Rain* (1952) takes it for granted in recounting the ground-breaking moment when, as its trailer declares, "the screen learned to talk," moving the medium beyond its infancy. Many critics and fans alike consider this Gene Kelly–Stanley Donen film to be the best musical ever made, and it is the one which even those who do not like the genre as a rule have usually seen and enjoyed. *Singin' in the Rain* has consequently helped to fix a certain history of the musical's origins in people minds. According to this history, *The Jazz Singer*'s unexpected success in 1927 brought silent film production to a halt, requiring the industry's immediate conversion to sound recording while also causing artistic chaos as filmmakers and performers struggled to adapt the techniques of silents to talkies. Throughout all this uncertainty, musicals began to be produced almost the day after the Jolson movie premiered—or at least *Singin' in the Rain* represents it this way in a montage showing the immediate impact of *The Jazz Singer*: lots of movie musicals.

Richard Barrios notes that, in recounting this historic moment in 1927, "*Singin' in the Rain* remains true to the spirit of its sources" (Barrios 1995: 5). The film's makers took pains to incorporate industry anecdotes about the coming of sound, even to use in the sets the very same cumbersome equipment from that era, such as the noisy, stationary camera fitted inside a booth for soundproofing (Wollen 1992: 54). Nonetheless, *Singin' in the Rain* takes some artistic liberties when depicting the conversion to talkies. The montage recording the emergence of full-blown musicals upon the heels of *The Jazz Singer*'s opening, for instance, affectionately parodies those early efforts by blending references to trends and styles from both the 1920s (flapper costumes, the Charleston, Jazz Age tunes) and 1930s (the mobile camera work and kaleidoscopic patterns associated with Busby Berkeley). Yet the "berkeleyesque" style being parodied was achieved only after modification of early sound technology allowed for the tracking crane shots with which Berkeley designed and photographed numbers at Warner Bros. beginning with *42nd Street* (1933). The very first musicals were much more static in their camera movement, framing and use of perspective within a shot, in large part because of the new technology's physical limitations. The camera was on occasion placed overhead for a novelty shot at a sudden point within a number, but dance routines were performed as if on a literal stage and filmed as if the camera were located in a front-row center seat (Delamater 1978: 17–18). Most likely Kelly and Donen assumed that, for their audiences in the 1950s, musicals of the mid-1930s like Berkeley's adequately signified examples of the new genre. But this foreshortening of the musical's development has the effect of portraying the arrival of sound as the abrupt yet progressive transformation of one film language into another, more superior one, an account consistent with that of early film historians (Crafton 1997: 1–4).

The course by which the various studios converted to sound, as scholars have now documented, was actually slower and more deliberated. From the start there were two technologies in competition, Warners' Vitaphone sound-on-disc process, the one shown in *Singin' in the Rain*, and Fox's more flexible Movietone sound-on-film process, which all the other studios used in one form or another (RKO's rival Photophone was compatible with Movietone in exhibition). Though it retained the Vitaphone label, Warners itself converted to sound-on-film recording in 1931. Vitaphone and Movietone were first tried out in various short subjects and compilation programs before being applied to feature-length movies, a more expensive and hence riskier prospect for smaller companies like Warner Bros. and Fox Films (which became Twentieth Century-Fox in 1935). For that matter, although *The Jazz Singer* still gets the credit, Warners' follow-up hits in 1928, *The Lights of New York* and Jolson's *The Singing Fool*, convinced the other studios to convert to sound (Crafton 1997: 275).

The very first responses of Warners' rivals were not musicals as we know them now, nor as we see them in *Singin' in the Rain*, but part-talkies: silent films with snatches of dialogue, sound effects, musical scores, perhaps some numbers. MGM's *Broadway Melody*, which premiered in February 1929, was "the first true musical film" (Barrios 1995: 59). In fact, it was advertised with the famous slogan that came to exemplify the genre's appeal, "ALL TALKING, ALL SINGING, ALL DANCING." While appearing clumsy today, *Broadway Melody* established many of the narrative conventions, protocols for using sound musically, and production practices that would remain central to the genre, albeit refined and taken further. What immediately followed *Broadway Melody*'s success, not to mention its Academy Award for Best Picture, were many backstage musicals imitating it. Further exploiting the new genre's popularity, the studios transferred Broadway musical comedies and operettas to the screen, more or less as filmed stageplays. Another common type of early musical were revues such as MGM's *Hollywood Revue of 1929* and Warners' *Show of Shows* (1929). These non-narrative musicals, modeled on vaudeville and more lavish Broadway variety shows such as the annual editions of *Ziegfeld Follies*, capitalized on sound's ability to present an assortment of musical styles from various walks of the entertainment world, and they tended to show off or audition the voice of a studio's present or future stars.

Although these first "all talking, all singing, all dancing" musicals attracted public interest in 1929, their box-office appeal did not hold up when audiences tired of hastily produced, poorly staged and statically edited imitations of earlier successes, particularly the revues. Beginning in 1930, just three years after the introduction of sound, and "contrary to the general belief that hard times generated a desire for escapist fare" (Crafton 1998: 359), the musical was already considered a recipe for box-office failure, so studios rethought the genre's viability. For instance, in 1929 Paramount released Ernst Lubitsch's *The Love Parade*, a sexy, tongue-in-cheek operetta. Its success prompted the studio to repeat the formula with the two stars, Maurice Chevalier and Jeanette MacDonald, either together or paired with someone else. By 1932, this cycle failed to sustain audience interest beyond large cities, and the risqué script, faux-European aristocratic setting, and operetta-style were presumed to be the reason for the disappointing returns of the best and most innovative musical in this cycle, Rouben Mamoulian's *Love Me Tonight* (1932) (Balio 1993: 213–14). Paramount ceased production of its fairy-tale operetta musicals, concentrating instead on comedies with songs that featured stage stars such as the Marx Brothers in film versions of their Broadway successes minus many of the numbers. Other studios had similar results with their musicals, still producing a few but canceling others or converting some properties into straight comedies. Studio as well as audience interest in the genre was then renewed in 1933 when Warners, responding to the competition from radio and the failure of its own filmed revues, dusted off the backstage plot in *42nd Street* (Balio 1993: 214). Warners' success inspired the other studios to begin producing musicals again in large numbers, sustaining their investment in the genre at a relatively constant level until the mid-1950s.

The studio system

Despite its knowing, satiric references to movie production in 1927, *Singin' in the Rain*'s condensed account of the simultaneous arrival of sound and musicals, like other popular histories of the film medium that tell a comparable story, has the additional effect of making the musical genre seem to transcend its industrial origins in the studio system. Sound technology was surely an indispensable condition for the musical's emergence as a major genre, and musicals just as surely played a crucial role in the industry's conversion to sound. However, forgotten or downplayed in this abbreviated tale of the musical's origin is how the introduction of the new technology was equally instrumental in the process by which the five major studios (MGM, Paramount, Warner Bros., Fox, and RKO) achieved their control of filmmaking in the United States through vertical integration of production, distribution, and exhibition. These five companies maintained their economic dominance of the industry until the federal government successfully forced them to spin off their theater chains, beginning in 1948. When that happened, the economic conditions of film production altered since the studios lost their most consistent source of income—theater holdings in large numbers—which provided their economic incentive for maintaining production facilities in Los Angeles on a large scale.

One thinks of the old studios primarily as companies devoted to filmmaking, but they were more precisely "diversified theater chains, producing features, shorts, cartoons, and newsreels to fill their houses" (Gomery 1986: 8). The studios concentrated each of their chains in different regions of the country while maintaining a downtown flagship theater for first-run exhibition in most cities even when it was their sole venue in the area. The three secondary or "minor" companies—Universal, Columbia, and United Artists—did not own theaters and so relied on the five majors for exhibition of their comparable output. The major studios were much like the corporations of any other big industry: well-run factories turning out product on a weekly basis for exhibition in their theaters. The studios manufactured films through streamlined work practices and specialized labor (contracted workers responsible for various tasks, from performing and directing to set designing and building), and distinguished this product as a particular studio's own according to a consistent filmic style, the repeated presence of certain stars, generic specialization, deployment of production values (selective use of color, for instance), and advertising. The musical was one of this industry's most prestigious and reliable products.

The studio system was already in place during the silent era at Paramount, the first fully integrated major, and MGM, formed in 1924 to provide product for the Loew's theater chain. However, it was through the introduction of sound that Warners, Fox, and RKO achieved parity with MGM and Paramount in the late 1920s (Gomery 1985). Exploiting sound technology allowed those three smaller companies to achieve greater product differentiation and increased profits, giving Paramount and MGM a run for their money and requiring all the studios to retool to keep up with the competition. The conversion of the five major theater chains to sound effectively standardized it for independent theater owners and producers as well. Buttressed by the boom economy of the mid-1920s, the competition further instigated a flurry of mergers or acquisitions involving all five companies as they expanded. Warners, for instance, purchased the First National production company and enlarged its theater holdings, and Fox bought controlling interest in MGM until the government stepped in and forbade the merger. By 1930 the worsening effects of the Depression made the studios' finances more precarious because of the enormous debts incurred by their expansion. At that point, with some studios like Paramount on a course toward receivership, the industry cut expenses as much as possible, and its practices were set in place with regard to the technical, narrative, and aesthetic deployment of sound technology.

The introduction of sound had other consequences for the industry. It resulted in alliances between the film companies and media-communications corporations such as Western Electric (the manufacturing arm of American Telegraph and Telephone) and Radio Corporation of America (co-owned by General Electric and Westinghouse, and a parent company of RKO, created to make sound films with RCA's own sound system). The two companies researched and made the technology needed for production and exhibition of talkies, such as microphones and amplifiers. In addition, the advent of sound led to various studio investments in or ownership of other entertainment industries related to the new product in an early form of synergy: radio or experimental televison stations, music publishing firms, record labels, Broadway productions. Economic participation in these other industries allowed the studios to avoid some of the expenses involved in making musicals, such as the costly royalties to music publishers for songs not directly written for a particular film. By the same token, these competing industries allowed the studios access to profitable ancillary markets in which to promote musicals through their songs. Crossover success, in fact, was a consideration of every original score. Broadway shows could have a dozen or more songs, out of which one or two became standards, whereas film musicals typically had fewer songs but each was meant to be a hit (Croce 1972: 117). *Top Hat* (1935) has only five Irving Berlin songs but they all did their job to support the theatrical exhibition of the film through radio play, sheet music sales, and recordings.

Financial involvement in the other entertainment industries was by no means across the board and the same for each studio. Even without direct economic ties, though, all the studios eyed these other media as sources of new musical talent. One may usually think of Hollywood performers being discovered at an early age and then groomed by a studio into major stardom, as was the case with Judy Garland at MGM, but most stars of movie musicals (Fred Astaire at RKO, Eleanor Powell and Gene Kelly at MGM, Alice Faye and Carmen Miranda at Fox, Bing Crosby and Betty Hutton at Paramount, Dick Powell and Doris Day at Warners), first found renown in another entertainment industry, if not radio, then Broadway, records, or one of the big bands. Even Judy Garland's career began in vaudeville as the youngest member of a touring sister act. The same held true of supporting players or speciality acts (Charlotte Greenwood, Virginia O'Brien, the Nicholas Brothers, Benny Goodman and his band, Harry James and his). Likewise, directors (Busby Berkeley, Vincente Minnelli, Charles Walters), choreographers (Robert Alton, Jack Cole), screenwriters (Betty Comden and Adolph Green), songwriters (Cole Porter, Irving Berlin, the Gershwins), all were imported to Hollywood after finding success in New York, furthering the interest, financial or otherwise, of the studios in the other entertainment industries. To be sure, some talent came and left: Ethel Merman (at both Paramount and Fox in the 1930s) and Mary Martin (at Paramount in the 1940s) never found the stardom in movie musicals that they achieved initially and afterward on the Broadway stage.

Once signed by a studio, these talents worked with production units that functioned more or less like stock repertory companies, giving each studio's product its distinct "look," with reference not only to a studio's own house style but also to the kind of musical it produced. A comparative glance at Warners' backstage musicals of the 1930s, which revived the genre's popularity after that momentary lull at the decade's start, and RKO's dance musicals with Astaire and Rogers can illustrate. Each series was crafted as distinct studio product, yet each was also ground-breaking, both in giving the genre its renewed box-office clout during the mid-1930s and in shaping its dominant aesthetic protocols overall.

Warner Bros. clearly plotted an effort to revive the musical in 1933 since, under Darryl F. Zanuck's guidance, the studio released three backstage musicals in succession during that year: *42nd Street* was followed by *Gold Diggers of 1933* and *Footlight Parade*. The films were all major hits, with *Gold Diggers* the most successful of the trio. The three musicals comprise an identifiable cycle. Each has a similar backstage story and contemporary Depression setting, snappy dialogue, fast paced direction and editing, and those extravagant, eye-popping Busby Berkeley numbers. Berkeley did the production numbers but someone else directed the narrative portions, and all three musicals share a common formal structure related to this division of labor: a narrative about putting on a show is segmented by a handful of numbers. As the film progresses, the numbers, first motivated in the plot as rehearsals or song try-outs, become increasingly longer and more impossible in their size, scope, and temporality. Exploding the coherence of diegetic time and space, visualizing the bodies of the chorus in abstract patterning, obscuring the focus on the solo star performer, the big production numbers exceed the limitations of a theatrical stage and overwhelm their ostensible purpose as show numbers happening within the world of the story. These spectacular numbers, moreover, are typically "stacked," placed in sequence at or toward the finale, which further "overbalances the narrative" (Rubin 1993: 98–99).

The many backstage musicals Warners made over the next five years to capitalize on its three successive hits followed this formula, with the studio even titling some later musicals *Gold Diggers of 1935* and *Gold Diggers of 1937* in order to mark a franchise just as numerical sequels do today. Further standardizing this series as identifiable Warners product, the same people were involved in making it. Berkeley did only the numbers to begin with but later directed some entire films. Dick Powell, usually opposite Ruby Keeler, starred in most of them with support from the same contracted players time and again. Al Dubin and Harry Warren wrote songs for many of these musicals. The production staff at the studio maintained a consistent style of photography, editing, costuming, set designing, with artists and technicians going from one musical to the next.

Along with shared formal elements and Berkeley's innovations in filming big, lavish production numbers, consistency of studio labor gave this backstage cycle its distinctive Warner Bros. stamp in comparison with musicals that the other studios made in the 1930s with their own production units, such as MGM's *Broadway Melody* and Paramount's *Big Broadcast* series. All three studios turned out musicals in their respective series that did not carry the brand title *per se* but clearly belonged. MGM's *Born to Dance* (1936), for instance, could have easily been given the *Broadway Melody* title since, with its featured star (Eleanor Powell), supporting cast, Broadway plot, and visual style, it so closely resembles the musicals bearing the series name released the year before and after. The brand title itself, though, encapsulates how studios used their own backstage cycles to distinguish one another's musicals; each new musical in a studio series was just like others but an updated version—this year's *Gold Diggers*, or *Big Broadcast*, or *Broadway Melody*.

The nine Astaire–Rogers musicals made by RKO between 1933 and 1939, while never given a brand name, similarly recycled their materials year in and year out due to the requirements of the studio's producing these films as a series of star vehicles for the team. Astaire came to RKO as a Broadway star, though at first the studio was not sure how to use his talents, loaning him to MGM for a bit part and then teaming him with contract player Ginger Rogers as a secondary couple in *Flying Down to Rio* (1933). Their dancing stole the picture, so the studio began crafting musicals to build upon this new star attraction, rather quickly turning out two Astaire–Rogers musicals each year when the series was at the height of its popularity in the mid-1930s. As with the Warners' musicals, consistency of studio personnel helped to standardize the RKO series while differentiating it through emphasis on the star couple and their dancing. Pandro S. Berman produced all eight Astaire–Rogers musicals that followed *Flying Down to Rio*; Mark Sandrich directed five of them; Allen Scott collaborated with other writers on six; David Abel was cinematographer on five; Van Nest Polglase designed the sets of eight. Most important, Astaire worked with his assistant, Hermes Pan, on the choreography throughout the series' run. Astaire contractually maintained control over the filming of his numbers. His insistence on shooting and editing in a way that respects the choreographic logic of dancing allowed him and his production team to move the genre in a different direction than where Berkeley was going with the big production numbers at Warners.

The RKO series of dance musicals with Astaire and Rogers is as formulaic as any other studio's of this era. Needing to craft new scripts at a fast clip to keep up with the pace of production, the studio writers "looked back to what had worked before" and recycled plot ideas from previous films (Croce 1972: 74). What may have been lack of inspiration on the writers' part helped to join each new Astaire–Rogers musical to the series format as a whole. At its peak, the series alternated between two formulas: the two stars as a romantic couple opposite an older comic pair, as in

Top Hat and *Swing Time* (1936), and the two stars as a youthful comic couple opposite a less interesting romantic pair of similar age, as in *Roberta* (1935) and *Follow the Fleet* (1936) (Croce 1972: 33). When Astaire and Rogers played the romantic leads they were supported by many of the same actors in the same stock roles each time out: Edward Everett Horton, Eric Blore, Eric Rhodes, Helen Broderick. When the stars played the comic couple the cast was filled out by other RKO stars, such as Irene Dunne and Randolph Scott. Another signature element of the series derived from its production values; the musicals were designed to feature the star team in what came to be called the B.W.S. or "Big White Set"—for instance, Venice in *Top Hat*—the architectural set piece designed and photographed to take advantage of the rich contrasts of black and white film, and to which the largest part of the budget for the physical production was devoted (Croce 1972: 25). The scores, written by leading Broadway talents such as Irving Berlin, were likewise composed to repeat similar functions and through a similar sequence: Astaire in a solo, the two stars in a challenge dance, Astaire in a speciality dance, the two stars in a romantic duet, the two stars in a novelty dance incorporating them into a big production number on the Big White Set that tries to compete with Berkeley's style. "So formulaic does the pattern become," Rick Altman observes of the numbers' sequencing, "that by *Top Hat* a routine is established which is rarely varied throughout the remainder of the series" (Altman 1987: 164).

These two series of musicals, produced within the industrial constraints of the studio system, dominate histories of the genre because each redefined the visual discourse of a filmed musical, in particular showing how numbers could be imagined and then rendered cinematically. Both series were as influential as they were popular because of the eventual standardization of their styles by other producers and directors. At Warners, Berkeley exploited the possibilities of cinematic space, subordinating dance to the spectacle, so the choreography itself is secondary to camera movement and editing. At RKO, Astaire's more intimate choreography required—and, as the series hit its stride, quickly found—a correlative in "camerawork and editing [that] are fashioned to enhance the flow and the continuity of the dance, not to undercut or overshadow it" (Mueller 1981: 137).

In each series the numbers' functional relation to narrative differs too. Befitting both the division of labor that went into their production and their close stacking toward the climax, the big production numbers in the Warners/Berkeley musicals are rarely thematically irrelevant to what is happening elsewhere in the film's narrative, but they do exceed their plot functions, often appearing to set up a parallel universe of pure spectacle. In the RKO musicals, just as Astaire had the numbers shot and edited according to the rhythm of his choreography, so too their formulaic sequencing follows the plot's development, outlining the romantic couple's progress. The numbers do not recount or fill out the romance narrative so much as reorient attention to its major turning points for the couple through song and dance.

The two series, in sum, followed and perfected different aesthetic standards for a musical. The RKO/Astaire musicals approach the genre as more of an *integrated* form, with "song, dance, and story . . . artfully blended to produce a combined effect" (Mueller 1984: 28). The Warner/Berkeley musicals, on the other hand, treat the genre as more of an *aggregate* form, with numbers functioning "as a series of self-contained highlights that work to weaken the dominance of a homogenous, hierarchical narrative continuity" (Rubin 1993: 18). Although integration has traditionally been valued as the more desirable standard, affirming the genre's maturation as a popular art form in many critical accounts, what that term describes is a particular aesthetic practice in the industry which was by no means universal to all musicals. Fox's Betty Grable musicals of the 1940s are more characterized by an aggregate use of musical numbers than

MGM's Judy Garland musicals of the same period, say, which appear more integrated in their placement of numbers in relation to narrative. Nonetheless, while MGM is known for perfecting the integrated musical begun at RKO, notably through its production unit headed by Arthur Freed, MGM musicals display the influences of *both* Berkeley's and Astaire's styles, a dynamic interaction of integration and aggregation already apparent in the studio's *Broadway Melody* series.

After their respective contracts at Warners and RKO ended in the late 1930s, in fact, Berkeley and Astaire moved on to MGM, and on many occasions they worked for Freed, albeit never on the same project. However, in contrast with what he did at Warners, Berkeley's musicals at MGM, as in *For Me and My Gal* (1942) and *Girl Crazy* (1943), seem more regulated by a studio-imposed aesthetic of integration. By the same token, Astaire's musicals at this studio more readily accommodate a greater drive toward aggregation, as in the fantasy romance *Yolanda and the Thief* (1945) and the plotless revue *Ziegfeld Follies* (1946). Generally speaking, MGM musicals show that great care was paid to planning numbers so that they serve narrative progression, but they also regularly feature star solos, specialty acts and dream ballets that can stop the story cold. For that matter, quite often a lavish production number overwhelms or substitutes for the plot's resolution, as in Berkeley's finales to the Mickey Rooney–Judy Garland musicals or the "Begin the Beguine" sequence near the end of Astaire's *Broadway Melody of 1940*. The direct participation of Berkeley or Astaire in a particular film notwithstanding, integration and aggregation contributed equally to establishing the genre's selling points as far as the studio was concerned. MGM musicals are not exceptional in this regard since, in one way or another, most musicals register the value of both aesthetics as each helped to determine the generic shape of this studio product.

Protocols of the studio-era musical

The Warners/Berkeley and RKO/Astaire series illustrate how musicals thrived during the studio era because the factory system allowed for production units dedicated to turning out this specific genre. Studios had the economic resources to bring together various talents who not only worked together to develop musicals on a consistent basis but then collaborated with the specialized craft and technological departments when making them. As already mentioned, producers found much of the talent in front of and behind the camera from other entertainment industries, which also supplied ideas for plots, themes, choreography, and songs; studio production teams then used the talent and revised the ideas in specifically cinematic ways. After Gene Kelly moved to Hollywood from Broadway, where he had established himself as dancer and choreographer, he had to reimagine dancing for the camera, a lesson he claims to have learned right away from working with Busby Berkeley on *For Me and My Gal*. Studios imported talents from entertainment venues besides Broadway that, on the face of it, may not have seemed potentially cinematic, but more often than not the translation to film worked. Fox had great success in the late 1930s fashioning musicals around ice-skating star Sonja Henie, so in the early 1940s MGM signed swimmer Esther Williams and turned her into an even bigger box-office attraction. The studios likewise capitalized on fads in music. Fox and MGM exploited the popularity of big band orchestras and the craze for South American dance styles in the 1940s, incorporating the bands and the choreography into production numbers.

When it came to producing the genre, then, most of the creative attention and studio financing went to the numbers, which distinguished a particular musical through their execution. The studio-era musical could be highly imaginative in its deployment of the film medium. Planning numbers fostered artistic innovation and, as often, encouraged technical experimentation in order to realize the filmmaker's ideas for a routine. Numbers could push the proverbial envelope with their sophisticated orchestral and vocal arrangements, physically demanding choreography, imaginative set designs, and inventive manipulations of space in their staging, cinematography, and editing. Gene Kelly's solo in Columbia's *Cover Girl* (1944) used trick photography in order to have him dance with his alter-ego, so his next MGM film, *Anchors Aweigh* (1945), went one better by having Kelly dance with a cartoon mouse. The segment on Esther Williams' musicals in *That's Entertainment* gives the impression that her swimming numbers were all the same, yet the need each time out to top what she had previously done meant that the numbers increasingly became more spectacular and technically complex, and required more daring stuntwork on her part.

For all the innovation that could occur in the execution of numbers, however, the musical was still a highly regulated generic format. Innovation and conformity went hand-in-hand. The industrial need to make each new musical appear "new" while remaining the same fundamental product allowed for ongoing innovation on the part of the artists and craftspeople involved when planning and shooting a routine (this commonly used term, in fact, implies the conventionality regulating the singularity of a number's execution). Individual artists could aim high but as far as studios were concerned the musical remained an industrial product, its value assured through its standardization, and numbers served this aim. In promoting an upcoming musical, a studio's theatrical trailers often focused more on the film's musical spectacle—Gene Kelly's dancing, Esther Williams' water ballets—than its story. Trailers highlighted a musical's stars and featured specialty acts, its lavish production numbers, the quantity of its songs, all to show how this new film contained the same attractions as the studio's or star's previous hits while surpassing them.

From this perspective, plot was of secondary importance to many musicals. Although the series brand was primarily a studio ploy in the 1930s, musicals afterward continued to recycle plot elements even when not linked to a series. Every studio-era genre was reiterative when it came to plot, but the musical more so because of the need to include numbers within the standard two-hour running time of features; musicals thus had to condense their narratives. Recycling plot situations functioned as generic shorthand, allowing for narrative conflict and characterization but with enough economy to leave room for the requisite singing and dancing. Just as it did not necessarily need good songs, merely serviceable ones with an "autonomy and clarity of musical form" that would make them memorable (Williams 1981: 156), a musical did not need original or complex stories as long as they allowed for the inclusion of numbers. Narrative on its own did not typically make a musical seem "new," nor was it expected to do so.

The many musical biographies of famous show business personalities or composers—such as Warners' *Rhapsody in Blue* (1945), the story of George Gershwin, and MGM's *Words and Music* (1948), that of Richard Rodgers and Lorenz Hart—typify how plot could function simply to link numbers together. This cycle of show musicals began in the 1930s but became more popular and formulaic in the 1940s, and it was not unique to any one studio. Musical biographies shared a standard rags to riches plot line, usually beginning in an ethnic enclave of New York City and moving the protagonist to fame and high society via Broadway or vaudeville; these scenarios usually bore little if any relation to the person's actual life and came to resemble each other with their comparable "and then I wrote (or sang)" narrative structure. What distinguished one "biopic" (as they have since been dubbed) from another was its subject, whose career provided an occasion for basing a musical on a familiar set of songs. The plot served more than anything else as a structuring device for moving from number to number, and the numbers, recognizable old songs associated with or written by the film's subject, often featured specialty acts or guest appearances by the studio's stars. *Words and Music* even bills the many stars doing just a number or two—Judy Garland, Gene Kelly, June Allyson, Lena Horne—over Tom Drake, who plays Richard Rodgers yet gets a secondary costarring credit below the film's title.

Related to the biopic were catalogue musicals like *An American In Paris* (1951) and *Singin' in the Rain*, which fabricated plots to showcase numbers by a famous songwriter or songwriting team. The song catalogue was the inspiration for doing the film in the first place, and the songwriter's name a major marketing tool when it came to promoting it. The Irving Berlin catalogue in particular seemed limitless. MGM starred Judy Garland and Fred Astaire in a backstage plot with new and old Berlin songs in *Easter Parade* (1948). Paramount did the same with Bing Crosby and Danny Kaye in Berlin's *White Christmas* (1954), the title song recycled from the studio's earlier hit with Crosby and Astaire, *Holiday Inn* (1942). Twentieth Century-Fox cast Ethel Merman along with Marilyn Monroe, Dan Dailey, and Donald O'Connor in still another backstage plot with a Berlin score, *There's No Business Like Show Business* (1954), the title song carried over from *Annie Get Your Gun* (1950), which Merman did on stage but not on screen. Merman, for that matter, also costarred with Alice Faye in an earlier Fox musical built around Berlin songs, *Alexander's Ragtime Band* (1938), which purported to be a fictionalized biopic of the songwriter.

The various examples of catalogue musicals and biopics suggest as well the extent to which the musical was a star-driven genre above all else. The close affiliation of certain stars with their home studio helped to establish the company brand for product differentiation, so much so that the chronological history of the movie musical at a particular studio can be charted through its major stars. Fox's output of musicals during the studio era, for instance, was designed to feature Shirley Temple, Sonja Henie, and Alice Faye in the 1930s, Faye, Carmen Miranda, Vivian Blaine, and most of all, Betty Grable in the 1940s, and Grable and Marilyn Monroe in the early 1950s. MGM similarly planned its musicals around Eleanor Powell and the team of Jeanette MacDonald and Nelson Eddy in the 1930s, Frank Sinatra, Judy Garland, Gene Kelly, and Esther Williams in the 1940s, and Kelly, Williams, Kathryn Grayson, Jane Powell, and Howard Keel in the 1950s. As star vehicles, musicals in large part derived their coherence from their leading players. The films were crafted to reiterate the star's persona not simply by having her or him play a certain type of character in the plot, but through the numbers. Scores and choreography were tailored to suit the star's special abilities, with plots designed primarily to offer ready excuses for a song or dance number in the distinct style associated with the star. Garland's persona as the unglamorous small-town girl with loads of pep and even more talent was achieved and, while at MGM, stabilized through the numbers assigned to her. Songs such as "Over the Rainbow," "In Between," "You Made Me Love You," and "The Trolley Song" articulated and gave emotionality to the persona which her films repeated, but they go further to complicate the ordinariness she represents on screen in ways that the plots themselves seldom do (Dyer 1986: 156–68).

Conventions standardizing the filming of numbers further emphasized the significant role of stardom for the genre. Whenever musical performers do a number they usually "shift their identities from being actors in a drama to entertainers addressing the audience directly" (Schatz 1981: 217). Slippage between fictional character and star persona occurs because of the performing style fostered by the protocols of shooting and editing musicals to make stars the main attraction. Plot scenes follow the custom of Hollywood cinema generally; whether in long shot or closeup, the stars are photographed at an angle, facing the camera indirectly to indicate the spatial boundaries of the diegesis. When it comes to numbers, on the other hand, stars typically face the camera to sing or dance, readjusting the film's register to a more direct address (Feuer 1993: 35–42).

A shift from indirect to direct address is most apparent in show numbers. Usually handled with a minimum of editing and maximum of camera movement, the star performer—whether doing a solo, duet, or a full production number—looks directly at a diegetic audience, shown in a reverse shot at some early point in the routine; a combination of camerawork and editing then slyly reorients the spatial perspective of the number so that it seems to be addressed directly to the extradiegetic moviegoer. Although a show number naturalizes the shifts in address because the diegetic audience initially appears as a stand-in for the actual film spectator, direct address occurs in numbers placed in other diegetic contexts as well, as in Garland's numbers in *Meet Me in St. Louis* (1944) or Kelly's in *An American in Paris*. As a musical moves back and forth between the diegetic realism of story and extradiegetic awareness of the star's performance in numbers, the oscillation between indirect and direct address heightens the audience's sense of not observing the star play a character so much as witnessing her or his own authenticity, charisma, and talent without the mediation of fictional narrative or cinematic technology.

Other protocols of studio production reinforced what the direct address of numbers imply. Because it involved large casts, elaborate costumes and sets, more off-camera personnel, extensive preparation time, and longer-than-usual shooting schedules, a musical required major expenditures of labor and capital, which resulted in industrial practices designed to insure greater studio control. Most important to the production of numbers was the prerecording of vocal tracks. First tried on *Broadway Melody* when MGM, needing to redo a big production number, wanted to avoid the expense of bringing the full orchestra back to the set for the new shoot and hit upon the strategy of reusing the soundtrack from the first version, prerecording quickly became the industry standard. The soundtrack of numbers was recorded first, oftentimes edited from more than one take to achieve the best vocal performance, then played back on the set for the singer to lip-synch or, as was Garland's method, to sing over during shooting.

Prerecording manufactured a perfected vocal track for filming, so it allowed numbers to be shot in segments more easily, as determined by the camera angles to be used for the sequence and the routine's difficulty. The practice cut down on costly mistakes that could occur—from a singer missing lyrics or losing a breath, say, or having to sing while dancing. Prerecording also made it easier for non-singers to do musicals, either by allowing the vocal performance to be edited from various takes done at recording sessions or, as in the case of dancers like Cyd Charisse and Vera-Ellen, by facilitating use of a voice double. Orchestral accompaniments for dances were handled much like the singing, with the music prerecorded for the shooting. Postproduction editing then put together the filmed footage with the prerecorded track and postrecorded dance sound effects, such as taps.

In distinguishing a filmed performance from a live one, the practice of prerecording gave a specific materiality and meaning to the act of performing in the musical. Prerecording technically enhanced the singer's voice, regulating what aurally signified as a natural, effortless vocal performance on screen, while masking the labor and technology that enabled the performance. The same logic extended beyond production of the soundtrack. As Jane Feuer explains, "engineering is a prerequisite for the creation of effects of utter spontaneity in the Hollywood musical" (Feuer 1993: 5). This paradox—central to what a movie musical can do that a live performance on stage cannot—accounts for the conventionalized numbers that, by design, efface the "work . . . involved in producing dance routines" (Feuer 1993: 10). For instance, in the prop dance, a set piece of many musicals which Feuer calls the "bricolage" or tinkering solo, a performer such as Astaire or Kelly makes props out of ordinary things at hand in the setting, creating an impression of spontaneity despite the number's carefully planned choreography or its special effects. Though more subtle, the same impression of spontaneous yet virtuoso dancing occurs whenever a couple strolls onto a nightclub floor and ends up doing a polished routine, which frequently happens in the Astaire–Rogers series. Likewise, every time a musical's backstage story motivates the inclusion of an obviously perfected number by treating it as a rehearsal, this convention effaces the labor involved in bringing the routine to its finished state. Beyond a show setting, apparently simple folk dance elements can effectively disguise the intricate and well-rehearsed choreography of production numbers meant to demonstrate communal unity, as when Garland, siblings, and friends dance to "Skip to My Lou" in *Meet Me in St. Louis*.

These recurring types of numbers represent "*as* entertainment the work that goes into producing entertainment" (Feuer 1993: 12). The genre's repeated comparison in dialogue or song of the troupe backstage with an idealized view of community outside the theater makes the same point, as does the frequency with which stars like Garland, professional entertainers in reality, play characters who are amateurs performing in the home or kids with native talent struggling for that one big break, driven by their sheer love of singing and dancing and not by desire for fame or a huge salary. This does not mean that the genre fails to represent the extent to which entertainment is work, stars are career-minded professionals, and show business just that, the business of putting on shows. As Feuer points out, some musicals, such as *The Band Wagon* (1953), self-reflexively call attention to the labor of putting on a show in order to demystify "the making of entertainment" through a privileged view of "the other side of the curtain," which reveals quarreling performers, a star supposedly past his or her prime, malfunctioning stage machinery, an opening night that lays an egg. However, this demystifying exposure is, as *The Band Wagon* well illustrates, just as routinely "followed by a new mystification, the seamless final show or placing back on the pedestal of a disgraced performer" (Feuer 1993: 43–44).

The genre's highly conventionalized representation of performing reinforces its populist view of entertainment more generally. Musicals repeatedly quote from show business; again and again plots and numbers refer to its institutions (minstrelsy, vaudeville, Tin Pan Alley, jazz, swing) and then as often valorize them as a refreshing, vital contrast with the stuffier, more elitist world of "high art" (opera, ballet, classical music and theater). This referential field claims an unbroken continuity with the traditions of entertainment in American culture as a means of demonstrating that the genre's own mass-produced form of entertainment speaks as authentically to a mainstream audience, the nation unified through its history of popular music. In this respect, the flip side of the studio-era musical's profitable interaction with other entertainment industries, whose talents the genre borrows and which it represents on screen every time the show must go on, whether in Broadway or in a barn, is an ideological investment in representing show business as the perfect embodiment of communal values and social coherence—the quintessential expression of Americanness.

Studying the musical as popular entertainment

Recalling the industrial context in which musicals were produced only begins to account for the genre's cultural significance as mainstream entertainment during the studio era, and the essays collected in this reader begin, in effect, where this introduction breaks off. A commercial product designed to appeal to a mass audience, the musical clearly reproduced the values of the mainstream culture it addressed, as evident in the fetishizing exhibition of female bodies in production numbers, the central role given to the heterosexual couple in fashioning a romance narrative around the numbers, the whitening of ethnic music and marginalization of African-American performers. Yet the musical's history betrays a much more problematic and certainly fascinating relation between the genre and the culture which watched it as escapist fare.

The essays that follow—all originally published as articles or book chapters, most of which are excerpted for reasons of length—explore this complexity with subtlety and insight. As a means of sketching the range of their approaches, the reader is divided into four parts. The first, "Generic Forms," examines how musicals achieved their cultural currency through their form. Part II, "Gendered Spectacles," interrogates the genre's representation of sexual difference in spectacle. Part III, "Camp Interventions," reads against the grain of the genre's outward appearance of wholesome—and "straight"—entertainment. Finally, Part IV, "Racial Displacements," traces the significance of race in the genre's quotation of entertainment traditions.

The essays themselves, however, are not as single-minded as this organization may outwardly suggest; for instance, questions about the genre's cultural politics are by no means limited to Part IV, just as issues of gender are not confined to Part II. Indeed, each part features discussion of *Gold Diggers of 1933* as a means of illustrating how a musical opens itself up to multiple critical viewpoints which intersect. But the interconnection of all these pieces should be evident throughout as the writers cite, build upon, and at times disagree with each other's arguments; taken together, the work reprinted in this reader shows why certain topics, films, and stars have become central to studies of the musical, in effect recording an exciting, still unfinished dialogue about the genre and its importance. My selection has therefore been guided by the goal of representing key issues, influential arguments, and ongoing debates. As well as putting together in a single volume diverse examinations of the musical, I have also wanted to pay special attention to new scholarship from the past decade. Consideration of length has been yet another factor in the selection, limiting the number of pieces to these fourteen and ultimately determining the volume's exclusive focus on the studio era in the United States. The bibliography appended in the back refers to the larger critical context for the essays included here while also providing resources for further study.

When all is said and done, among the essays collected here each asks how best to make sense of a musical, this impossible yet once hugely popular genre. That fundamental question, in fact, is the overriding concern of this reader, which aims to introduce students to musicals by demonstrating how much more there is to the genre than may first dazzle the eye and please the ear. The musical was a cornerstone of the studio system, but its considerable pleasures should not be taken lightly. For to assume from its function as studio product that the musical was simply entertainment does not mean as a consequence that it was *simple* entertainment. That is far from the case, as all of these essays demonstrate.

Steven Cohan
May, 2001

PART ONE

GENERIC FORMS

Introduction

The essays in this section explore the musical's significance as a form, paying particular attention to the relation of narrative and number, but going further to consider how and why a genre combining story and spectacle for purposes of entertainment can also function as a mode of cultural representation with ideological and historical implications. In the first piece, "Entertainment and Utopia," Richard Dyer argues that, far from being escapist, the musical is responsive to history through its form, which articulates in non-representational terms what utopia feels like. This emotional register characterizes what the genre offers as entertainment; that is, through its numbers the musical makes evident the contradictions of a capitalist, patriarchal society by recasting them as ahistorical needs, such as "abundance," "intensity," "transparency," and "community." Looking at several exemplary musicals in illustration, Dyer points out how the genre's utopian sensibility is inflected differently when a musical's plot is segmented from its utopian numbers, as in *Gold Diggers of 1933*; set in tension with them, as in *Funny Face* (1957); or fully integrated with them, as in *On the Town* (1949).

Dyer's article considers how the musical's utopian ethos has ideological weight because forms of entertainment are culturally grounded. In "The Self-reflective Musical and the Myth of Entertainment," Jane Feuer argues that the genre can even mythify its own entertainment values. Raising many points that anticipate her later book, *The Hollywood Musical*, Feuer focuses on several celebrated MGM backstage musicals, such as *The Band Wagon* and *Singin' in the Rain*. These films are self-reflective, giving every appearance of commenting critically on their own formal status as musicals, because they take the production of popular entertainment as their central thematic. This concern drives their plots and accounts for the way their numbers differentiate authentic from inauthentic performing according to three myths about the ameliorating value of entertainment—the myths of spontaneity, integration, and the audience—which the films all ultimately endorse as a means of effacing the ideological contradictions arising from their industrial production.

Like Dyer's discussion, Feuer's account of the self-reflective musical explores how the genre structurally acknowledges cultural contradictions but makes them appear reconcilable. According to Rick Altman, the genre as a whole operates toward this end. In "The American Film Musical as Dual-Focus Narrative," a chapter from his book on the genre, Altman claims that all musicals have the same underlying structure: a dual focus privileging the couple downplays the plot's linear progression by heightening paralleled elements (comparable numbers, scenes, settings, values, etc.). Using *New Moon* (1940) and *Gigi* (1958) as his examples, Altman shows how this dual focus encourages a lateral rather than linear reading of a musical around oppositional elements which each half of the couple locates; their successful pairing then achieves the formal appearance of resolution, which is to say that the male–female dualism makes other, more irreconcilable dichotomies secondary to achieve a concluding vision of social harmony in the guise of courtship.

The first three essays in Part I view musicals through the premise that their own formal orchestrations of narrative and number function, in Altman's phrase, as a "cultural problem-solving device." It is therefore worth pointing out that these essays also approach musicals through their numbers more than their plots, and that each piece presumes, in one way or another, that formal integration works to contain ideological contradiction as a means of resolution. These essays, in sum, implicitly understand the musical's form as a dialectic operation; numbers do not simply serve narrative progression but interact with and comment upon it. In Part I's fourth piece, "Busby Berkeley and the Backstage Musical," Martin Rubin historically reexamines the film musical's dialectical form by returning to the genre's stage sources in what he calls "a tradition of spectacle," the tradition of the music hall, minstrelsy, and revues.

While recognizing the importance of integration as an aesthetic standard in both the production and critical valorization of certain musicals, Rubin argues that, with their contrasting aesthetic of aggregation, Berkeley's backstage musicals derive from that earlier tradition. They foreground an alternate view of the genre's form which places heterogeneity over homogeneity, spectacle over story, excess over restraint, delay over progression. Examination of Berkeley's style and its effects shows how his musicals build upon a tension between narrative and number which, Rubin posits, inheres in the genre's form overall. Although Rubin focuses primarily on the formal questions raised by the non-integrative impetus of Berkeley's musicals, his approach, when set alongside the arguments advanced by the other pieces in this section, has broader implications. For when the musical is placed within the "tradition of spectacle," any attempt to account for its form as a mode of potent cultural representation needs to consider the significance that numbers bear whether analyzed alone, in sequence, or as elements in a larger formal structure that includes but is not dominated by narrative.

Entertainment and Utopia 1

RICHARD DYER

This article is about musicals as entertainment. I don't necessarily want to disagree with those who would claim that musicals are also 'something else' (e.g. 'Art') or argue that entertainment itself is only a product of 'something more important' (e.g. political/economic manipulation, psychological forces), but I want to put the emphasis here on entertainment as entertainment. Musicals were predominantly conceived of, by producers and audiences alike, as 'pure entertainment'—the *idea* of entertainment was a prime determinant on them. Yet because entertainment is a common-sense, 'obvious' idea, what is really meant and implied by it never gets discussed.

Musicals are one of a whole string of forms—music hall, variety, TV spectaculars, pantomime, cabaret, etc.—that are usually summed up by the term 'show biz'. The idea of entertainment I want to examine here is most centrally embodied by these forms, although I believe that it can also be seen at work, *mutatis mutandis*, in other forms and I suggest below, informally, how this might be so. However, it is probably true to say that 'show biz' is the most thoroughly entertainment-oriented of all types of performance, and that notions of myth, art, instruction, dream and ritual may be equally important, even at the conscious level, with regard to, say, Westerns, the news, soap opera, or rock music.

It is important, I think, to stress the cultural and historical specificity of entertainment. The kinds of performance produced by professional entertainment are different in audience, performers and above all intention to the kinds of performance produced in tribal, feudal, or socialist societies. It is not possible here to provide the detailed historical and anthropological argument to back this up, but I hope the differences will suggest themselves when I say that entertainment is a type of performance produced for profit, performed before a generalized audience (the 'public'), by a trained, paid group who do nothing else but produce performances which have the sole (conscious) aim of providing pleasure.

Because entertainment is produced by professional entertainers, it is also largely defined by them. That is to say, although entertainment is part of the coinage of everyday thought, none the less how it is defined, what it is assumed to be, is basically decided by those people responsible (paid) for providing it in concrete form. Professional entertainment is the dominant agency for defining what entertainment is. This does not mean, however, that it *simply* reproduces and expresses patriarchal capitalism. There is the usual struggle between capital (the backers) and labour (the performers) over control of the product, and professional entertainment is unusual in that: (1) it is in the business of producing forms not things, and (2) the workforce (the performers themselves) is in a better position to determine the form of its product than are, say, secretaries or car workers. The fact that professional entertainment has been by and large conservative in this century should not blind us to the implicit struggle within it, and looking beyond class to divisions of sex and race, we should note the important role of structurally subordinate groups in society—women, blacks, gays—in the development and definition of entertainment. In other words, show business's relationship to the demands of patriarchal capitalism is a complex one. Just as it does not simply 'give the people what they want' (since it actually defines those wants), so, as a relatively autonomous mode of cultural production, it does not simply reproduce unproblematically patriarchal-capitalist ideology. Indeed, it is precisely on seeming to achieve both these often opposed functions simultaneously that its survival largely depends.

Two of the taken-for-granted descriptions of entertainment, as 'escape' and as 'wish-fulfilment', point to its central thrust, namely, utopianism. Entertainment offers the image of 'something better' to escape into, or something we want deeply that our day-to-day lives don't provide. Alternatives, hopes, wishes—these are the stuff of utopia, the sense that things could be better, that something other than what is can be imagined and maybe realized.

Entertainment does not, however, present models of utopian worlds, as in the classic utopias of Thomas More, William Morris, *et al.* Rather the utopianism is contained in the feelings it embodies. It presents, head-on as it were, what utopia would feel like rather than how it would be organized. It thus works at the level of sensibility, by which I mean an affective code that is characteristic of, and largely specific to, a given mode of cultural production.

This code uses both representational and, importantly, non-representational signs. There is a tendency to concentrate on the former, and clearly it would be wrong to overlook them—stars are nicer than we are, characters more straightforward than people we know, situations more soluble than those we encounter. All this we recognize through representational signs. But we also recognize qualities in non-representational signs—colour, texture, movement, rhythm, melody, camerawork—although we are much less used to talking about them. The nature of non-representational signs is not, however, so different from that of representational. Both are, in Peirce's terminology, largely iconic; but whereas the relationship between signifier and signified in a representational icon is one of resemblance between their appearance, their look, the relationship in the case of the non-representational icon is one of resemblance at the level of basic structuration.

This concept has been developed (among other places) in the work of Susanne K. Langer, particularly in relation to music. We are moved by music, yet it has the least obvious reference to 'reality'—the intensity of our response to it can only be accounted for by the way music, abstract, formal though it is, still embodies feeling.

> The tonal structures we call 'music' bear a close logical similarity to the forms of human feeling—forms of growth and of attenuation, flowing and stowing, conflict and reso-lution, speed, arrest, terrific excitement, calm or subtle activation or dreamy lapses—not joy and sorrow perhaps, but the poignancy of both—the greatness and brevity and eternal passing of everything vitally felt. Such is the pattern, or logical form, of sentience; and the pattern of music is that same form worked out in pure measures, sound and silence. Music is a tonal analogue of emotive life.

Such formal analogy, or congruence of logical structures, is the prime requisite for
the relation between a symbol and whatever it is to mean. The symbol and the object
symbolized must have some common logical form.

(Langer 1953: 27)

Langer realizes that recognition of a common logical form between a performance sign and
what it signifies is not always easy or natural: 'The congruence of two given perceptible forms
is not always evident upon simple inspection. The common *logical* form they both exhibit may
become apparent only when you know the principle whereby to relate them' (ibid.). This
implies that responding to a performance is not spontaneous—you have to learn what
emotion is embodied before you can respond to it. A problem with this as Langer develops
it is the implication that the emotion itself is not coded, is simply 'human feeling'. I would
be inclined, however, to see almost as much coding in the emotions as in the signs for them.
Thus, just as writers such as E.H. Gombrich and Umberto Eco stress that different modes of
representation (in history and culture) correspond to different modes of perception, so it is
important to grasp that modes of experiential art and entertainment correspond to different
culturally and historically determined sensibilities.

This becomes clear when one examines how entertainment forms come to have the
emotional signification they do: that is, by acquiring their signification in relation to
the complex of meanings in the social-cultural situation in which they are produced. Take the
extremely complex history of tap dance—in black culture, tap dance has had an improvisatory,
self-expressive function similar to that in jazz; in minstrelsy, it took on an aspect of jolly
mindlessness, inane good humour, in accord with minstrelsy's image of the Negro; in
vaudeville, elements of mechanical skill, tap dance as a feat, were stressed as part of vaudeville's celebration of the machine and the brilliant performer. Clearly there are connections
between these different significations, and there are residues of all of them in tap as used in
films, television and contemporary theatre shows. This has little to do, however, with the
intrinsic meanings of hard, short, percussive, syncopated sounds arranged in patterns and
produced by the movement of feet, and everything to do with the significance such sounds
acquire from their place within the network of signs in a given culture at a given point of
time. Nevertheless, the signification is essentially apprehended through the coded non-
representational form (although the representational elements usually present in a
performance sign—a dancer is always 'a person dancing'—may help to anchor the necessarily
more fluid signification of the non-representational elements; for example, a black man, a
white man in blackface, a troupe, or a white woman tap-dancing may suggest different ways
of reading the taps, because each relates to a slightly different moment in the evolution of
the non-representational form, tap dance).

I have laboured this point at greater length than may seem warranted partly with polemic
intent. First, it seems to me that the reading of non-representational signs in the cinema is
particularly undeveloped. On the one hand, the *mise-en-scène* approach (at least as classically
developed in *Movie*) tends to treat the non-representational as a function of the representational, simply a way of bringing out, emphasizing, aspects of plot, character, situation,
without signification in their own right. On the other hand, semiotics has been concerned with
the codification of the representational. Second, I feel that film analysis remains notoriously
non-historical, except in rather lumbering, simplistic ways. My adaptation of Langer seeks to
emphasize not the connection between signs and historical events, personages, or forces, but

rather the history of signs themselves as they are produced in culture and history. Nowhere here has it been possible to reproduce the detail of any sign's history (and I admit to speculation in some instances), but most of the assertions are based on more thorough research, and even where they are not, they should be.

The categories of entertainment's utopian sensibility are sketched in the accompanying Table 1, together with examples of them. The three films used will be discussed below; the examples from Westerns and television news are just to suggest how the categories may have wider application; the sources referred to are the cultural, historical situation of the code's production.

The categories are, I hope, clear enough, but a little more needs to be said about 'intensity'. It is hard to find a word that quite gets what I mean. What I have in mind is the capacity of entertainment to present either complex or unpleasant feelings (e.g. involvement in personal or political events; jealousy, loss of love, defeat) in a way that makes them seem uncomplicated, direct and vivid, not 'qualified' or 'ambiguous' as day-to-day life makes them, and without intimations of self-deception and pretence. (Both intensity and transparency can be related to wider themes in the culture, as 'authenticity' and 'sincerity' respectively—see Trilling 1972.)

The obvious problem raised by this breakdown of the utopian sensibility is where these categories come from. One answer, at a very broad level, might be that they are a continuation of the utopian tradition in western thought. George Kateb describes what he takes to be the dominant motifs in this tradition, and they do broadly overlap with those outlined above. Thus:

> when a man [sic] thinks of perfection . . . he thinks of a world permanently without strife, poverty, constraint, stultifying labour, irrational authority, sensual deprivation . . . peace, abundance, leisure, equality, consonance of men and their environment.
>
> (1972: 9)

We may agree that notions in this broad conceptual area are common throughout western thought, giving it, and its history, its characteristic dynamic, its sense of moving beyond what is to what ought to be or what we want to be. However, the very broadness, and looseness, of this common ground does not get us very far—we need to examine the specificity of entertainment's utopia.

One way of doing so is to see the categories of the sensibility as temporary answers to the inadequacies of the society which is being escaped from through entertainment. This is proposed by Hans Magnus Enzensberger in his 'Constituents of a theory of the media'. He takes issue with the traditional left-wing use of concepts of 'manipulation' and 'false needs' in relation to the mass media:

> The electronic media do not owe their irresistible power to any sleight-of-hand but to the elemental power of deep social needs which come through even in the present depraved form of these media.
>
> (1972: 113)

> Consumption as spectacle contains the promise that want will disappear. The deceptive, brutal and obscene features of this festival derive from the fact that there can be no

question of a real fulfilment of its promise. But so long as scarcity holds sway, use-value remains a decisive category which can only be abolished by trickery. Yet trickery on such a scale is only conceivable if it is based on mass need. This need—it is a utopian one—is there. It is the desire for a new ecology, for a breaking-down of environmental barriers, for an aesthetic which is not limited to the sphere of the 'artistic'. These desires are not—or are not primarily—internalized rules of the games as played by the capitalist system. They have physiological roots and can no longer be suppressed. Consumption as spectacle is—in parody form—the anticipation of a utopian situation.

(ibid.: 114)

This does, I think, express well the complexity of the situation. However, Enzensberger's appeal to 'elemental' and 'physiological' demands, although we do not need to be too frightened by them, is lacking in both historical and anthropological perspectives. I would rather suggest, a little over-schematically, that the categories of the utopian sensibility are related to specific inadequacies in society. I illustrate this in Table 2.

The advantage of this analysis is that it does offer some explanation of why entertainment *works*. It is not just left-overs from history, it is not *just* what show business, or 'they', force on the rest of us, it is not simply the expression of eternal needs—it responds to real needs *created by society*. The weakness of the analysis (and this holds true for Enzensberger too) is in the give-away absences from the left-hand column—no mention of class, race, or patriarchy. That is, while entertainment is responding to needs that are real, at the same time it is also defining and delimiting what constitute the legitimate needs of people in this society.

I am not trying to recoup here the false needs argument—we are talking about real needs created by real inadequacies, but they are not the only needs and inadequacies of the society. Yet entertainment, by so orienting itself to them, effectively denies the legitimacy of other needs and inadequacies, and especially of class, patriarchal and sexual struggles. (Though once again we have to admit the complexity and contradictions of the situation—that, for instance, entertainment is not the only agency which defines legitimate needs, and that the actual role of women, gay men and blacks in the creation of show business leaves its mark in such central oppositional icons as, respectively, the strong woman type, e.g. Ethel Merman, Judy Garland, Elsie Tanner, camp humour and sensuous taste in dress and decor, and almost all aspects of dance and music. Class, it will be noted, is still nowhere.)

Class, race and sexual caste are denied validity as problems by the dominant (bourgeois, white, male) ideology of society. We should not expect show business to be markedly different. However, there is one further turn of the screw, and that is that, with the exception perhaps of community (the most directly working-class in source), the ideals of entertainment imply wants that capitalism itself promises to meet. Thus abundance becomes consumerism, energy and intensity personal freedom and individualism, and transparency freedom of speech. In other (Marcuse's) words, it is a partially 'one-dimensional' situation. The categories of the sensibility point to gaps or inadequacies in capitalism, but only those gaps or inadequacies that capitalism proposes itself to deal with. At our worse sense of it, entertainment provides alternatives *to* capitalism which will be provided *by* capitalism.

However, this one-dimensionality is seldom so hermetic, because of the deeply contradictory nature of entertainment forms. In Variety, the essential contradiction is between comedy and music turns; in musicals, it is between the narrative and the numbers. Both these contradictions can be rendered as one between the heavily representational and

Table 1

	Energy	Abundance	Intensity	Transparency	Community
	Capacity to act vigorously; human power, activity, potential	Conquest of scarcity; having enough to spare without sense of poverty of others; enjoyment of sensuous material reality	Experiencing of emotion directly, fully, unambiguously, 'authentically', without holding back	A quality of relationships—between represented characters (e.g. true love), between performer and audience ('sincerity')	Togetherness, sense of belonging, network of phatic relationships (i.e. those in which communication is for its own sake rather than for its message)
Show-biz forms	Dance—tap, Latin-American, American Theater Ballet; also 'oomph', 'pow', 'bezazz'—qualities of performance	Spectacle; Ziegfeld, Busby Berkeley, MGM	'Incandescent' star performers (Garland, Bassey, Streisand); torch singing	'Sincere' stars (Crosby, Gracie Fields); love and romance	The singalong chorus numbers
Sources of show-biz forms	Tap—black and white folk culture; American Theater Ballet—modern dance plus folk dance plus classical ballet	Court displays; high art influences on Ziegfeld, Cedric Gibbons (MGM); *haute couture*	Star phenomenon in wider society; the Blues	Star phenomenon in wider society; eighteenth-century sentimental novel	Pub entertainment *and* parlour balladry; choral traditions in folk and church
Gold Diggers of 1933	'Pettin' in the Park' (tap, roller skates; quick tempo at which events are strung together)	'Pettin' . . .' (leisure park) 'We're in the Money' (showgirls dressed in coins) 'Shadow Waltz' (lavish sets; tactile, non-functional, wasteful clothing; violins as icon of high culture, i.e. expense)	'Forgotten Man' 'I've Got to Sing a Torch Song' (Blues inflections)	'Shadow Waltz' (Keeler and Powell as couple in eye-to-eye contact).	Showgirls (wise-cracking interaction, mutual support—e.g. sharing clothes)

Funny Face	'Think Pink' 'Clap Yo' Hands' (tap) 'Let's Kiss and Make Up' (tap, and Astaire's longevity) Cellar dance	'Think Pink' (use of materials and fabrics) 'Bonjour Paris' 'On How to be Lovely' (creation of fashion image)	'How Long Has This Been Going On?'	'Funny Face' 'He Loves and She Loves' ''S Wonderful'	(?) Cellar dance
On the Town	'New York, New York' 'On the Town' 'Prehistoric Man' 'Come up to My Place'	'New York, New York' (cf. 'Bonjour Paris') 'Miss Turnstiles' (woman as commodity fantasy)	'A Day in New York' ballet; climatic chase	'You're Awful' (insult turned into declaration of love) 'Come up to My Place' (direct invitation)	'You Can Count on Me'
Westerns	Chases, fights, bar-room brawls; pounding music (1960s onwards)	Land—boundlessness and/or fertility	Confrontation on street; suspense	Cowboy as 'man'— straight, straightforward, morally unambiguous, puts actions where his words are	Townships; cowboy camaraderie
TV news	Speed of series of sharp, short items; the 'latest' news; hand-held camera	Technology of news-gathering—satellites, etc.; doings of rich; spectacles of pageantry and destruction	Emphasis on violence, dramatic incident; selection of visuals with eye to climactic moments	(?) 'Man of the people' manner of some newscasters, celebrities and politicians (?) simplification of events to allow easy comprehension	The world rendered as global village; assumptions of consensus

Table 2

Social tension/inadequacy/absence	Utopian solution
Scarcity (actual poverty in the society; poverty observable in the surrounding societies, e.g. Third World); unequal distribution of wealth	Abundance (elimination of poverty for self and others; equal distribution of wealth)
Exhaustion (work as a grind, alienated labour, pressures of urban life)	Energy (work and play synonymous), city-dominated (*On the Town*) or pastoral return (*The Sound of Music*)
Dreariness (monotony, predictability, instrumentality of the daily round)	Intensity (excitement, drama, affectivity of living)
Manipulation (advertising, bourgeois democracy, sex roles)	Transparency (open, spontaneous, honest communications and relationships)
Fragmentation (job mobility, rehousing and development, high-rise flats, legislation against collective action)	Community (all together in one place, communal interests, collective activity)

verisimilitudinous (pointing to the way the world is, drawing on the audience's concrete experience of the world) and the heavily non-representational and 'unreal' (pointing to how things could be better). In musicals, contradiction is also to be found at two other levels—within numbers, between the representational and the non-representational, and within the non-representational, due to the differing sources of production inscribed in the signs.

To be effective, the utopian sensibility has to take off from the real experiences of the audience. Yet to do this, to draw attention to the gap between what is and what could be, is, ideologically speaking, playing with fire. What musicals have to do, then, (not through any conspiratorial intent, but because it is always easier to take the line of least resistance, i.e. to fit in with prevailing norms) is to work through these contradictions at all levels in such a way as to 'manage' them, to make them seem to disappear. They don't always succeed.

I have chosen three musicals (*Gold Diggers of 1933*, *Funny Face*, *On the Town*) which seem to me to illustrate the three broad tendencies of musicals—those that keep narrative and number clearly separated (most typically, the backstage musical); those that retain the division between narrative as problems and numbers as escape, but try to 'integrate' the numbers by a whole set of papering-over-the-cracks devices (e.g. the well-known 'cue for a song'); and those which try to dissolve the distinction between narrative and numbers, thus implying that the world of the narrative is also (already) utopian.

The clear separation of numbers and narrative in *Gold Diggers of 1933* is broadly in line with a 'realist' aesthetic: the numbers occur in the film in the same way as they occur in life, that is, on stages and in cabarets. This 'realism' is of course reinforced by the social-realist orientation of the narrative, settings and characterization, with their emphasis on the Depression, poverty, the quest for capital, 'golddigging' (and prostitution). However, the numbers are not wholly contained by this realist aesthetic—the way in which they are opened out, in scale and in cinematic treatment (overhead shots, etc.) represents a quite marked shift from the real to the non-real, and from the largely representational to the largely non-representational (sometimes to the point of almost complete abstraction). The thrust of the narrative is towards seeing the show as a 'solution' to the personal, Depression-induced problems of the characters; yet the non-realist presentation of the numbers makes it very hard to take this solution seriously. It is 'just' escape, 'merely' utopian.

If the numbers embody (capitalist) palliatives to the problems of the narrative—chiefly, abundance (spectacle) in place of poverty, and (non-efficacious) energy (chorines in self-enclosed patterns) in place of dispiritedness—then the actual mode of presentation undercuts this by denying it the validity of 'realism'.

However, if one then looks at the contradiction between the representational and non-representational within the numbers, this becomes less clear-cut. Here much of the representational level reprises the lessons of the narrative—above all, that women's only capital is their bodies as objects. The abundant scale of the numbers is an abundance of piles of women; the sensuous materialism is the texture of femaleness; the energy of the dancing (when it occurs) is the energy of the choreographic imagination, to which the dancers are subservient. Thus, while the non-representational certainly suggests an alternative to the narrative, the representational merely reinforces the narrative (women as sexual coinage, women—and men—as expressions of the male producer).

Finally, if one then looks at the non-representational alone, contradictions once again become apparent—e.g. spectacle as materialism and metaphysics (that is, on the one hand, the sets, costumes, etc., are tactile, sensuous, physically exhilarating, but on the other hand, are associated with fairyland, magic, the by-definition immaterial), dance as human creative energy *and* sub-human mindlessness.

In *Funny Face*, the central contradiction is between art and entertainment, and this is further worked through in the antagonism between the central couple, Audrey Hepburn (art) and Fred Astaire (entertainment). The numbers are escapes from the problems, and discomforts, of the contradiction—either by asserting the unanswerably more pleasurable qualities of entertainment (e.g. 'Clap Yo' Hands' following the dirge-like Juliette Greco-type song in the 'empathicalist', i.e. existentialist, *soirée*), or in the transparency of love in the Hepburn–Astaire numbers.

But it is not always that neat: In the empathicalist cellar club, Hepburn escapes Astaire in a number with some of the other beats in the club. This reverses the escape direction of the rest of the film (i.e. it is an escape from entertainment/Astaire into art). Yet within the number, the contradiction repeats itself. Before Hepburn joins the group, they are dancing in a style deriving from Modern Dance, angular, oppositional shapes redolent in musical convention of neurosis and pretentiousness (cf. Danny Kaye's number, 'Choreography', in *White Christmas*). As the number proceeds, however, more show-biz elements are introduced—use of syncopated clapping, forming in a vaudeville line-up, and American Theater Ballet shapes. Here an 'art' form is taken over and infused with the values of entertainment. This is a contra-diction between the representational (the dreary night club) and the non-representational (the oomph of music and movement), but also within the non-representational, between different dance forms. The contradiction between art and entertainment is thus repeated at each level.

In the love numbers, too, contradictions appear, partly by the continuation in them of troubling representational elements. In 'Funny Face', photographs of Hepburn as seen by Astaire, the fashion photographer, are projected on the wall as background to his wooing her and her giving in. Again, their final dance of reconciliation to "'S Wonderful' takes place in the grounds of a château, beneath the trees, with doves fluttering around them. Earlier, this setting was used as the finish for their fashion photography sequence. In other words, in both cases, she is reconciled to him only by capitulating to his definition of her. In itself, there is nothing contradictory in this—it is what Ginger Rogers always had to do. But here the mode of reconciliation is transparency and yet we can see the strings of the number being pulled. Thus the representational elements, which bespeak manipulation of romance, contradict the non-representational, which bespeak its transparency.

The two tendencies just discussed are far more common than the third, which has to suggest that utopia is implicit in the world of the narrative as well as in the world of the numbers.

The commonest procedure for doing this is removal of the whole film in time and space—to turn-of-the-century America (*Meet Me in St Louis*, *Hello Dolly!*), Europe (*The Merry Widow*, *Gigi*, *Song of Norway*), cockney London (*My Fair Lady*, *Oliver!*, *Scrooge*), black communities (*Hallelujah!*, *Cabin in the Sky*, *Porgy and Bess*), to places, that is, where it can be believed (by white urban Americans) that song and dance are 'in the air', built into the peasant/black culture and blood, or part of a more free-and-easy stage in American development. In these films, the introduction of any real narrative concerns is usually considerably delayed and comes chiefly as a temporary threat to utopia—thus reversing the other two patterns, where the narrative predominates and numbers function as temporary escapes from it. Not much happens, plot-wise, in *Meet Me in St Louis* until we have had 'Meet Me in St Louis', 'The Boy Next Door', 'The Trolley Song' and 'Skip to My Lou'—only then does father come along with his proposal to dismantle this utopia by his job mobility.

Most of the contradictions developed in these films are overridingly bought off by the nostalgia or primitivism which provides them with the point of departure. Far from pointing forwards, they point back, to a golden age—a reversal of utopianism that is only marginally offset by the narrative motive of recovery of utopia. What makes *On the Town* interesting is that its utopia is a well-known modern city. The film starts as an escape—from the confines of navy life into the freedom of New York, and also from the weariness of work, embodied in the docker's refrain, 'I feel like I'm not out of bed yet', into the energy of leisure, as the sailors leap into the city for their day off. This energy runs through the whole film, *including the narrative*. In most musicals, the narrative represents things as they are, to be escaped from. But most of the narrative of *On the Town* is about the transformation of New York into utopia. The sailors release the *social* frustrations of the women—a tired taxi driver just coming off shift, a hard-up dancer reduced to belly-dancing to pay for ballet lessons, a woman with a sexual appetite that is deemed improper—not so much through love and sex as through energy. This sense of the sailors as a transforming energy is heightened by the sense of pressure on the narrative movement suggested by the device of a time-check flashed on the screen intermittently.

This gives a historical dimension to a musical, that is, it shows people making utopia rather than just showing them from time to time finding themselves in it. But the people are men—it is still men making history, not men and women together. And the Lucy Schmeeler role is unforgivably male chauvinist. In this context, the 'Prehistoric Man' number is particularly interesting. It centres on Ann Miller, and she leads the others in the takeover of the museum. For a moment, then, a woman 'makes history'. But the whole number is riddled with contradictions, which revolve round the very problem of having an image of a woman acting historically. If we take the number and her part in it to pieces (Table 3), we can see that

Table 3

Self-willed	Mindless
Miller as star (R)	Miller's image ('magnificent animal') (R)
Miller character—decision-maker in narrative (R)	Number set in anthropology museum—associations with primitivism (R)
Tap as self-expressive form (NR)	Tap as mindless repetitions (NR)
Improvisatory routine (R/NR)	

it plays on an opposition between self-willed and mindless modes of being; and this play is between representational (R) and non-representational (NR) at all aesthetic levels.

The idea of a historical utopianism in narrativity derives from the work of Ernest Bloch. According to Fredric Jameson, Bloch

> has essentially two different languages or terminological systems at his disposition to describe the formal nature of Utopian fulfilment: the movement of the world in time towards the future's ultimate moment, and the more spatial notion of that adequation of object to subject which must characterise that moment's content ... [These] correspond to dramatic and lyrical modes of the presentation of not-yet-being.
>
> (1971: 146)

Musicals (and Variety) represent an extra ordinary mix of these two modes—the historicity of narrative and the lyricism of numbers. They have not often taken advantage of it, but the point is that they could, and that this possibility is always latent in them. They are a form we still need to look at if films are, in Brecht's words on the theatre, to 'organize the enjoyment of changing reality'.

Note

This chapter was originally published in spring 1977 in *Movie* 24.

References

Enzensberger, Hans Magnus (1972) 'Constituents of a theory of the media', in Denis McQuail (ed.) *Sociology of Mass Communications*, Harmondsworth: Penguin, 99–116.
Jameson, Fredric (1971) *Marxism and Form*, Princeton, NJ: Princeton University Press.
Kateb, George (1972) *Utopia and its Enemies*, New York: Schocken.
Langer, Susanne K. (1953) *Feeling and Form*, London: Routledge & Kegan Paul.
Trilling, Lionel (1972) *Sincerity and Authenticity*, London: Oxford University Press.

Further Reading

Altman, Rick (ed.) (1981) *Genre: The Musical*, London: Routledge & Kegan Paul.

Altman, Rick (1987) *The American Film Musical*, Bloomington, IN: Indiana University Press.

Feuer, Jane (1982) *The Hollywood Musical*, London: Macmillan.

Gaines, Jane and Herzog, Charlotte (eds) (1990) *Fabrications: Costume and the Female Body*, London and New York: Routledge.

Geraghty, Christine (1991) *Women and Soap Opera*, Cambridge: Polity Press.

Lovell, Terry (1980) *Pictures of Reality*, London: British Film Institute.

Modleski, Tania (1982) *Loving with a Vengeance*, New York: Methuen.

Williams, Linda (1990) *Hard Core: the Frenzy of the Visible*, Berkeley, CA: University of California Press.

The Self-reflective Musical and the Myth of Entertainment

2

JANE FEUER

Within the musical film the most persistent subgenre has involved kids (or adults) "getting together and putting on a show." The Jazz Singer (1927) featured a show business story, and during the talkie boom that followed (1929–30), a large percentage of the early musicals took for their subjects the world of entertainment: Broadway, vaudeville, the Ziegfeld Follies, burlesque, night clubs, the circus, Tin Pan Alley, and, to a lesser extent, mass entertainment media in the form of radio or Hollywood itself. Warner Brothers' Forty Second Street (1933) precipitated a second cycle of musicals. The Forty Second Street spinoffs tended to feature a narrative strategy typical of the backstage musical: musical interludes, usually in the form of rehearsal sequences detailing the maturation of the show, would be interspersed with parallel dramatic scenes detailing maturation of the off-stage love affairs. Even a radio story such as Twenty Million Sweethearts (1934) took its narrative structure from this paradigm. Perhaps these "art" musicals fulfilled a need for verisimilitude; perhaps the audience felt more comfortable viewing musical numbers within the context of a show than seeing fairytale queens and princes suddenly feel a song coming on in the royal boudoir. Whatever the explanation for its origins, the backstage pattern was always central to the genre. Incorporated into the structure of the art musical was the very type of popular entertainment represented by the musical film itself. The art musical is thus a self-referential form.

All art musicals are self-referential in this loose sense. But given such an opportunity, some musicals have exhibited a greater degree of self-consciousness than others. Dames (1934) climaxes its show-within-the-film with an apology for its own mode of entertainment, appropriately entitled "Dames." Moreover, the "Dames" number resolves a narrative in which the forces of Puritanism do battle with the forces of entertainment. It is the victory of what might be termed the "prurient ethic" over the Puritan ethic that the final show celebrates within the film, and that the "Dames" number celebrates within that show. In similar fashion, the Fred Astaire–Ginger Rogers cycle at RKO (1933–39) began to reflect upon the legends created in its dancing stars.[1]

Shall We Dance (1937) culminates in a show merging popular dancing with ballet. Yet that merger consists not in an equal union but rather in the lending of youth, rhythm, and vitality to the stiff, formal, classical art of ballet. Once again, a musical film has affirmed its own value for the popular audience.

Dames and *Shall We Dance?* are early examples of musicals that are self-*reflective* beyond their given self-referentiality. Historically, the art musical has evolved toward increasingly greater degrees of self-reflectivity. By the late forties and into the early fifties, a series of musicals produced by the Freed Unit at MGM used the backstage format to present sustained reflections upon, and affirmations of, the musical genre itself. Three of these apologies for the musical (all scripted by Betty Comden and Adolph Green), *The Barkleys of Broadway* (1949), *Singin' in the Rain* (1952), and *The Band Wagon* (1953) involve contrasts between performances that fail to please audiences and performances that are immediately audience-pleasing.[2] Performances in these films are not restricted to onstage numbers. Multiple levels of performance and consequent multiple levels of audience combine to create a myth about musical entertainment permeating ordinary life. Through the work of these filmic texts all successful performances, both in art and in life, are condensed into the MGM musical.

To say that entertainment is "mythified" is to institute a triple play upon conventional meanings of the word "myth." Most simply, it means that entertainment is shown as having greater value than it actually does. In this sense musicals are ideological products; they are full of deceptions. As students of mythology have demonstrated, however, these deceptions are willingly suffered by the audience. In *American Vaudeville as Ritual*, Albert F. McLean attempts to explain this contradiction in his definition of myth as:

> a constellation of images and symbols, whether objectively real or imaginary, which brings focus and a degree of order to the psychic (largely unconscious) processes of a group or society and in so doing endows a magical potency upon the circumstances of persons involved.[3]

McLean's notion of myth as "aura" occupies a pole opposite that of myth as "untruth" in constituting the myth of entertainment.

According to Claude Lévi-Strauss, the seemingly random surface structure of a myth masks contradictions which are real and therefore unresolvable.[4] Art musicals are structurally similar to myths, seeking to mediate contradictions in the nature of popular entertainment. The myth of entertainment is constituted by an oscillation between demystification and remythiciza-tion.[5] Musicals, like myths, exhibit a stratified structure. The ostensible or surface function of these musicals is to give pleasure to the audience by revealing what goes on behind the scenes in the theater or Hollywood, that is, to demystify the production of entertainment. But the films remythicize at another level that which they set out to expose. Only unsuccessful performances are demystified. The musical desires an ultimate valorization of entertainment; to destroy the aura, reduce the illusion, would be to destroy the myth of entertainment as well.[6] For the purpose of analysis, the myth of entertainment can be subdivided into three categories: the myth of spontaneity, the myth of integration, and the myth of the audience. In the films, however, the myth makes its impact through combination and repetition. Thus, a single musical number can be highly overdetermined and may be discussed under all three categories.

The myth of spontaneity

Perhaps the primary positive quality associated with musical performance is its spontaneous emergence out of a joyous and responsive attitude toward life. The musical buffs' parlor game which attempts to distinguish Fred Astaire's screen persona from Gene Kelly's ignores the overriding similarities in both dancers' spontaneous stances.[7] The Barkleys of Broadway, Singin' in the Rain, and The Band Wagon contrast the spontaneity of Astaire or Kelly with the prepackaged or calculated behavior of other performers.

In Singin' in the Rain, spontaneous talent distinguishes Don, Cosmo, and Kathy from Lina Lamont. Lina's laborious attempts to master basic English are followed by Don Lockwood's elocution lesson. Don and Cosmo seize upon the tongue-twister to turn the lesson into a spontaneous, anarchic dance routine, "Moses Supposes." Spontaneous self-expression through song and dance characterizes the three Positive performers: Cosmo in "Make 'Em Laugh," Don in "Singin' in the Rain," and all three in "Good Mornin'," which evolves out of their collective solution to the problems of the "Dueling Cavalier."

In addition, the impression of spontaneity in these numbers stems from a type of *bricolage*; the performers make use of props-at-hand—curtains, movie paraphernalia, umbrellas, furniture—to create the imaginary world of the musical performance. This *bricolage*, a hallmark of the post-Gene Kelly MGM musical, creates yet another contradiction: an effect of spontaneous realism is achieved through simulation.

The Barkleys of Broadway opposes strained, artificial "serious" performances to spontaneous and natural musical comedy performances. Dinah Barkley's sparkling costume and demeanor in the title sequence with Astaire ("Swing Trot") contrasts with her subdued garb and sullen demeanor as a dramatic actress. Early in the film we see Dinah truncating her understudy's carefully calculated audition, doing a brief warm-up, and going into a perfectly executed rehearsal of a tap routine with her husband. The rehearsals of "Young Sarah" (a play about Sarah Bernhardt's *struggle* to become an actress) are quite the opposite. Josh (Astaire), the musical comedy director-performer, is always spontaneous and natural. In the parallel sequence to Dinah's labors over "Young Sarah," we see Josh doing a completed number from his new show. "Shoes With Wings On" presents musical comedy dancing as an involuntary response, like breathing. Dancing is so spontaneous for Josh that animated shoes pull him into performance. The Astaire character never changes; he is presented as an utterly seamless monument of naturalness and spontaneity. Others must adapt to his style. Dinah can succeed as a performer only in a musical setting with Josh. Even their offstage performances stem from a spontaneous responsiveness to ordinary life, as when their dance to "You'd Be Hard to Replace" evolves out of the natural movements of putting on robes.

Similar oppositions between spontaneous and canned performers structure Singin' in the Rain and The Band Wagon. Astaire's trademark, "reflex" dancing, has its counterpart in the "Gotta Dance" motif which informs Kelly's "Broadway Ballet," part of the ultimately successful film-within-the-film. The Band Wagon cuts from Tony Hunter's (Astaire's) spontaneous eruption into song and dance at the penny arcade to Jeffrey Cordova in Oedipus Rex. The moaning sounds in the background of this production are later associated with the reactions of an audience to Cordova's laborious musical version of Faust. We are shown Cordova from the point of view of Tony and the Martons in the wings (almost always a demystifying camera position), as he segues from his curtain calls as Oedipus into his offstage pomposity. Although Cordova's Oedipus is said to be successful with audiences in the film the extent to which it is demystified for us undercuts its status as a successful show. Cordova is characterized throughout the first half of the film by the mechanical nature of his actions and utterances. He continually gives rehearsed speeches such as the one about Bill Shakespeare's immortal lines and Bill Robinson's immortal feet. On the first day of rehearsals, Cordova tells the cast exactly what will happen to them before the show opens. Not until he dances with Astaire (and in Astaire's style) in the top-hat, white tie, and tails soft-shoe number in the second "Band Wagon" does Cordova achieve true spontaneity as a performer.

Almost every spontaneous performance in *The Band Wagon* has a matched segment which parodies the lack of spontaneity of the high art world. Tony drops Gaby while attempting a lift during the rehearsal of a ballet number for the first show; later in "The Girl Hunt," a jazz ballet, he lifts her effortlessly. Tony and Gaby's relaxed offstage rehearsal of a dance to "You and the Night and the Music" literally explodes on stage at the dress rehearsal. A prepackaged orchestral rendition of "Something to Remember You By" at the official New Haven cast party dissolves into a vocal version of the same song spontaneously performed by the "kids" at the chorus party. Spontaneity thus emerges as the hallmark of a successful performance.

The myth of spontaneity operates through what we are shown of the work of production of the respective shows as well as how we are shown it. In *Singin' in the Rain*, we see the technical difficulties involved with filming and projecting "The Dueling Cavalier," including Lina's battle with the microphone and the failure of the film when its technological base is revealed to the preview audience. "The Dancing Cavalier," in contrast, springs to life effortlessly. The film shows an awareness of this opposition between the foregrounding of technology in "The Dueling Cavalier" and the invisibility of technology in the "Dancing Cavalier." "The Broadway Ballet" is presented in the context of an idea for a production number, and one of the biggest jokes in the film concerns the producer's inability to visualize what we have just been shown, elaborate and complete. Yet at many other points in *Singin' in the Rain* this awareness is masked, often in quite complex ways.[8] In "You Were Meant for Me" the exposure of the wind machine figures prominently in the demystification of romantic musical numbers. Yet in a dialogue scene outside the soundstage just prior to this number, Kathy's scarf had blown to the breeze of an invisible wind machine. Even after we are shown the tools of illusion at the beginning of the number, the camera arcs around and comes in for a tighter shot of the performing couple, thereby remasking the exposed technology and making the duet just another example of the type of number whose illusions it exposes. Demystification is countered by the reassertion of the spontaneous evolution of musical films. Perhaps the ultimate in spontaneous evolution of a musical number occurs in *The Barkleys*. At the end of the film, the couple decides to do another musical. Josh describes a dance routine which, unlike "Young Sarah," will have *tempo*, and the couple goes into a dance, framed to the right of a curtain in their living room. As they spin, there is a dissolve to the same step as part of an elaborate production number in the new show.

In *The Band Wagon* the labor of producing the first show eclipses the performances. Never do we see a completed number from the first show. Technical or personal problems prevent the completion of every number shown in rehearsal, as when Tony walks out or when Cordova is levitated by the revolving stage. It is not because high art (ballet) and popular art (musical comedy) are inherently mutually exclusive that Cordova's show fails. After all, it is Tony's Impressionist paintings which pay for the successful show. Rather, the film suggests that Cordova fails because he has been unable to render invisible the technology of production in order to achieve the effect of effortlessness by which all entertainment succeeds in winning its audience.

Of course, spontaneous performances that mask their technology have been calculated too—not for audiences within the films but for audiences *of* the film. The musical, technically the most complex type of film produced in Hollywood, paradoxically has always been the genre which attempts to give the greatest illusion of spontaneity and effortlessness. It is as if engineering were to affirm *bricolage* as the ultimate approach to scientific thought. The self-reflective musical is aware of this in attempting to promulgate the myth of spontaneity. The heavily value-laden oppositions set up in the self-reflective films promote the mode of expression of the film musical itself as spontaneous and natural rather than calculated and technological. Musical entertainment thus takes on a natural relatedness to life processes and to the lives of its audiences. Musical entertainment claims for its own all natural and joyous performances in art and in life. The myth of spontaneity operates (to borrow Lévi-Strauss's terminology) to make musical performance, which is actually part of culture, appear to be part of nature.

The myth of integration

Earlier musicals sometimes demonstrated ambiguous attitudes toward the world of musical theater, perceiving conflicts between success on the stage and success in the performers' personal lives. In *Ziegfeld Girl* (1941), Lana Turner is destroyed when she forsakes the simple life in Brooklyn for the glamour of the Follies. In *Cain and Mabel* (1936), Marion Davies has to be physically dragged onto the stage after deciding to retire to a garage in Jersey with prize fighter beau Clark Gable. But the self-reflective musical asserts the integrative effect of musical performance. Successful performances are intimately bound up with success in love, with the integration of the individual into a community or a group, and even with the merger of high art with popular art.

In *Singin' in the Rain*, the success of the musical film brings about the final union of Don and Kathy. This consummation takes place on the stage at the premier in front of a live audience and in the form of a duet. The music is carried over to a shot of the lovers embracing in front of a billboard of Don and Kathy's images. But the successful show on the billboard is no longer "The Dancing Cavalier"; it is *Singin' in the Rain*, that is, the film itself. This hall-of-mirrors effect emphasizes the unity-giving function of the musical both for the couples and audiences *in* the film and for the audience *of* the film. In *The Barkleys*, Josh and Dinah are reunited when she realizes she wants "nothing but fun set to music," that is, the type of performance associated with the MGM musical. Gaby, in *The Band Wagon*, learns the value of popular entertainment as she learns to love Tony. "Dancing in the Dark" imitates the form of a sexual act as it merges two kinds of dancing previously set in conflict. The number combines the ballet movements associated with Gaby and her choreographer beau Paul Byrd with the ballroom dancing associated with Astaire. At the end of the film the long run of their successful show is used by Gaby as a metaphor for her relationship with Tony.

The right kind of musical performance also integrates the individual into a unified group just as the wrong kind alienates. *The Band Wagon* traces Tony's repeated movements from isolation to the joy of being part of a group. At the beginning of the film, Tony sings "By Myself" isolated by the tracking camera; as he enters the crowded terminal, the camera stops moving to frame him against the crowd, a mass that becomes an audience for Tony's antics with the Martons. The arcade sequence repeats this opening movement. Once again Tony overcomes his sense of isolation by reestablishing contact with an audience through spontaneous musical performance. The "?" machine at the arcade symbolizes the problem/solution format of the narrative. When Tony answers the question of how to make a comeback by dancing with a shoeshine man, the machine bursts open and his audience rushes to congratulate him. Another such movement occurs when, after the failure of the first show, Tony finds himself the only guest at the official cast party. "I Love Louisa" marks his renewal of contact with yet another audience—this time the common folk of the theater itself. At the end of the film, Tony moves from a reprise of "By Myself" into the final integration—a symbolic marriage to Gaby and to the rank and file of the theater. The myth of integration makes itself felt through the repetitive structure of the film.

Paralleling Tony's movement from isolation to integration and also paralleling the integration of the couple, is Gaby's integration into the populist world of musical theater from the elitist world of high art. We first see Gaby in a ballet performance in which she functions as prima ballerina backed by the corps. At Cordova's, the two worlds are spatially isolated as the representatives of high art (Gabrielle and Paul) and those of popular art (Tony and the Martons) occupy separate rooms. The possibility of movement between the two worlds is stressed by the precisely parallel actions taking place in each room as well as by Cordova's role as mediator between the two rooms (worlds). Cordova prevents a terminal clash between Tony and Gaby by rushing into the neutral space of the front hall and drawing the representatives of both worlds back into his own central space.

Gabrielle begins her integration into the world of popular art through a renewal of contact with the common folk in Central Park, a process which culminates in "I Love Louisa" with Gaby serving as part of the chorus. Paul Byrd draws Gaby away from the group into an isolated space symbolic of the old world of ballet; the camera frames the couple apart from the mass. The colors of their isolated space—subdued shades of brown and white—contrast with the vibrant colors of the chorus' costumes which have just filled the frame. In leaving this isolated space to return to the group, Gaby has taken the side of the collective effort which will produce the successful musical. "New Sun in the Sky," the first number in the new show, again finds Gaby backed up by a chorus, but this time the mood is celebratory—the bright golds and reds as well as the lyrics of the song emphasize Gaby's rebirth. Even the musical arrangement of the song—upbeat and jazzy—contrasts with the more sedate balletic arrangement we heard in that rehearsal for the Faustian *Band Wagon* in which Tony dropped Gaby. At the end of the film, Gaby expresses her feelings for Tony by speaking for the group, the chorus framed in back of her as she speaks.

Everyone knows that the musical film was a mass art produced by a tiny elite for a vast and amorphous consuming public; the self-reflective musical attempts to overcome this division through the myth of integration. It offers a vision of musical performance originating in the folk, generating love and a cooperative spirit which includes everyone in its grasp and which can conquer all obstacles. By promoting audience identification with the collectively produced shows, the myth of integration seeks to give the audience a sense of participation in the creation of the film itself. The musical film becomes a mass art which aspires to the condition of a folk art—produced and consumed by the same integrated community.

The myth of the audience

It follows that successful performances will be those in which the performer is sensitive to the needs of his audience and which give the audience a sense of participation in the performance. Josh Barkley berates Dinah for her performance in the subway scene because "the audience wants to cry there and you won't let them." Cordova is more concerned with the revolving stage than with delivering audience-pleasing performances; his canned speeches of solidarity with the cast are undercut by his delivering them with his back to the group, oblivious to their response. Tony Hunter, on the other hand, is willing to leave the self-enclosed world of the theater to regain contact with the folk who make up his audience. "Dancing in the Dark" is precipitated by observing ordinary people dancing in Central Park.

The insensitive performer also attempts to manipulate his audience. Cordova wants to control the timing of the curtain, the actress's exit pace, and the placing of an amber spot in *Oedipus*. Lina Lamont masks the fact that she is unable to speak for herself either on stage or on screen.

Yet while setting up an association between success and lack of audience manipulation, the musicals themselves exert continuous control over the responses of their audiences. The film musical profits rhetorically by displacing to the theater the myth of a privileged relationship between musical entertainment and its audience. Popular theater can achieve a fluidity and immediacy in this respect that the film medium lacks. The out-of-town tryout, the interpolation of new material after each performance, the instantaneous modulation of performer to audience response—none of these common theatrical practices is possible for film. Hollywood had only the limited adaptations made possible by the preview system and the genre system itself which accommodated audience response by making (or not making) other films of the same type. The backstage musical, however, manages to incorporate the immediate angle, and we see the couple taking a bow before a live audience. The audience in the film is there to express the adulation the number itself sought to arouse from the film's audience.

MGM musicals make use of natural, spontaneous audiences which form around offstage performances.[9] "Shine on Your Shoes" in *The Band Wagon* demonstrates Astaire's ability to adapt his dancing to any occasion and any audience, as he incorporates the shoeshiner into his performance. The spontaneous audience which forms around the duo provides a point of identification for the film audience as well. In "I Love Louisa" the chorus serves first as an audience for Tony and the Martons's clowning, and then participates in the dance, providing a vicarious sense of participation for the film audience. Audiences in the films suggest a contagious spirit inherent in musical performance, related to the suggestion that the MGM musical is folk art; the audience must be shown as participating in the production of entertainment.

Intertextuality and star iconography can be a means of manipulating audience response. Many of the later MGM musicals play upon the audience's memories of earlier musicals. *The Barkleys* plays on the Astaire–Rogers legend from its first shot of the couple's feet, which echoes the title sequence of *Top Hat* (1935). The couple's reunion performance to "You Can't Take That Away From Me" harks back to *Shall We Dance* (1937), with the dance itself reminiscent of one of their old routines. Such attempts to evoke nostalgia play on the star system's desire to erase the boundaries between star persona and character, between onscreen and offscreen personalities. *The Barkleys* thus celebrates Ginger Roger's return to musical comedy after a series of straight dramatic films, suggesting that the only way she can succeed with an audience is by dancing with Astaire in musicals.[10]

Other self-reflective musicals make use of audience response to songs from previous stage musicals or films. Most of the songs in *Singin' in the Rain* were written for the earliest MGM film musicals. *The Band Wagon* takes its music from stage reviews of the same period (late twenties to early thirties). In the interim many of these songs had become standards, and the films were able to play upon the audience's familiarity with the lyric. "Dancing in the Dark," for example, is used only in instrumental arrangement, thus inviting the audience to participate by supplying the lyric. Two related practices of the Freed Unit—biopics fashioned around a composer's hit songs, and the purchase of a song catalog around which to construct an original musical—depended upon audience familiarity (through both filmic and nonfilmic intertexts) for their effectiveness.

Conclusion

Self-reflective musicals mediate a contradiction between live performance in the theater and the frozen form of cinema by implying that the MGM musical *is* theater, possesses the same immediate and active relationship to its audience. Both the myth of integration and the myth of the audience suggest that the MGM musical is really a folk art, that the audience participates in the creation of musical entertainment. The myth of integration suggests that the achievement of personal fulfillment goes hand-in-hand with the enjoyment of entertainment. And the myth of spontaneity suggests that the MGM musical is not artificial but rather completely natural. Performance is no longer defined as something professionals do on a stage; instead, it permeates the lives of professional and nonprofessional singers and dancers. Entertainment, the myth implies, can break down the barriers between art and life.

The myth of entertainment, in its entirety, cannot be celebrated in a single text or even across three texts. Different aspects of the myth achieve prominence in different films but the myth is carried by the genre as a whole. The notion of breaking down barriers between art and life, for example, is more prominent in Minnelli's *The Pirate* (1947) than in any of the films discussed here. It might be said that the elements of the myth of entertainment constitute a paradigm which generates the syntax of individual texts.

Ultimately, one might wonder why these films go to such lengths to justify the notion that all life should aspire to the condition of a musical performance. That is, why expend so much effort to celebrate mythic elements the audience is likely to accept anyway? Answering this question involves an awareness both of the function of ritual and of the ritual function of the musical. All ritual involves the celebration of shared values and beliefs; the ritual function of the musical is to reaffirm and articulate the place that entertainment occupies in its audience's psychic lives. Self-reflective musicals are then able to celebrate myths created by the genre as a whole.

Yet the extremes of affirmation in *The Band Wagon* need further justification in terms of its function for MGM as well as for the popular audience. At a time when the studio could no longer be certain of the allegiance of its traditional mass audience, *The Band Wagon*, in ritual fashion, served to reaffirm the traditional relationship. For the musical was always the quintessential Hollywood product: all Hollywood films manipulated audience response, but the musical could incorporate that response into the film itself; all Hollywood films sought to be entertaining, but the musical could incorporate a myth of entertainment into its aesthetic discourse. As Thomas Elsaesser says, "The world of the musical becomes a kind of ideal image of the [film] medium itself."[11]

Nowhere is Lévi-Strauss's notion of myth more applicable to the musical than in the relationship of the genre to the studio system which produced it. Faced with declining attendance due to competition from television, the studio could suggest, through *Singin' in the Rain*, that making musicals can provide a solution to any crisis of technological change. Faced with charges of infantilism from the citadels of high art, the studio could suggest, through *The Barkleys of Broadway*, that all successful performances are musical performances. Faced with the threat of changing patterns of audience consumption, the studio could suggest, through *The Band Wagon* that the MGM musical can adapt to any audience. *The Band Wagon* ends where the films *That's Entertainment I* and *II* commence, in an attempt to recapture the aura of the "Golden Age" of the Freed/MGM musicals. It is not surprising that the "That's Entertainment" number from *The Band Wagon* should have been inserted into the contemporary sequences of the nostalgia compilations. For the ending of *The Band Wagon* already marked the genre's celebration of its own (and Hollywood's) economic death and ritual rebirth.

Self-reflexivity as a critical category has been associated with films, such as those of Godard, which call attention to the codes constituting their own signifying practices. The term has been applied to aesthetically or politically radical films which react against so-called classical narrative cinema by interrogating their own narrativity. Thus we tend to associate reflexivity with the notion of deconstruction within filmmaking practice. The MGM musical, however, uses reflexivity to perpetuate rather than to deconstruct the codes of the genre. Self-reflective musicals are conservative texts in every sense. MGM musicals have continued to function both in the popular consciousness and within international film culture as representatives of the Hollywood product at its best. I hope to have shown that this was the very task these texts sought to accomplish.

Notes

1 See Leo Braudy, *The World in a Frame* (New York: Anchor Press/Doubleday, 1976), pp. 143–147, for a discussion of self-consciousness in *Shall We Dance?*

2 *The Barkleys of Broadway* presents Josh and Dinah Barkley (Fred Astaire and Ginger Rogers) as the Lunts of musical comedy. Dinah leaves musical comedy to do a serious play ("Young Sarah"), and finally learns the lesson that there's no difference between serious acting and musical comedy acting. She returns to do a musical at the end of the film. *Singin' in the Rain* depicts the coming of sound to Hollywood. An early talkie which fails ("The Dueling Cavalier") is remade as a musical which succeeds ("The Dancing Cavalier"). *The Band Wagon* also involves the re-production of a show that flops (a musical version of the Faust story called "The Band Wagon") into a musical revue which succeeds (again called "The Band Wagon").

3 University of Kentucky Press, 1965, p. 223.

4 "The Structural Study of Myth" in *Structural Anthropology* (New York: Basic Books, 1963), p. 220. I am also indebted to Lévi-Strauss for other ideas contained in the same essay: first, that a myth works itself out through repetition in a number of texts; second, that myth works through the mediation of binary oppositions.

5 These terms are taken from Paul Ricoeur, *Freud and Philosophy* (New Haven: Yale University Press, 1970), p. 54. Ricoeur uses them to refer to two schools of hermeneutics which nevertheless constitute "a profound unity." I find them equally applicable to texts which seek to interpret themselves.

6 The inseparability of demystification from its opposite (remythicization) is best illustrated by A *Star is Born* (Warners, 1954), at once the last bearer of the studio's myth of entertainment and the first of the antimusicals. Even the supposedly Brechtian antimusical *Cabaret* (1972) merely inverts the backstage paradigm, while maintaining its narrative strategy.

7 See Braudy, p. 147 ff. for a discussion of the function of spontaneity in the Astaire and Kelly personas.

8 See David Lusted, "Film as Industrial Product—Teaching a Reflexive Movie." *Screen Education* 16 (Autumn 1975) for detailed examples of the mystification–demystification dynamic in *Singin' in the Rain*.

9 Other good examples of "natural audiences" in the MGM musical include "By Strauss," "I Got Rhythm," and "S'Wonderful" in *An American in Paris* (1951); "Nina" in *The Pirate* (1947); and "I Like Myself," Gene Kelly's dance on roller skates in *It's Always Fair Weather* (1955). The history of this device in the musical film may be traced from Jolson to Chevalier to Astaire to Kelly and back to Astaire, spontaneity of performance providing the link among the major male musical stars.

10 The extreme example of this phenomenon is A *Star is Born* (1954) the signification of which depends upon the audience's knowledge of Judy Garland's offscreen life as the negation of her MGM onscreen image.

11 "The American Musical," *Brighton Film Review* 15 (December 1969), p. 13.

The American Film Musical as Dual-Focus Narrative

3

RICK ALTMAN

When we look at a narrative film or read a novel, what do we tend to see? All our experience predisposes us toward a particular way of viewing. We expect certain character relationships and plot patterns just as surely as we expect a film to have a specific shape on the screen. The very vocabulary we use to describe narrative reveals a great deal about our presuppositions. We speak, for example, of the hero or protagonist of a film as if a film always had a single central character, around whom all other activity revolves. Indeed, all our notions about narrative structure seem to support this proposition. When we speak of a plot we usually mean the hero's (or heroine's) trajectory from the beginning of the text to the end; alternately acting and acted upon, he (she) ties the plot together by providing a psychological bridge between each action and the next. The concept of motivation is thus essential to this standard view of narrative structure. An event takes place, it motivates a second event, which in turn occasions a third, and so on until the necessary chain of causality has been extinguished and the film draws to a close.

It is of course not possible to *prove* that one event causes another, any more than we can prove that a moving billiard ball striking a stationary ball causes the stationary one to move. The traditional approach to narrative solves this problem by postulating psychological motivation as a necessary and sufficient connector. When we watch a character read a telegram, then see him grab his hat and coat, rush out the door, and head for the police station, we assume that his actions are motivated by the telegram, that something in his synapses or his brain *causes* him to react in a specific way to a specific stimulus. As spectators of commercial cinema, we have acquired the habit of linking one segment of a traditional film to another by postulating such an intermediary psychological motivation. From this point of view each plot looks more or less the same. An initial impulse sets in motion a series of causally related events, each one closely tied to the preceding and following events:

$$a \longrightarrow b \longrightarrow c \longrightarrow d \longrightarrow e \longrightarrow \ldots x$$

Why belabor these apparently obvious notions about narrative? It seems clear that most films follow the destiny of a single character, integrate other characters and happenings into his/her career, motivate the plot by reference to his/her psychology, and depend on the twin chains of chronological progression and causal sequence.[1] Attempts to analyze the musical following these principles have consistently come up short, however, for like many popular genres the musical operates only in part according to the model of psychological motivation. To be sure, the musical *looks* as if it can be properly defined by a linear, psychological model, but this impression is created by no more than a veneer, a thin layer of classical narrativity which we must learn to look beyond, discovering instead the radically different principles of organization which lie just beneath the surface.

Let us take as an extremely clear example the first two sequences of MGM's 1940 version of *New Moon*. The first few shots set the scene: the French ship Marseilles in 1789 en route to New Orleans, carrying a group of extremely well-dressed society ladies. The older ladies in the group soon pressure one of the younger members to share her operatic talents, a typical method of introducing Jeanette MacDonald's first song. As MacDonald holds forth on deck, demonstrating her appetizing physical features along with her well developed voice, her song is slowly drowned out by muffled male voices. The camera immediately cuts to the source of this second song: imprisoned in the hold, a group of disheveled young Frenchmen about to be sold into slavery sing of their plight. Their leader, played by Nelson Eddy, is introduced in the same shot sequence previously used for MacDonald's song: full shot for the first two lines, cut to medium shot at line three, then to a close-up at line seven. At the request of the ladies on deck, an emissary soon appears to order the men in the hold to cease their singing or suffer the consequences.

These first two scenes appear to correspond quite closely to the characteristics of classical narrative outlined above. An event within scene one (the voices drowning out MacDonald's song) motivates a cut to scene two, where we witness the logical consequences of the first scene (Eddy and friends are told to reduce the "noise"). What this chronological approach ignores, however, are the careful parallels set up between Jeanette MacDonald and Nelson Eddy. Tied together by similar shot scale, mise-en-scène, and domination of the sound track, the two stars are nevertheless implicitly contrasted in numerous ways. *She* sings on deck, *he* sings in the hold; *she* sings to entertain a bevy of society women, *he* sings to relieve the misery of a group of penniless men; *she* is free, *he* is behind bars. The first two scenes must be visualized not one after the other but one balanced against the other. Now classical narrative analysis would make the chronological relationship primary, relegating the simultaneity and parallelism of the scenes to the shadows of stylistic analysis or theme criticism. In order to understand the musical, however, we must learn to do just the opposite; we must treat the conceptual relationships as fundamental, assuming that the rather tenuous cause-and-effect connections are in this case secondary, present only to highlight the more important parallelisms which they introduce. Instead of stressing a causal progression, the first two sequences of *New Moon* present and develop the two centers of power on which the film depends: *the female*—rich, cultured, beautiful, easily offended; *the male*—poor, practical, energetic, tenacious. Yet they share one essential attribute: they both sing.

Two centers of power, two sexes, two attitudes, two classes, two protagonists. We seem to be traveling not on the Marseilles in 1789 but on Noah's Ark many millennia earlier. Instead of focusing all its interest on a single central character, following the trajectory of her progress, the American film musical has a dual focus, built around parallel stars of opposite sex and radically divergent values.[2] This dual-focus structure requires the viewer to be sensitive not so much to chronology and progression—for the outcome of the male/female match is entirely conventional and thus quite predictable—but to simultaneity and comparison. We construe the first two sequences of *New Moon* not according to their syntagmatic ties but

While Jeanette MacDonald warbles a well-known song on deck, Nelson Eddy and his henchmen belt out their frustrations in the hold. Courtesy of BFI Stills, Posters and Designs

in the light of their paradigmatic relationship; that is, we subordinate their sequential connection to their parallelism. The principle which holds for the paired initial scenes also applies to the following scene which joins Eddy and MacDonald for the first time. In terms of traditional plot analysis we might say that this scene serves to initiate the love plot, which will eventually culminate in the couple's final embrace. If this, however, is the sole function of the scene, then it is wasted indeed. What moviegoer in 1940 needed a preliminary infatuation scene to inform him that Eddy and MacDonald would ultimately fall in love? New Moon was the seventh movie in five years to pair the two as lovers. In short, the matched scenes that open New Moon are sufficient to suggest the course which the plot will take.

What then *is* the purpose of the stars' first meeting in New Moon? Having simultaneously decided to visit the captain, both Eddy and MacDonald at first seem simply to continue the thematics of the original balanced sequences. He is still concerned about the fate of his singing friends; *she* still wants to be able to sing without interruption. He is all rebellious energy, caring little for social mores as long as the cause of freedom is served; *she* is all properness, expecting the dictates of society to be obeyed even on the high seas. It is in this context that we must interpret the simple but significant clothing motif developed during this first meeting. When Eddy first sees MacDonald he forgets his revolutionary purpose for a moment in order to don the nearest coat; even then he apologizes for having appeared in shirt sleeves before a lady. By the end of the scene, MacDonald has reversed the process; she arrived bundled up, but she is so captivated by Eddy that she soon removes her shawl, and with it some of the propriety which has thus far defined her. If the initial paired scenes define Eddy as energy, MacDonald as restraint, this first joint scene moves each of the prospective lovers a step toward the other, Eddy demonstrating his civility and MacDonald her desire. As this analysis suggests, the plot of New Moon depends not on the stars falling in love (they do that early on) nor even on their marriage (even that takes place well before the end), but on the resolution of their differences. Each must adopt the characteristics of the other: Eddy must exercise restraint and MacDonald must learn to reveal her desire before the love story—and the film—can end.

This simple analysis is given not as an interpretation of the film, but as an example of how the American film musical must be construed. Those aspects which form the heart of traditional narrative analysis—plot, psychology, motivation, suspense are to such an extent conventional in the musical that they leave little room for variation: we alternate between the male focus and the female focus, working our way through a prepackaged love story whose dynamic principle remains the difference between male and female. *Each segment must be understood not in terms of the segments to which it is causally related but by comparison to the segment which it parallels.* The first three sequences of New Moon are thus not to be construed in traditional terms:

$$A \longrightarrow B \longrightarrow C$$

but in a radically modified fashion:

$$A/B, C/C'$$

The first two paired scenes (on deck, in the hold) are balanced; they are meant to be measured against each other. The third scene (in the captain's cabin) can be understood only when we

Male and female, dark and light, bondsman and aristocrat—all are brought together in *New Moon*'s romantic conclusion. Courtesy of BFI Stills, Posters and Designs

divide it in half, comparing Eddy's conduct to MacDonald's. *New Moon* is thus seen not as a continuous chain of well-motivated events but as a series of nearly independent fragments, each a carefully constructed duet involving the two principal personages. The presence of Jeanette MacDonald and Nelson Eddy predetermines the plot of *New Moon*, forces it to conform to certain definite criteria, even makes it stoop to the most unlikely combinations in order to set up repeated confrontations or parallels between the two stars. Whereas the traditional approach to narrative assumes that structure grows out of *plot*, the dual-focus structure of the American film musical derives from *character*.

An extended example from a well-known film should help demonstrate the importance of this new method of viewing the musical. Vincente Minnelli's *Gigi* (MGM, 1958) borrows from the French novelist Colette a story about a young girl on the verge of becoming a woman. During the course of the film, Gigi (Leslie Caron) changes from an impish girl into a dazzling beauty capable of exciting the interest of Gaston Lachaille (Louis Jourdan). Very few scenes in the film actually advance this plot, however, and those that do are singularly lacking in motivation. Gaston leaves Gigi's apartment one lovely Paris night, he stops on a bridge, looks pensive, the music swells, and presto! he suddenly realizes that his young friend has changed. To judge from the point of view of the plot, *Gigi* is a remarkably unimpressive affair: it wastes time, motivates little, seems more concerned to paint representative days in the lives of its characters than to fashion the kind of tightly knit fabric that characterizes masterful narrative. But if we inspect the film from the vantage point of dual-focus structure we find that from its very first words it creates an organized and compact whole.

"Bonjour Monsieur, bonjour Madame," says Gaston's Uncle Honoré (Maurice Chevalier) as the film opens, thus dividing the world from the very beginning into two groups, the very groups that will preside over the film's structure. The film's first song, "Thank Heaven for Little Girls," demonstrates the extent to which even the youngest members of society are defined by gender. In fact, the scenes which follow make no sense at all unless we see them as outgrowths of the basic sexual parameter introduced by Chevalier. We first see Gigi at home, where she is told by her grandmother to change her clothes, comb her hair, and hurry to the lessons in femininity which her Aunt Alicia gives her once a week. Over the music of "Thank Heaven" we then dissolve to Gaston receiving a visit from his uncle; while Gaston buys two cars and admits having recently bought an entire railroad, his uncle reminds him that he is expected at an embassy tea. It is not the plot that justifies Gaston's appearance here, but the extended series of parallels linking these two scenes. We observe Gigi at home, then Gaston at home; Gigi is with an older relative, so is Gaston; Gigi has no great desire to keep her appointment, neither does Gaston; Gigi is defined by female preoccupations (looks, clothes, manners), Gaston by their turn-of-the-century male counterparts (business, politics, riches). Before they have even met on screen, Gigi and Gaston are linked in the viewer's mind by these parallel scenes, thus initiating the duality which will inform the film's structure.

The following sequences further develop this paradigm. Gaston's song "It's a Bore," which emphasizes his profound disgust with Parisian life, is matched by Gigi's "I Don't Understand the Parisians." While Gigi endeavors to learn the manners of Gaston's world, Gaston enjoys the camomile tea and cookies to which Gigi is accustomed. Each scene involving only one of the lovers is invariably matched by a parallel scene (song, shot, event) featuring the other lover. From this rather simple discovery about the *structure* of *Gigi* we can deduce certain important attributes of the *interpretation process* appropriate for *Gigi* and the American film musical in general. In any film a given scene, in order to be properly understood, must be set in its proper context. Traditional narrative analysis usually stresses other scenes involving the same character, but *in the musical the basic context is constituted by a parallel scene involving the other lover*. When Gaston wanders through the park singing "Gigi" he sits down on a park bench. Not just any bench, however; it is the very same bench used by Gigi during her earlier song. She sang "I Don't Understand the Parisians;" now he insists that he doesn't understand Gigi. Objects, places, words, tunes, positions—everything becomes colored with the other person's actions and values.

It is this aspect of *Gigi*'s structure that Raymond Bellour misses in his influential analysis of *Gigi*.[3] Building his interpretation around segments which "rhyme"—i.e., which rework the same material—Bellour limits his examples to situations where a character repeats in modified fashion an action which he/she performed earlier. Bellour is unable to capture the text's dialectic, paradigmatic structure because he does not recognize that the musical uses one character's actions to establish the context for the other character's parallel activities. His presuppositions about the linear, cause-and-effect, psychological nature of classical narrative have blinded him to the structural patterns particular to the musical.

a) Female occupations: Gigi primping

b) Male occupations: Gaston buying

c) While Gigi learns the manners of Gaston's world

d) Gaston helps himself to another of Mamita's cookies

e) Two songs culminate on the same park bench: Gigi sings "I Don't Understand the Parisians"

f) In front of a family of swans Gaston sings that Gigi is no longer an ugly duckling

g) Juxtaposition of similar mirror shots highlights Gigi's and

h) Gaston's divergent attitudes toward love. (Collection of the author)

When Gaston returns home from Honfleur, where he punishes his mistress's infidelity, his uncle informs him that he must not leave Paris. "Male patriotism" requires that he give a series of parties to celebrate his triumph. The episodic sequence that follows reveals Gaston performing his masculine duty, hosting party after party. How do we interpret this short but effective sequence? From a psychological point of view it is all but useless, since it tells us nothing about Gaston which we do not already know; it motivates nothing which is not already motivated in a number of other ways. If we wait a few minutes, however, we soon find this episodic sequence matched by another, this time on Gigi's side. When Gigi returns from Trouville (the next resort down the coast from Honfleur), Aunt Alicia insists that her education be speeded up. Gigi is no more enchanted by her aunt's lessons than Gaston by his uncle's parties, but follow the dictates of the older generation they must, and so we are given the only other episodic sequence in the entire film, in which Gigi is forced to serve tea, to sip wine, to choose cigars, to select a dress. Throughout these parallel sequences we recall the worldly wisdom of Gigi's aunt and Gaston's uncle: if the function of men in society is to collect women, the role of women is to collect jewels. A role for men, a symmetrical role for women: such is the vision of the world which Minnelli's dual-focus editing constantly produces. Each pairing of shots reinforces the notion that men and women alike play predetermined parts in an already written scenario. Individuals have responsibilities to their sex; the older generation must remind the younger of these responsibilities. Older characters serve not so much as go-betweens but as symbols of the conduct expected of their younger charges. This symbolic function reaches its height when Gigi's grandmother and Gaston's uncle sing "I Remember It Well" against the setting sun. This dialogue-song recapitulates in miniature the film's characteristic alternation between the sexes, demonstrating the extent to which love is an eternal and unchanging part of the human scene, ever the same from generation unto generation.

We have seen thus far how every aspect of *Gigi* obeys a principle of duality. Instead of the traditional pattern whereby a cause calls forth an effect, we have a less linear configuration whereby each male aspect seems to call for a parallel female one, and vice-versa. This rule is by no means limited to actual events. It includes paired songs ("It's a Bore", "I Don't Understand the Parisians"), paired montage segments (the episodic sequences), paired roles (collecting women/ collecting jewels), paired trips (to Honfleur/to Trouville), paired locations (Gigi's and Alicia's apartments/Gaston's and Honoré's rooms), as well as paired activities (Gigi's lessons/Gaston's embassy tea), paired feelings (Gigi's exasperation with her aunt/Gaston's boredom), and paired scenes (Gigi at home with her grandmother/Gaston at home with his uncle). The technique even extends to paired shots and objects: just before the couple's first "date" we are given a single shot of Gaston in front of his mirror (choosing a jewel) from which we cut directly to Gigi in front of her mirror (dressing and primping).

What conclusions can we reach about Gigi based on comparison of these various pairings? The question is an essential one; on our answer rests the very variety of the American film musical. If we can say only that Gigi's pairings divide the world into male and female in order ultimately to bring the two sexes together again in matrimony, then all musicals will seem identical, for nearly every American film musical sets up a series of male/female oppositions, eventually resolving them to harmonious unity through the device of marriage. On careful inspection, however, we can distinguish in any musical a secondary but essential opposition alongside the primary sexual division: each sex is identified with a particular attitude, value, desire, location, age, or other characteristic attribute. These secondary attributes always begin diametrically opposed and mutually exclusive.

If sexual differentiation represents Gigi's major duality, then what will its minor opposition be? What characteristics constantly inform the opposition of Gaston to Gigi? Two answers to this question are immediately apparent. First, we have learned that both sexes are collectors, men collecting women and women amassing jewels. This simple opposition remains important throughout the history of the American film musical, from the Gold Diggers series of the thirties (where man is seen as an endless source of gold, while woman is identified by her beauty) to the tongue-in-cheek extravaganzas of the fifties (e.g., Howard Hawks's 1953 Gentlemen Prefer Blondes, which turns on this simple principle: "Don't you know that a man being rich is like a girl being pretty?"). Marriage is seen, according to this view, as the only way to join beauty and riches, to effect not a compromise but a merger between the *dulce* and the *utile*. And no wonder, for in the sexually differentiated climate of the three decades in which the musical flourished a woman could by and large become rich in only one way: marry for money. Similarly, a man could not fully enjoy the charms of feminine beauty without marrying. Sexual stereotyping and a strict moral code went hand in hand, leaving only one solution for young men and women alike: marriage. In this sense Gigi, like many other musicals, is an apology for traditional mores, an ode to marriage as the only way to combine riches and beauty.

The beauty/riches motif is a common one, however; we must search further if we are to understand the specificity of Gigi as a functional mechanism, one which overcomes the very contradictions on which society is founded. When we first see Gigi and then Gaston, she is preparing for her "femininity" lessons with Aunt Alicia, while he is about to leave with his uncle for an embassy tea; she must change clothes and brush her hair, while he is buying cars and railroads. At first I characterized these activities as typically female and male: she is concerned with beauty, he with riches. On second glance, however, a minor premise of some importance becomes apparent. *She* skips and hops, plays tag and eats candy; *he* is reserved, serious, moody. *She* wears a brightly colored pinafore; *he* has formal attire and a cane. In short, *she* is a child and *he* is a man. The initial paired sequences clearly stress the stars' respective female and male qualities, yet simultaneously create a generation gap between Gigi and Gaston. This impression is reinforced at their first meeting, when Gigi speaks to Gaston as a naive child would speak to a favorite uncle; Gaston returns the compliment, treating Gigi as he would a daughter, even threatening to spank her. When they go off to the ice palace together he orders champagne for himself and the turn-of-the-century French equivalent of a milkshake for her.

Now there is nothing problematic about an intergenerational relationship—unless, that is, the members of different generations suddenly develop a romantic interest in each other. And that, of course, is just what happens in Gigi. We even find out that Gigi's grandmother and Gaston's uncle are former lovers who might have been married were it not for his infidelity. There is something vaguely incestuous about the Gigi–Gaston relationship (since they could, indeed, be related by blood). One minute she is sitting in his lap, cheating at cards and munching on caramels, the next she is being eyed, invited, and embraced as a potential sexual partner. The point here is not that Gaston and Gigi violate society's prohibition against incest. In fact, quite to the contrary, their love affair serves to gloss over the very oppositions on which the incest taboo is based.

In many societies a specific ceremony or ritual process marks the passage of the child into adulthood. In American society more than any other, however, such rites of passage have been minimized, thus depriving society of a convenient way in which to handle the child/adult opposition. We act as if the dichotomy were a mutually exclusive one (for movie ratings, air fares, drinking and driving ages, and so forth). Children and adults are conceived as two diametrically opposed groups that allow no overlapping. Yet in order to reach maturity every individual within our society must violate the seemingly airtight partition separating the two categories. Children are not adults, yet at some indefinite point they become adults. It is this problematic relationship between childhood and adulthood that *Gigi* mediates, with the marriage model providing the resolution: the distinction between the generations is leveled by a merging of adult and childlike qualities within the couple. As Gigi for the first time gains the right to engage in adult activities, Gaston progressively refuses to carry out the petty duties to which adulthood condemns him. Now *he* eats the caramels he brings to Gigi, dances wildly around the room with Gigi and her grandmother, plays leap-frog on the beach at Trouville. While she is becoming an adult, he is recapturing some of the excitement of youth. Instead of simply making Gigi into an adult and thus creating an adult couple, the film operates a merger of the generations through the couple's marriage. In this sense Maurice Chevalier is a perfect symbol of the film's attempt to bridge the generation gap: he is both young and old, both living in the past and constantly creating new memories, glad that he's "Not Young Any More" and yet able to "Thank Heaven for Little Girls."

Gigi thus appears as a series of paired segments built around a fundamental duality, that of sexual differentiation, and two minor oppositions, beauty/riches and child/adult, both of which represent problematic dichotomies for society. Beauty and riches are treated like sex-linked chromosomes, with each quality allotted to a single sex. Yet both qualities are desirable; society's ideal individual has both. The child/adult pairing causes difficulties because it treats a dynamic, diachronic process as a stable, synchronic opposition. These problematic dichotomies are eventually resolved only when the resolution of the sexual duality (marriage) is used as a non-rational mediatory model for the attendant thematic oppositions, bringing together categories and individuals that seemed irreconcilably opposed. The only way for the same individual to enjoy both riches and beauty is to marry. The only way to save both childlike and adult qualities is through a merger, thus blurring the barrier between the generations, thereby erasing the spectre of incest.

Though extremely simple, this method must radically change our understanding of the American film musical. No longer can we point to the musical's conventional plot, call it gauche and episodic, and walk away satisfied. Once we have understood the dual-focus approach we easily grasp the importance of the many set pieces or production numbers which some see as cluttering the musical's program and interrupting its plot. The plot, we now recognize, has little importance to begin with; the oppositions developed in the seemingly gratuitous song-and-dance number, however, are instrumental in establishing the structure and meaning of the film. Only when we identify the film's constitutive dualities can we discover the film's function.

Seen as a cultural problem-solving device, the musical takes on a new and fascinating identity. Society is defined by a fundamental paradox: both terms of the oppositions on which it is built (order/liberty, progress/stability, work/entertainment, and so forth) are seen as desirable, yet the terms are perceived as mutually exclusive. Every society possesses texts which obscure this paradox, prevent it from appearing threatening, and thus assure the society's stability. The musical is one of the most important types of text to serve this function in American life. By reconciling terms previously seen as mutually exclusive, the musical succeeds in reducing an unsatisfactory paradox to a more workable configuration, a concordance of opposites. Traditionally, this is the function which society assigns to myth.

Indeed, we will not be far off the mark if we consider that the musical fashions a myth out of the American courtship ritual.

Notes

1   On the causal model of narrative structure, see Roland Barthes' influential introduction to *Communications* 8 (1966), entitled "Introduction à l'analyse des récits," as well as any current manual of literary terms, e.g., Sylvan Barnet, Morton Berman, and William Burto, *The Study of Literature: A Handbook of Critical Essays and Terms* (Boston: Little, Brown, 1960). On the notion of "classical Hollywood narrative" and its adoption of this causal model, see my "Classical Narrative Revisited: *Grand Illusion*," *Purdue Film Studies Annual* I (1976), 87–98.

2   Further theoretical considerations regarding dual-focus narrative may be found, with medieval examples, in my "Medical Narrative vs. Modern Assumptions: Revising Inadequate Typology," *Diacritics* 4 (1974), 12–19; "Two Types of Opposition and the Structure of Latin Saints' Lives," *Medievalia et Humanistica*, New Series 6 (1975), I–II; "Interpreting Romanesque Narrative: Conques and the *Roland*," *Olifant* 5, no. I (Oct. 1977), 4–28.

3   Raymond Bellour, "Segmenting/Analysing," in *Genre: The Musical*, ed. Rick Altman (London and Boston: Routledge and Kegan Paul, 1981), 102–33.

Busby Berkeley and the Backstage Musical

4

MARTIN RUBIN

The distinctive qualities of Busby Berkeley's production numbers are usually thought of as essentially cinematic, representing a decisive break from the stage-bound camera style of early talkie musicals. Equally important, and often overlooked, is the *continuity* between Berkeley's film style and preceding theatrical forms—particularly those forms deriving from a certain stage tradition, designated here the "Tradition of Spectacle." This is a primarily nineteenth-century tradition of popular entertainment: the tradition of P.T. Barnum's American Museum, the minstrel show, vaudeville, burlesque, the three-ring circus, and Buffalo Bill Cody's Wild West Show. It is a tradition based on creating feelings of abundance, variety, and wonder. Stressing aggregation rather than integration, it offers a fundamentally different approach to entertainment from those more modern forms that are oriented toward unity, continuity, and consistency.

The musical genre is in large part a holdover from such archaic entertainment forms. The genre remains in a state of unresolved suspension between spectacle and narrative, between aggregation and integration. A major aesthetic choice in a musical concerns the type of relationship it develops between these two sides of the genre.

During the early twentieth century, the form of musical theater in which the spectacle side flourished most was the revue. Like such earlier entertainment forms as vaudeville, burlesque, and minstrel show (especially its final section, known as the "olio"), the revue was a mélange of self-contained acts, with a general emphasis on music and comedy. However, the format of the revue was more solid and anchored than that of its predecessors, and it offered greater opportunities for spectacle.

On the one hand, the revue was not bound by the constraints of narrative consistency. The most elaborate production concepts could be fully indulged with a minimal regard for integration, plot sequence, or simple logic. A revue could mount a Parisian number and follow it with an Arabian number, without bothering to connect the two via any narrative framework.

On the other hand, a revue had available to it all the scenic and production resources of the mainstream dramatic stage. A vaudeville show might have as flexible a format as a revue, but, thrown together with little advance preparation and constantly on the move, it could not afford to be encumbered with ambitious, large-scale production elements.

The period of the First World War and the early 1920s was the heyday of the spectacular revue on Broadway (as well as in Paris and London). This era saw the flourishing of the great annual series, led by the *Ziegfeld Follies* and also including *The Passing Show, George White's Scandals,* the *Earl Carroll Vanities,* and the *Greenwich Village Follies.* Becoming increasingly unfashionable and insolvent, the big revues lumbered through the end of the 1920s, when the Crash and talking pictures sent them on the road to extinction.

During his career as a Broadway dance director (1925–30), Busby Berkeley first achieved fame for his work in musical comedies such as *A Connecticut Yankee* (1927), *Present Arms* (1928), and *Good Boy* (1928). His early acclaim was based on qualities remarkably different from those for which he is now known. By mid-1928, Berkeley had acquired a reputation as an innovator of intricate and offbeat rhythms, an apostle of new integrated musical comedy forms, and a leader in the break away from the more primitive traditions of external novelty, gratuitous spectacle, and regimented "precision dancing."

It was only in the latter part of his Broadway career, beginning with the *Earl Carroll Vanities of 1928* and continuing through *Pleasure Bound* (1929), *A Night in Venice* (1929), *Broadway Nights* (1929), *Ruth Selwyn's Nine Fifteen Revue* (1930), and *Lew Leslie's "International Revue"* (1930), that Berkeley began to work primarily in the revue form. It is at that point that one finds, recognizably and consistently, a predominance of the "Berkeleyesque"—i.e., those elements of spectacle that would later become identified with Berkeley's name, such as large-scale chorus formations, geometric patterns, and giant props.

Berkeley came on the scene of the big Broadway revue during the period of its overripe maturity and imminent decline. As it had done for the stage melodrama in the age of Griffith, the cinema gave a new lease on life to a waning theatrical form—in this case, the spectacular production number and the revue form that nurtured it. The first major wave of talking pictures in 1929–30 saw the screen inundated with musical films, more than in any other period of American film history. Some of the most important early movie musicals were pure plotless revues: *The Hollywood Revue of 1929, The Show of Shows* (1929), *King of Jazz* (1930), *Paramount on Parade* (1930). Others, such as *The Broadway Melody* (1929, winner of the Academy Award for Best Picture) and *Glorifying the American Girl* (1929, produced under the nominal supervision of Florenz Ziegfeld), employed backstage plots concerning the production of a spectacular stage revue.

The place of the plotless musical revue is an extremely minor one in the narrative-dominated history of American film, limited mainly to the anything-goes, music-crazy period of the conversion to sound. The temporary decline in popularity of the movie musical in 1931–32 brought with it a general demise of the pure plotless revue on the screen. However, this fact does not diminish the importance of the revue tradition in the development of Berkeleyesque spectacle on the screen. The revue impulse also extends to a range of adulterated forms that incorporate narrative while at the same time maintaining a pronounced autonomy of the musical passages. There are several precedents for this in the history of the musical theater.

Early revues, especially in the pre-1915 era, commonly incorporated flimsy plots to string together their specialty acts. This structure, although less popular during the era of the big annual revues, was still practicable enough to be employed when Berkeley worked on such late twenties Broadway revues as *A Night in Venice, Pleasure Bound,* and *Broadway Nights.*

Other lightly narrativized musical forms preceded the advent of the revue proper. One such form was the "tour-of-the-town" show, introduced to New York by the successful 1823 importation of Pierce Egan's London hit, *Tom and Jerry; or, Life in London. Tom and Jerry* centered loosely on a country cousin's adventures during a whirlwind tour of the big city. The show's peripatetic structure allowed for "rapidly shifting scenes, great diversity of city types and of character, and a large amount of consequent spectacle, song and dance."[1]

The success of the first *Tom and Jerry* show led to a number of variations on the tour-of-the-town format over the next half-century, including *A Glance at New York in 1848* (1848), *The World's Fair: or, London in 1851* (1851), *Apollo in New York* (1854), *Life in New York, or, Tom and Jerry on a Visit* (1856), *Round the Clock, or New York by Dark* (1872), and Harrigan & Hart's *The Donovans* (1875). The celebrated 1875 spectacle *Around the World in 80 Days* extended the tour-of-the-town format on a global scale. *Good Boy* (1928), one of the most important shows that Berkeley worked on during his Broadway period, was substantially in the tour-of-the-town tradition, utilizing the basic Tom-and-Jerry format of a country bumpkin's visit to the city as the pretext for a series of rapidly shifting scenes filled with song and dance.

A later form closely related to the tour-of-the-town was the "farce-comedy." This form employed a rudimentary plot, usually just enough to bring the characters into a setting, such as a theater or cabaret or ocean-liner salon, where they could watch and/or perform a program of specialty and musical acts, much like the olio of a minstrel show. Farce-comedies appeared regularly on the New York stage from 1879 until well into the 1890s. Charles Hoyt's *A Trip to Chinatown* (1891), one of the most successful and important nineteenth-century musicals, was largely derived from the farce-comedy mode.[2]

The final example of these narrative forms with revue tendencies is the backstage musical. The previous two forms—tour-of-the-town and farce-comedy—bring the narrative from someplace outside into a place or places where a show can be performed. The backstage musical, on the other hand, works primarily from the inside, originating from the venue where the show is made and centering on the relationships between the performers who make it.

The backstage musical has always been far more popular and important on the screen than on the stage. The predominance of the form in the film musical was established virtually from the beginning. *The Jazz Singer* (1927), the first movie musical, contains strong backstage elements. Several movie musicals of 1929—including *The Broadway Melody*, *Syncopation*, *Close Harmony*, *William Fox Movietone Follies of 1929*, *Glorifying the American Girl*, *Broadway*, *Broadway Babies*, *Dance of Life*, *Broadway Scandals*, *Gold Diggers of Broadway*, *On with the Show*, and *Footlights and Fools*—make significant use of the backstage structure.

It is remarkable how quickly the backstage form achieved maturity in the movie musical. *The Broadway Melody* (released in February, 1929) still holds up as a classic of its form. The lesser-known *On with the Show* (May, 1929) demonstrates a strikingly assured use of the show-within-a-show structure, resulting in an enhanced dynamism of the film's style. Even though it employs only a few camera movements, *On with the Show* rarely seems static in the manner of many early talkies, mainly because of the fluid interplay it sets up between onstage performance and backstage action through crosscutting and foreground/background relationships. Although not as accomplished as *On with the Show*, *Broadway* (May, 1929) uses its backstage framework (here applied to a nightclub setting) as an excuse to send the cinema's first bonafide camera-crane soaring self-indulgently skyward for every song-and-dance number. In these pioneer musical films, the backstage/show-within-a-show structure has a liberating effect on film technique and on opportunities for spectacle, setting a pattern that would be continued in the subsequent history of the movie musical.

The major Warner Brothers/Berkeley musicals of the early 1930s—*42nd Street* (1933), *Gold Diggers of 1933* (1933), *Footlight Parade* (1933), *Dames* (1934), and *Gold Diggers of 1935* (1935)—are widely acknowledged (especially the first three) to be pinnacles of the backstage form, which flourished throughout the 1930s at all studios. The backstage form continued to thrive in the 1940s, often overlapping with the musical-biography (e.g., *Rhapsody in Blue*, 1945; *Till the Clouds Roll By*, 1946) and wartime-rally (e.g., *Star-Spangled Rhythm*, 1942; *This is the Army*, 1943) modes. In the 1950s, it provided a refuge for the spectacular, semi-autonomous production number, even in the face of a growing trend toward integrated, plot-oriented musicals: "Broadway Rhythm" in *Singin' in the Rain* (1952), "Girl Hunt" in *The Band Wagon* (1953), "Born in a Trunk" in *A Star is Born* (1954). After 1960, the backstage form was used occasionally for spectacle-oriented purposes, often with a nostalgic or parodic inflection, as in *Funny Girl* (1968), *The Producers* (1968), *The Boy Friend* (1971), and *Funny Lady* (1975).

The backstage form's relationship to spectacle-oriented and integration-oriented modes of the musical is shifting and analogical; it may lean toward one mode or the other, or it may be open to both within a single film. For example, backstage musicals like *Glorifying the American Girl*, *Footlight Parade*, and *The Boy Friend* are mainly spectacle-oriented (i.e., based on a marked distinction—both qualitative and quantitative—between the discourse of the narrative and the discourse of the production numbers). On the other hand, *Babes in Arms* (1939), *The Barkleys of Broadway* (1949), and *Cabaret* (1972) are more integration-oriented (i.e., based on a tighter and more consistent relationship between numbers and narrative), while backstagers such as *Gold Diggers of 1935*, *Folies Bergère* (1935), and *The Band Wagon* are more open to both modes.

By the same token, forms such as tour-of-the-town, farce-comedy, and backstage musical are by no means mutually exclusive; they easily combine and blend into one another. For instance, the Warner Brothers/Berkeley classic *Footlight Parade* contains elements of all three forms: whirling passage from venue to venue (tour-of-the-town), progress of the narrative toward the place of serial, olio-like performances (farce-comedy), and the narrative's concentration on behind-the-scenes preparations and the relationships between show people (backstage musical).

The common denominator that seems to be essential to the establishment of spectacle in the backstage musical is primarily a *spatial* one rather than a musical or narrative one. The film must work to establish a space (or a series of homologous spaces) that are, to a certain extent, self-enclosed and independent of the surrounding narrative. This renders the space accessible to spectacular expansions and distortions that can be clearly in excess of the narrative without necessarily disrupting it. The main requirement is that this space be a special or bracketed space, adjoining the primary space of the narrative but not completely subordinated to it.

The strong demarcation of the space of the numbers as distinct from that of the offstage narrative is an essential ingredient of Berkeleyesque cinema. In the classic Warner Brothers/Berkeley musicals of the early 1930s, this spatial demarcation of the musical numbers takes on a special intensity and a special inflection. It is overdetermined in a very particular way.

In his 1974 article "Realism and the Cinema: Notes on Some Brechtian Theses," Colin MacCabe defines the classic realist text as one in which the various discourses in the text form a hierarchy. This hierarchy is surmounted by a dominant discourse that resolves or rationalizes all the other discourses and provides a frame of reference off which they can be read. In classical narrative cinema, this dominant discourse is the main narrative line.[3]

A simple example of the operation of the dominant discourse is the inclusion within the narrative of dream and fantasy sequences (comprising different "discourses" or modes of address), which are ultimately referred back to the dominant "reality" of the surrounding narrative framework. This type of discursive divagation might be kept more deliberately ambiguous or outright contradictory in other forms of cinema, such as European art cinema, politically radical cinema, and avant-garde cinema. MacCabe writes, 'The classic realist text cannot deal with the real as contradictory."[4]

The musical genre constitutes something of a special case within the institution of classical narrative cinema, because musicals are based on a central contradiction between the discourse of the narrative and the discourse of at least a significant portion of the musical numbers. The narrative and the musical numbers appear to be based on different laws or ground rules. This contradiction is never (or, at best, only weakly) resolved in the musical, so that the narrative's status as the dominant discourse remains excessively problematic.

One way of stating this concept is to say that many of the numbers in a musical are "impossible"—that is, impossible from the standpoint of the realistic discourse of the narrative. Typical examples of this impossibility include:

1   Gaylord Ravenal (Allan Jones) and Magnolia Hawks (Irene Dunne), meeting for the first time, spontaneously perform the beautiful duet, "Only Make Believe" (*Show Boat*, 1936).
2   Pete Peters (Fred Astaire) and Linda Keene (Ginger Rogers), previously established as having had no experience with roller skates, flawlessly execute the great roller-skate number, "Let's Call the Whole Thing Off" (*Shall We Dance* 1937).
3   Unknown singer Lily Mars (Judy Garland) stumbles accidentally onto a bandstand and immediately launches into a perfect vocal arrangement of "Tom, Tom, The Piper's Song" with the orchestra (*Presenting Lily Mars*, 1943).
4   Ninotchka (Cyd Charisse), a Russian envoy with no apparent composing talents or familiarity with popular music, bursts into the song, "Love's a Chemical Reaction, That's All" (*Silk Stockings*, 1957).

A possible working definition of the musical (at least in its traditional form) is: a musical is a film containing a significant proportion of musical numbers that are impossible—i.e., persistently contradictory in relation to the realistic discourse of the narrative. This definition is useful for distinguishing bonafide generic musicals from movies that are merely films with musical performances in them—films like *She Done Him Wrong* (1933), *Young Man with a Horn* (1950), *The Glenn Miller Story* (1954), *River of No Return* (1954), *Nashville* (1975), *Coal Miner's Daughter* (1980), and *Dirty Dancing* (1987). These films all feature several musical numbers, but the numbers do not create sustained problems in terms of a dominant realistic discourse. There are no (or hardly any) impossible numbers; the numbers can all be rationalized on the level of the narrative as professional stage performances or prerehearsed routines.[5]

In most traditional musicals, this requisite impossibility is concentrated along the transitional points between narrative and performance—that is, at those points where the character "feels a song (or dance) coming on" and bursts into spontaneous, purportedly unrehearsed, but perfectly executed performance. However, the classic Warner Brothers/ Berkeley musicals of the early 1930s are based on a significantly different configuration.

With a few exceptions (all of which occur in *Dames* and *Gold Diggers of 1935*, transitional films between the declining Warner Brothers/Berkeley and ascendant R-K-O/Astaire formulas), the numbers in the major Warner Brothers/Berkeley musicals do not create discursive difficulties in terms of the numbers' placement within the narrative. In other words, there is no impossibility at the points of transition from narrative to performance—no bursts into magically spontaneous, unrehearsed, perfectly and elaborately executed song-and-dance. In almost every case, the numbers in these films are realistically established as performances taking place on a theatrical stage, their previous origination painstakingly developed in the backstage plot, which shows (or, at least, frequently refers to) the preparation, rehearsal, and execution of those numbers. Even when Brad (Dick Powell) spontaneously sings "I've Got to Sing a Torch Song" to express his romantic feelings toward Polly (Ruby Keeler) in *Gold Diggers of 1933*, there is no rupture of discourse. It has already been clearly established in the narrative that Brad is a songwriter engaged to write tunes for the show and that he has been working on this and other songs. He performs the number seated at his piano, with a music sheet in front of him and a pencil, presumably still warm with inspiration, lodged behind his ear.

However, this does not mean that the numbers in the Warner Brothers/Berkeley musicals are realistically aligned in relation to the discourse of the narrative, with no consequent problematization or impossibility, and that these films therefore fall into the category of films with music rather than that of full-scale generic musicals. The major shift in discourse in these films occurs not in the transition from narrative to performance but within the performance itself.

Although the introduction of the numbers into the narrative in the Warner Brothers/Berkeley musicals creates no impossibility, the numbers themselves (as many commentators have noted) are blatantly and audaciously impossible in terms of the theatrical space in which they are supposedly taking place.

These impossibilities occur on two main levels: the level of scale and the level of effects. On the level of scale, the numbers create a constant and rapid progress into new and enormous spaces that could not all (and often individually) be contained on any theatrical stage, not even that of New York's mammoth Hippodrome. Examples include: the huge stucco pool in "By a Waterfall" (*Footlight Parade*), the enormously long bar set (complete with backroom opium den) and even more enormous street set in "Shanghai Lil" (*Footlight Parade*), the movement from street set to subway to abstract dream space in "I Only Have Eyes for You" (*Dames*), the infinitely expanding abstract spaces in "Dames" (*Dames*), the fifty-two pianos that appear out of nowhere in 'The Words Are in My Heart" (*Gold Diggers of 1935*), the Grand Central-sized nightclub (plus apartment house plus street sets) in "Lullaby of Broadway" (*Gold Diggers of 1935*).

In terms of effects, the numbers create configurations that are feasible only with a movie camera, on an editing table, or in a special effects lab, and that would be either impossible or incomprehensible on a theatrical stage. Examples include: the kaleidoscopic overhead shots and location-shifting concealed cuts in many Berkeley numbers, the underwater shots in "By a Waterfall," the crowds that "all disappear from view" in "I Only Have Eyes for You," the reverse-motion effects in "Dames" and "Lullaby of Broadway," the face of Wini Shaw looming up to fill the screen and then dissolving into the New York skyline in "Lullaby of Broadway."

Spatial elements are exactly aligned with discursive elements in the Warner Brothers/Berkeley backstage musicals. Unlike in a typical film musical, the impossible discourse of the numbers does not encroach on the realistic discourse of the narrative. This distinction is then doubled and reinforced in spatial terms: performance space is kept separate from narrative space, with each having its own qualities, laws, and modes of address. The rigid alignment of performance space and performance discourse imparts to the musical numbers a revue-like autonomy, freed from the demands of even the most tenuous narrative-to-numbers consistency. This allows full, unrestrained indulgence and extension of the impulse toward spectacle, toward the Berkeleyesque.

In effect, Berkeley is allowed to operate his own musical sideshow within the context of a narrative film. As stated (undoubtedly with some exaggeration) in a 1970 interview/article by William Murray in the *New York Times*,

> Berkeley himself never cared much about the story line and regarded it merely as a convenient skeleton on which to flesh out his fantasies, much in the manner of Rossini draping his gorgeous solos, duets and ensembles all over the framework of whatever hack libretto an impresario handed him. "I did my numbers and the director did the story," Berkeley recalls. "Sometimes I'd even forget who was directing."[6]

This central strategy of the Warner Brothers/Berkeley musicals can be contrasted with that of the next dominant mode of the movie musical: the Fred Astaire/Ginger Rogers musicals produced at R-K-O, especially those directed by Mark Sandrich. In the Warner Brothers/Berkeley musicals of the early 1930s, the world of the numbers is compartmentalized and set apart from the world of the narrative. This separation occurs not only spatially and discursively, but also economically, presenting a world of opulence and excess in contrast to the world of struggling chorus girls and Depression hard times in the narrative passages. In the R-K-O/Astaire musicals of the mid- and late 1930s, the world of the musical numbers and the world of the narrative are made more homogenous and more continuous with each other.

This is accomplished by two complementary strategies: (1) by making the world of the musical numbers more natural and restrained (rather than a radically excessive world with its own laws of time and space, à la Berkeley), and (2) by making the world of the narrative more artificial and stylized. The former effect is accomplished by a reduction of scale and a naturalizing of musical performance style. The latter effect is enhanced by the use of polished dialogue and syncopated line deliveries that seem almost as stylized as song lyrics. In addition, everyday activities and environments are sometimes denaturalized by being set to choreographed rhythms (e.g., the "Walking the Dog" scenes in 1937's *Shall We Dance*, or the rhythmic engine-room pistons mimicked by Astaire's dance steps in the "Slap That Bass" number from the same film). As a result, the gap between the performance world and the narrative world, though not eliminated, is narrowed and smoothed over.

Performance space in the R-K-O/Astaire musicals is not confined to a separate, compartmentalized domain such as a theatrical stage. Instead, any place becomes a potential performance space: a roller-skating rink, a bedroom, a nightclub, a park, a ship's deck, a city street, a foggy woods, a ferry boat. Transitions from narrative to performance are stylized and impossible in the I-feel-a-song-coming-on mode, leading to an encroachment of performance discourse into narrative discourse. However, this discursive rupture is then smoothed over by the consistencies of tone, style, and scale between the narrative and the musical-performance passages. Mark Sandrich, the crucial director involved in the series (Freeland, Seiter, Stevens, and Potter were never able to match Sandrich's impeccably superficial touch), disliked numbers that were cut off from the narrative in the Warner Brothers/Berkeley manner. For instance, "The Continental" in *The Gay Divorcee* (1934) was originally conceived as a totally self-enclosed Berkeley-like spectacle, but Sandrich insisted on breaking up the number and interweaving it with narrative passages.[7]

In the R-K-O/Astaire musicals, the non-musical passages are virtually as stylized and artificial as the musical numbers, and the two blend together into a smoothly syncopated surface—an unbroken, swanky, bon ton world of luxury hotels, ocean-liners, deco nightclubs, and country estates. In the key Warner Brothers/Berkeley musicals, the production numbers are transcendent episodes in an otherwise gritty, wisecracking, hard-bitten Depression context.

The segregation of the production numbers from the body of the film occurs on three interlocking and mutually reinforcing levels in the Warners/Berkeley musicals of the early 1930s: narrative (they bear little relation to the surrounding plot), spatial (the space of the musical numbers is a separate domain from that of the narrative), and discursive (the impossible discourse of the musical numbers does not impinge on the realistic discourse of the narrative). Largely liberated from the necessities of serving plot, characterization, and cause-and-effect logic, with little or no obligation to maintaining the consistency of a fictional world, spectacle in Berkeley's numbers becomes an end in itself. Of crucial importance to the creation of Berkeleyesque spectacle is a sense of gratuitousness, extravagance, over-indulgence, flaunting—of display for the sake of display.

This notion of segregated, autonomous spectacle extends, in Berkeley's case, not only to mise-en-scène elements such as props, sets, and chorus girls, but also to the camera itself. In effect, Berkeley *spectacularizes the camera*. Just as the structure of the Berkeleyesque musical severs the domain of the production numbers from that of the narrative, the camera itself is liberated from the demands of narrativity (and, to a degree, from the demands of any form of subordinate expressivity) in order to assert its own presence as an element of autonomous display—that is, of spectacle. As Jean-Louis Comolli has written, Berkeley's cinema is a "cinema that resolves itself totally into spectacle, these images, these shots, these scenes . . . have no other function, no other meaning and no other existence but visual beauty."[8]

This concept of "spectacularization of the camera" refers not only to the camera apparatus itself. It also applies more generally to those situations where realistic consistency is violated for the sake of producing a cinematic effect. These include the intrusion into onstage numbers of purely cinematic configurations, such as trick cuts, reverse motion, and patterns visible only from certain camera angles. Also involved are those situations where the camera osten-tatiously asserts its presence (for instance, through an especially elaborate and massive camera movement) in a manner that seems totally arbitrary or, at least, greatly in excess of any possible function of displaying the performance, expressing the number's "inner feeling," and so on.

Technique in classical cinema is subordinated to and largely absorbed into the narrative. The Berkeleyesque camera, in contrast, affirms its power to inscribe itself directly into the film as an element of spectacular design. Editing, camera angle, camera movement, optical effects, and other cinematic devices are freed from the constraints of realistic, narrativized, cause-and-effect discourse and become liberated elements of play and display. Cut loose from the space and discourse of the narrative, they are free to soar into the realms of pure design and abstraction. This helps to account for the frequently drawn parallels between Berkeley's numbers and largely non-narrative modes of cinema such as abstract, surrealist, and avant-garde film. More crucial, however, was Berkeley's connection to a waning mode of popular entertainment. His contribution to the evolution of the movie musical can be seen not so much as the replacement of a theatrical mode by a cinematic one, but as the *extension* and *expansion* of a theatrical tradition—the Tradition of Spectacle—to include specifically cinematic elements.

Notes

1 George Odell, *Annals of the New York Stage*, quoted in David Bordman, *American Musical Theatre: A Chronicle* (New York: Oxford University Press, 1978), p. 7.

2 Bordman, p. 114.

3 Colin MacCabe, "Realism and the Cinema: Notes on Some Brechtian Theses," *Screen* 15, no. 2 (Summer 1974): 7–12.

4 Ibid., p. 12.

5 This definition is not airtight; it seems to work best at what might be called the musical genre's "center," both historically and qualitatively. It does not apply so well to some films—such as *A Star is Born* (1954), *Cabaret* (1972), and *All That Jazz* (1979)—that are included by consensus in the genre's canon. However, these examples (at least) can be distinguished by the fact that they are all explicitly "metamusicals"—i.e., films that reflect critically on the musicals/Hollywood/entertainment apparatus from positions that are (or at least purport to be) outside it to a certain extent.

6 William Murray, "The Return of Busby Berkeley," *New York Times Magazine*, 2 March 1969: 51–3.

7 Arlene Croce, *The Fred Astaire and Ginger Rogers Book* (New York: E.P. Dutton, 1972; reprint ed., New York: Vintage Books, 1977), p. 36.

8 Jean-Louis Comolli, "Dancing Images: Busby Berkeley's Kaleidoscope," *Cahiers du Cinéma* no. 174 (January 1966), reprinted in *Cahiers du Cinéma in English* no. 2 (1966): 24.

Notes:

PART TWO

GENDERED SPECTACLES

Introduction

As a genre of spectacle, the musical is renowned for the asymmetry with which it represents sexual difference in production numbers, encouraging the spectatorial position of a male voyeur. In backstage stories, directors, songwriters, and spectators are typically men, whereas women are objectified as the show, with the all-female chorus line, dressed in extravagant costumes, often made inseparable from the set. For example, "Cooking Up a Show," the opening number of *Billy Rose's Diamond Horseshoe* (1945), introduces showgirl after showgirl as different "herbs" and "spices," all reduced to ingredients in a nightclub revue; overseeing this "tasty" ensemble is the master of ceremonies, "chef" William Gaxton, whose culinary masterpiece is Betty Grable. But perhaps no musicals better illustrate, not to say exploit, the blatant display of the female body than Busby Berkeley's. For many critics and viewers, his overhead camera shots of women arranged to form abstract patterns epitomize the genre's ability to eroticize the female body, fragmenting and fetishizing it beyond recognition.

However, does it necessarily follow that, even in a Berkeley musical, the genre simply reproduces without problematizing a patriarchal ideology which subordinates the female body to the gaze of a male voyeur? The essays in this section argue for a more complex understanding of how the musical represents gender in spectacle. In "Sexual Economics: *Gold Diggers of 1933*," Patricia Mellencamp's analysis complements what Rubin claims about the aggregate form of a Berkeley musical but she is more attentive to the gender politics arising from the tension between narrative and the numbers' spectacle. According to Mellencamp, sexual difference organizes many other differences to sustain what she refers to as the textual economy of *Gold Diggers*. But this does not result in a unified text that successfully manages the ideological representation of gender. Rather, she examines how the film's narrative speaks to its historical setting in the Depression; although its closure is regulated by an ideology centered on the family through the formation of couples, the narrative establishes a counter-movement based in female friendships that trade on another system of currency: same-sex bonds. The Berkeley production numbers, by contrast, define heterosexuality through the female body, which they equate with technology and capital exchange. As a result, Mellencamp emphasizes, the film constructs a dual address that implies a doubling as well as differentiation of spectatorial investments according to gender and that epitomizes the genre's dominant representational strategies for containing female sexuality—the problematic of the *Gold Diggers* narrative, the preoccupation of its numbers.

Mellencamp's reading of *Gold Diggers* concludes that this musical conforms to the Depression era's dominant ideology even when the film exposes the contradictions reinscribing it; her analysis, moreover, tends to locate ideological conservation in the numbers and ideological disturbance in the narrative. In "Pre-Text and Text in *Gentlemen Prefer Blondes*," Lucie Arbuthnot and Gail Seneca treat another musical noted for its outright exploitation of female spectacle, but they reread it as a feminist text with the purpose of discovering how films supposedly conforming to the dominant ideology can nonetheless yield pleasures for female audiences. The authors look beyond what they call the "pre-text" of *Blondes*—that is, the generic conventions privileging a narrative of heterosexual romance as supported by a patriarchal gaze at the spectacle of Marilyn Monroe and Jane Russell—and discover in a close reading of the "text" a matrix of signs that resist the objectification of women and promote female friendship over heterosexual romance. Their reading draws implicit attention to the similarity of *Blondes* and *Gold Diggers*: the former film also has a golddigger plot stressing female bonds, at times its numbers parody the Berkeley style, and the numbers, primarily stacked in sequences at the beginning and toward the end of the film, are likewise segmented from the main narrative. However, in contrast with Mellencamp's analysis of the way narrative and number achieve diametrically opposed purposes in *Gold Diggers*, Arbuthnot and Seneca disregard form to find throughout the text of *Blondes* fissures in the ideological structure which the pre-text imports.

The first two pieces examine musicals centering on showgirls, that is, women who make their living performing in stage shows for the benefit of men. In "'Feminizing' the Song-and-Dance Man: Fred Astaire and the Spectacle of Masculinity in the Hollywood Musical," Steven Cohan examines what happens when a male performer turns upside down the supposed orthodoxy according to which the genre defines sexual difference by reducing women to spectacle. Although Astaire's musicals follow plot lines that reestablish the dominance of the male over the female, as spectacle his dance numbers disrupt this hierarchical arrangement. As Cohan demonstrates, an Astaire number, whether solo or duet, halts or exceeds the linearity of narrative to put the dancer in the position conventionally occupied by a female performer like Monroe or a Berkeley showgirl, but not with the effect of effeminizing him. On the contrary, in heightening a comparable theatricality, Astaire's dancing stages an alternative expression of masculinity in relation to spectacle because it is not reliant upon the support of narrative for its implications of agency and desire. Using *Royal Wedding* (1951) and *Silk Stockings* (1957) to illustrate, Cohan analyzes how the numbers in these films reinforce the unconventional masculine persona which Astaire projected as the leading male dancer in musicals. This discussion resists the premise of the integrated musical as another means of reading against the logic of what Arbuthnot and Seneca call the "pre-text" of heterosexual romance and male objectification of the female, which has determined how spectacle has been presumed to function in representing sexual difference for the genre.

Sexual Economics

Gold Diggers of 1933

PATRICIA MELLENCAMP

Containing social turmoil—containing women

On October 24, 1929, the U.S. stock market crashed. The crash resulted in a 1932 estimated unemployment figure of 13 million, out of a population of 123 million. Wages were 33 percent lower than in 1929. In spite of this decline in income, movie attendance was estimated at between 60 to 75 million per week.[1] The regular audience was attracted to codified genres (as well as sequels, series, and remakes) and the distinct styles of the five major studios.

To paraphrase one critic:

> At Warner Brothers . . . films were made for and about the working class. Their musicals, born of the depression, combined stories of hard-working chorus girls and ambitious young tenors with opulent production numbers. . . . Lighting was low key. . . . Cutting corners became an art. Stars were contracted at low salaries. . . . Directors worked at an incredible rate, producing as many as five features per year. The basic film at Warners . . . was a melodrama . . . which ran for 70 minutes. Pace was more than Warner's trademark—it was a necessity.[2]

If one momentarily accepts the undocumented assertion that Warner Brothers's films were made "for and about the working class," raising issues of address and enunciation, then labor's struggle to organize in the 1930s would be a critical context for reception.

Therefore, a few details are in order. Unions were just beginning to gain power and demand benefits. This was the era before Social Security, unemployment and health insurance, minimum wage, and other labor laws that prescribed working hours and conditions. Demonstrations by the employed occurred around the country, often involving violent encounters with the police. For example, thirty-five thousand demonstrators for unemployment insurance in New York were attacked by police, as were ten thousand protesters in Cleveland. On March 7, 1932, three thousand protesters marched on the Ford factory, demanding jobs. Police, armed with pistols and machine guns, fired; four protesters died and were declared Communists. In Toledo a large crowd of the unemployed marched on grocery stores and took food.[3]

The fear of the overthrow of capitalism, like the "red scares" of the twenties, was real. The Soviet revolution had occurred less than two decades earlier. The New Deal, with such versions of socialist practice as federally funded corporations (e.g., the Tennessee Valley Authority), helped to elect Franklin D. Roosevelt president. He enacted Social Security in 1934–35. Unions gained benefits, with collective bargaining granted in 1935.

The signs of economic chaos and poverty (like street people in the 1990s) visibly exposed the gap between rich and poor. An estimated seventy thousand children were homeless, living in shantytowns. William Wellman's film *Wild Boys of the Road* (Warner Brothers, 1933) portrayed their plight. Rather than interpreting these events as economically and socially determined, thereby questioning capitalism, some members of Congress viewed them as personal—inspired and instigated by Communists—and created a committee to investigate radical activities. Thus began the House Un-American Activities Committee, which would investigate Hollywood, particularly the screenwriters' guild, in the 1940s under its infamous acronym, HUAC. (It should be pointed out that Hollywood unionized early and thoroughly, with the exception of studio executives and producers; by the mid-1930s, there were guilds for writers, actors, directors, and cinematographers. Along the way, Prohibition was repealed in 1933, and the Catholic Legion of Decency was founded in 1934 to "select" [censor] movies for Catholic audiences.)

The 1933 Warner Brothers film *Gold Diggers of 1933* was listed by *Motion Picture Herald* as the second top moneymaker of 1933 (another Ruby Keeler-Dick Powell/Busby Berkeley extravaganza, *42nd Street*, was third). *Gold Diggers* is symptomatic of these issues of unemployment and homelessness. To start, there is the irony of the first spectacle, the musical number "We're in the Money." This is followed by the initial apartment sequence of unemployed chorus girls with the montage of unpaid bills and the theft of milk.

The film concludes with the "Remember My Forgotten Man" spectacle, which takes us on a theatrical 'Hale's Tour' of recent U.S. history. In this number, demarcating wipes, like stage curtains, separate the acts of history. Scenes of soldiers marching off to war transform into war's aftermath of wounded, bleeding, bandaged veterans of World War I, then segue into the breadlines and soup kitchens of the postwar years. This number explains the Depression as a product of World War I. As Carol (Joan Blondell) sings: "Remember my forgotten man. You put a rifle in his hand. You sent him away. You shouted hip-hooray. Just look at him today."

The film begins with the erotic spectacle of women as interchangeable with money in "We're in the Money": "Gone are my blues and gone are my tears. I've got good news to shout in your ears. The long lost dollar has come back to the fold. With silver you can turn your dreams to gold". It concludes with the dark blues of "Remember My Forgotten Man" and its backlit, tiered set of marching soldiers (which rhymes the women's silhouetted dressing rooms in "Pettin' in the Park").

Other signs of social unrest strangely permeate the opulently surreal world of the film. The circulating presence of police throughout the film is, perhaps, the most displaced image. The sheriff interrupts (censors) and stops "We're in the Money." This initiates the narrative pattern of interruption and delay of both story and show. He and his men literally strip the women of their costumes. Policemen are the roller-skating male chorus of "Pettin' in the Park," with Trixie, the comedienne (Aline MacMahon), cross-dressed as a policeman (although wearing a flower in her lapel). A policeman on the stage of "Forgotten Man" confronts a "bum," whom Carol reveals to be a war veteran. Near the end of the film, Barney, the producer, reveals the sheriff to be an out-of work actor. Thus police are rendered harmless, their image contained but still suggestive.

Alluding to Prohibition, Gigolo Eddy's guitar case (which is, like the violins in "Shadow Waltz," a female emblem) contains booze, which he dumps behind a backstage flat when the sheriff interrupts "We're in the Money." Two prohibitions are equated: women's bodies and sex with the illegality of alcohol. The speakeasies where Trixie and Carol seduce J. Lawrence Bradford and Fanuel Peabody also refer to Prohibition. Once the Legion of Decency began to condemn certain films for Catholic audiences in 1934, the scanty costumes and virtual nakedness of the "Pettin' in the Park" sequence were censored in the film's sequel.

Like classical Hollywood film and musical comedy in general, the film operates to proclaim, then contain, female sexuality. It moves from single women (and men, separated by class) to a triad of perfectly paired, married (classless) couples. This process takes women out of the erotic spectacle (and perhaps also the labor market) and into marriage and respectability. There is a moral for women in the last sequence: without men (or capitalism), women (the working class), including a black woman singing the blues, will be old, haggard, alone, and poor. For women, being without a man is indeed a barren fate, worse than death or high-contrast German expressionist lighting. For women, "alone" means living without men. Female friendship doesn't count.

Together and united, as they are in this film, women are not enough. They do not have access, except through sexual wiles, to the means of production, in this case financing for the show. They have the talent and the brains but not the bucks or the power. As the lyrics of "Remember My Forgotten Man" inform us: "And once he used to love me. I was happy then. He used to take care of me. Won't you bring him back again? 'Cuz ever since the world began, a woman's got to have a man. Forgetting him, you see, means you're forgetting me, like my forgotten man." Warner Brothers's explanation for social and economic ills resembles Congress's conspiracy theory, only with rampant female sexuality (elided with the effects of World War I on the family) rather than Communism as the guilty party.

Therefore, the film's solution to the Depression, unemployment, and unbridled, anxiety-provoking female sexuality is the family. This is narratively figured as marriage to Back Bay Boston investment bankers. Upper-class men save the show from bankruptcy with Brad's critical check of fifteen thousand dollars and his reluctant agreement to perform in the spectacle. This is paralleled by J. Lawrence's ten-thousand-dollar payment to Carol for nonsex, a check later transformed into a wedding gift. Thus the inequities of both class and gender are collapsed into marital salvation. The film equates marriage and the couple—the happy ending—with capitalism. By uniting the working-class chorus girls (Polly [Ruby Keeler] tells us in the upper-class nightclub scene on the balcony that her father was a postman) with upper-class, inherited wealth in a backstage triple whammy of Polly and Brad, Trixie and Fanuel, and Carol and J. Lawrence, presumably the nation will be restored.

Within the film's economy, the only significant "difference" is sexual difference. Other cultural, social differences—the inequities of class, race, politics, economics, and age—are secondary. While the female lead characters are represented as working-class, one must question the film's address to the working class; but the film addresses itself differently to women and men. Choreographer Berkeley's spectacles are addressed to the male spectator, literally a voyeur or fetishist, whereas the narrative sections directed by Mervyn Leroy demonstrate the pleasures of female friendship, the solidarity among Trixie, Carol, and Polly. These lively friends are infinitely more interesting, idiosyncratic, and clever than the wimpy men, particularly Warren William (who, as J. Lawrence, has top billing, albeit less screen time) and the eager tenor Dick Powell, in this instance portraying Brad Roberts or Robert Bradford.

(That the two investment bankers are parodied must also be taken into account. J. Lawrence and Fanuel are naive and inept, hardly savvy corporate scions. They are shown at their club, not at work. They are the representatives of inherited rather than earned wealth. What the film does value through the chorus girls and the character of Brad Roberts is working for a living.)

While the narrative is propelled by these fast-talking, inventive women, in the spectacles (which freeze the story's advance) they become identical, anonymous, Freudian symbols. In fact, their masquerade serves to make them so identical that Ruby Keeler, the film's star, is unnoticed in the anonymous chorus line of "We're in the Money." In one reading, the end functions as a resolute, albeit "logical," containment of women, which includes separating them. Or one can imagine marital rescue after a spending spree on luxury items as a fantasy of the historical women in the audience—with few other options available to them in the 1930s. The women use men's false (stereotypical) notions about women's character to get what they want. Masquerade and the double standard become story, with the audience keyed in on the deception, told from the women's point of view. The marital inevitability is manipulated by the women for economic pleasure and gain as much as, or more than, romance.

The narrative is thus an address and an appeal to women—who are let in on the joke, which is on J. Lawrence and Fanuel. These chorus girls are not stupid, inexperienced characters, particularly Trixie: "It's the Depression, dearie." However, knowledge, which the women have about men, is not power; money is. [. . .]

Techno-Freud: specialization, standardization, seduction

Psychoanalysis permeates *Gold Diggers*, particularly the symbolism of Berkeley's scenes. This is not surprising for 1933, given the influx of German and Austrian expatriates who were moving to Los Angeles and into the film industry. Many films had personal psychiatrists as consultants, often listed in the film's credits. Going to an analyst became de rigueur in the industry. The role of Hollywood (and Hitchcock) in popularizing psychoanalysis is incalculable, second only to that of feminist film theory and Woody Allen.

Taylorism, so important to studio business practices (as Janet Staiger's essays have shown), also resonates throughout *Gold Diggers*. Taylor's functional, scientific efficiency studies of management included timed descriptions of the body as (working in tandem with) a machine. The film echoes the assembly line, an invention of mass-production technology, in the symmetrical rows of matching chorus girls and the parading soldiers on conveyer belts in "Forgotten Man."

Like the Hollywood studio structure, with the vertically integrated monopolies of the Big Five, factory principles of standardization (and for the studios, specialization) operate in Berkeley's female formations of assembly-line symmetry, harmony, anonymity, perfection. The chorus lines are a combination of Freud's sexual fetish and Marx's commodity fetish, linking up with mechanical studies of human labor but taken into pleasure and leisure, like the history of cinema itself—popular culture as the flip side of industrial culture. The representation of women (and men) as types, for the show within the film and as characters, details the process of specialization: Polly, the sweet, young ingenue; Trixie, the older comedienne; Carol, the tough, ageless, sexy woman with the heart of gold; and Fay, the true gold digger. The changing physical fashions of women's bodies in the nineteen-twenties, thirties, and forties document the standardization of these types. The three couples represent three stages of romance, a marital typology that accords with character traits: Polly and Brad represent young, innocent, virginal love; Carol and J. Lawrence, middle-aged sexual desire and skepticism; and Trixie and Fanuel, asexual, older companionship.

Significantly, because all the women are young, the age of the man defines each relationship, suggesting that our interpretation of the women is, to a degree, determined by the men. The film upholds the double standard of chronological difference: women must forever be young, while men can vary in age and even grow old. The pairing of the older man and the younger woman is the norm for cinema, rarely the reverse.

Specialization also describes the film's (and Hollywood's) conditions of production, detailed in the credits according to department heads (design by Anton Grot and Carl Jules Weyl; costumes by John "Orry" Kelly; camera work by Gaetano Gardio, Barney McGill, and Sol Polito; music by Harry Warren and Al Dubin—mentioned in the film by Barney), with direction divided between Mervyn Le Roy, a contract studio director (like the rest of studio employees, on a monthly salary) who made over fifty films in eight years, and Berkeley. Standardization operates in the conventions of classical Hollywood style and genres, in this case the conventions of the musical comedy (with motifs and figures circulating throughout both spectacle and narrative segments, gluing them together despite their vastly different 'styles'). I examine this later in greater depth.

That these are capitalist, corporate practices is not without implication. In fact, the Berkeley sequences are spectacles of the glories of capitalist technique and hence visual demonstrations of the narrative—salvation via investment bankers. (This is a reference to and parody of the role such investment bankers as Waddill Catchings played in Warner Brothers's massive and expensive conversion to sound in 1927–28). Siegfried Kracauer argues this connection in a 1931 essay (whose thesis is later picked up in Bazin's essay on pinups), "Girls and Crisis":[4]

> In that postwar era, in which prosperity appeared limitless and which could scarcely conceive of unemployment, the girls were artificially manufactured in the USA and exported to Europe by the dozens. Not only were they American products; at the same time they demonstrated the greatness of American production. . . . When they formed an undulating snake, they radiantly illustrated the virtues of the conveyor belt; when they tapped their feet in fast tempo, it sounded like business, business; when they kicked their legs with mathematic precision, they joyously affirmed the progress of rationalization; and when they kept repeating the same movements without ever interrupting their routine, one envisioned an uninterrupted chain of autos gliding from the factories into the world, and believed that the blessings of prosperity had no end. (pp. 63–64)

Regarding the Rockettes and their sanitized routines, perhaps Kracauer is right. Equally, in the midst of the real and the film's Depression, Berkeley's scenes suggest that "prosperity had no end." Rather than operating technology, women are cogs of and for technology; like the machine they are submissive, dominated, usually by a male leader who can mold many into a singular uniformity. Although often treated as idiosyncratic and unique, Berkeley's girls were not new or unique. However, their B-movie versions demonstrate just how good and complex Berkeley's kaleidoscopic infinities are. Just see, for example, the chorus in *Stand Up and Cheer* (Fox, 1934): lead-footed chorus girls strut in costumes that just hang rather than reveal, awkwardly trying to move, let alone dance, with frontal, static, mid-height camera placement, virtually no moving camera shots, and editing void of any metric or rhythmic patterns.

Berkeley's scenes also celebrate technologies other than the body (or the female body as technology, a technology of gender in perfect historical harmony with cinema technology), including, in "Shadow Waltz," electricity in the neon-lighted violins and huge violin formation. Along with turning women into objects fraught with a Freudian symbolism so crassly obvious as to become parody and camp, his scenes depict the wonders of film technology and its ability to transform space and time—a very modern concern of painters, novelists and philosophers in the early twentieth century. As [Lucy] Fischer writes: "If the geography of the numbers is unchartable, their temporality is unmeasurable."[5] Berkeley combines the oldest technology, sex, with the modernist technology par excellence, cinema.

Carolyn Marvin argues in "Dazzling the Multitude" that around the turn of the century, engineers and entrepreneurs believed that electricity, particularly in manufacturing and transportation, would "heal the breach between classes . . . democratize luxury and eliminate conflict based on competition for scarce resources."[6] (The breach, it was at that time argued, was fostered by the inequities of steam power. The modernist belief that technology will bring social progress is an old and ongoing argument that can ignore social and political issues.) Along with its role in industry, electricity, like the automobile and cinema, was a novelty, spectacle, and a medium of entertainment. Electrical light shows were popular outdoor events, with elaborate performances against the sky at world's fairs and expositions.

However, even more directly pertinent as a forerunner to the electrical virtuosity of cinema is Marvin's description of the 1884 Electric Girl Lighting Company. They offered "to supply illuminated girls" for occasions and parties. These "fifty-candle power" girls were "fed and clothed by the company" (p. 260) and could be examined in the warehouse by prospective customers seeking waitresses or hostesses. Electric girls, their bodies adorned with light, made appearances at public entertainments as "ornamental objects" and performed electrical feats in revues. The term *ornamental* echoes Kracauer's use of the concept of mass ornament in relation to mass culture (a model arguing the existence of a mirroring relationship between the spectacle and the spectator).

What is intriguing to me is the persistent contradiction between yoking the female body to either nature or technology, presumably opposite interpretations. As I argued in 1981 regarding *Metropolis* (Fritz Lang, Germany, 1926), the historical equation of the female body with technology, including sex, represents the female body as a special effect, one that suggests both the danger and the fascination of spectacle, an aberration that must be held in check. However, whether as old-fashioned nature or modern high tech, the technology of gender functions to keep women in line, to serve their masters.[7]

As in most musicals, Berkeley combined techniques of the stage with cinematic technique. His girls were the modern, abstracted, often faceless descendants of revues, vaudeville (for example, Earl Carroll's "Vanities"), and, in England, music hall. Their exhausted reincarnations parade today at the Folies Bergère in Paris, aging women with sagging breasts; strut as imitations in glitzy Las Vegas shows; perform energetic holiday shows for families at Radio City Music Hall; do TV commercials for Leggs panty-hose; and appear on old TV reruns as the June Taylor dancers with Jackie Gleason.

As the story is told by John Lahr, the Rockettes were the U.S. version of England's Tiller Girls. They first performed in St. Louis in 1925 as the Missouri Rockets: "Sixteen dancers were strung out across the stage like beads on a necklace: thirty-two hands, thirty-two legs moving as one."[8] This sounds remarkably like Berkeley, as quoted by Fischer: "My sixteen regular girls were sitting on the side waiting; so after I picked the three girls I put them next to my special sixteen and they matched, just like pearls" (Fischer, p. 4). Russell Markert was the inventive, U.S. entrepreneur who "put the shortest dancers at the outside of the line and the tallest in the center to create the illusion of uniform size" (Lahr, p. 83). Installed in 1927 at the Roxy, the number of girls expanded to the thirty-two Roxiettes. then they moved to Radio City Music Hall they were renamed the Rockettes. Conformity was their forte; their "style was efficient, dehumanized, perfect, the last vestige of Twenties Bauhaus design in human form" (Lahr, p. 83).

The key was group discipline and submission. The worst thing a Rockette could do was "kick out," literally "step out of line." "If any girl got wide in the hips or thigh, I'd have the costume department measure her size . . . I'd tell her to reduce back to her original Rockette measurements" (Lahr, p. 83). Rockettes were not allowed to tan and were of the same color, white. Markert was the coach until he retired in 1971, the dance, with the trademark kick that still elicits applause, is the same, as is their rigid, upright posture and style of movement. They don't bump or wriggle (Lahr, p. 83). Berkeley's "girls" did not need to dance: "I never cared whether a girl knew her right foot from her left so long as she was beautiful" (Fischer, p. 6).

Interestingly enough, the analyses of various dance-line daddies are almost identical fantasies of power over women; their commentaries are as uniform as the precision female lines they order. A 1940 interview with Earl Carroll, remembering his "Vanities," could have been spoken by Markert or Berkeley (quoted in Fischer's opening epigram: "I love beautiful girls and I love to gather and show many beautiful girls with regular features and well-made bodies"):

> I soon realized that the most exciting thing one could put on a stage was a breathtakingly beautiful girl. She did not need to know how to dance or even sing . . . there were no talent requirements. . . . They are assembled on the stage and then segregated according to height. Then in lines of twenty, they step forward, count off, make quarter turns and face forward. . . . The following points of beauty are given careful consideration: color and texture of hair, brilliancy and size of eyes, regularity of teeth, general coloring, texture of skin, formation of hands and feet, posture and personality. . . . There are times (and this was particularly true during the war) when it was necessary to engage girls who do not have all the necessary qualifications. We replace them when it is possible.[9]

Carroll details an inch-by-inch ideal: a six-inch wrist, a twelve-inch neck, a nineteen-and-a-half-inch thigh, and a nine-inch ankle. He was also, in his way, a cultural historian: "Turnover is much greater than it used to be; those with talent go on to the films and those less gifted soon settle down into a quiet matrimony." As in the films, women have two choices: show-girl or wife and mother.

There is something truly perverse about creating beauty through precision control that abstracts women's bodies. I am reminded of Freud's remarks on beauty derived from vision, stated just prior to his discussion of scopophilia (the sexual pleasure of sight), and the relation between scopophilia with its active/passive components and Foucault's model of the panopticon with the see/seen dyad:

The progressive concealment of the body . . . keeps sexual curiosity awake. This curiosity seeks to complete the sexual object by revealing its hidden parts. [Think of the midget raising the curtain on the striptease in "Pettin' in the Park," the peeking intercuts of women dressing, changing costumes, backstage or in their apartments.] It can, however, be diverted (sublimated) in the direction of art, if its interest can be shifted away from the genitals on to the shape of the body as a whole."[10]

This perfectly describes *Gold Diggers'* structure.

Men transform female sex into art as an excuse, a cover-up for male desire. The film shifts from an emphasis on the women's genitals, the strategic coin placements of "We're in the Money," to the abstract shape of the female body as a neon violin, collectively bowed in "Shadow Waltz." The process of the film legitimizes, as art, a sublimation, making respectable what was illegal, uncivilized (at least for Freud and Berkeley)—women, female sexuality. Berkeley verges on real perversion, which, in history, has turned to parody in its excess. Now this film is just an example of the kind of movies "they" used to make.

Foucault's concepts of the surveyed, docile, disciplined body in *Discipline and Punish: The Birth of the Prison* are perfectly apt. He outlines tactics for subjecting bodies, taking his model from the military and pedagogy: "The individual body becomes an element that may be placed, moved . . . a fragment of mobile space . . . in order to obtain an efficient machine. . . . The body is constituted as a part of a multi-segmentary machine . . . [which] requires a precise system of command."[11] The contemporary version of precision dancing is aerobics, now step aerobics, with emphasis on taut, exercised buttocks rather than breasts.

The conventions of the classical text also function via the disciplinary techniques of repetition and difference. Moving inevitably to resolution through an intricate balancing of symmetry and asymmetry by constant petitions and rhymings on the sound and image tracks, classical narrative meticulously follows the disciplined rules of its game. The spectatorial play of these shared conventions provides pleasure: relays of anticipations and delays alternately create expectations and provide gratification for the audience.

Rhyming and repetition within *Gold Diggers*, as in many classical texts, is intricate. For example, Barney closes his office door "before the acrobats and midgets" arrive, which rhymes with the real midget of the "Pettin' in the Park" sequence. I have already mentioned the character of Gigolo Eddy and his guitar case containing booze; he appears in Barney's office while they await Brad's fifteen-thousand-dollar check. He is seen backstage rubbing alcohol on the "aging juvenile's" back. His guitar case is replicated by the Kentucky Hillbillies and is transformed into the neon image of women as violins. (The violin symbol is taken from vaudeville to the legit stage, from a lowly image to a lofty image.) In "Shadow Waltz," Polly wears a blond wig, resembling Carol; backstage we briefly glimpse her holding her blond wig. Through repetition with a difference, the work of the film is done for and with us. Like aerobics, repetition and careful instruction are as essential as the move toward closure and conclusion. From the very beginning, we await the pleasure of the end.

The narrative of musical comedy coincides with classical narrative.[12] In fact, musicals depict a literal version of "family romance," a theme often embedded within another story in other genres. Musicals virtually reenact the ritual of re-creation/procreation of privileged heterosexual couples. As in classical narratives, the work of musicals is the containment of potentially disruptive female sexuality, a threat to the sanctity of marriage and the family. However, musicals, and particularly Berkeley sequences, are set apart from other genres by the coded presence of spectacles, enclosed units within the larger narrative, set off by a system of visual and aural brackets. These spectacles mirror the narrative, have beginnings and endings, and presumably might rupture the filmic illusion of reality and halt the forward movement of the story.

First and foremost, spectacles are bracketed by complete musical scores. Thus it is significant that "We're in the Money" is not completed; it remains an interrupted spectacle. Music is a foregrounded code that symmetrically reoccurs as functional scoring in the narrative segments and under titles, thereby either anticipating or recalling the spectacle. "We're in the Money" occurs under the opening titles, then in the Fay Fortune spectacle; is played slowly during the "no jobs" montage, just prior to the decision to take the boys for an expensive ride; and is last heard when the orchestra plays it in the fancy nightclub. "Shadow Waltz" first emerges through the cute, cloying window when Brad plays it on the piano for Polly (the fun couple), resurfaces as a motif when they speak through the backstage door during the interruption of "Pettin' the Park" and then at the speakeasy, and later plays at the nightclub in a medley following "We're in the Money" and finally in the "Shadow Waltz" spectacle.

"I've Got to Sing a Torch Song" is played under titles; then Brad sings it in the apartment for Barney and the girls, and Trixie sings it in the bathtub before the first entrance of J. Lawrence and Fanuel Peabody. The melody is next heard on the balcony while J. Lawrence and Polly discuss her past and then in the apartment during the kissing sequences between Carol and J. Lawrence. Reportedly, this was another production number for Ginger Rogers (as Fay Fortune), just beginning her climb to stardom and top billing, here seventh in the credits. It was subsequently cut from the released version. It is the only song that does not have its own spectacle.

Brad first plays "Remember My Forgotten Man"; the song is repeated through the window and heard backstage when Brad is reluctantly assuming his place in the show, as well as at the end in its own spectacle. It is obviously a key thematic song, but more importantly, it is a stammer, a stutter; the film cannot end until Brad writes the lyrics. The conclusion, as in all good classical films, works via delay, with the end reiterating the beginning, circling back and tying up all the loose ends.

Remember the apartment scene with Barney and the girls. Brad Roberts says, "I've got something about a forgotten man, but I don't have the words to it yet. . . . I got the idea for it last night. I was down at Times Square, watching those men in the breadlines, standing there in the rain waiting for coffee and doughnuts, men out of a job, around the soup kitchen." In one of my favorite moments of cinema Barney says, "That's it! That's it! That's what the show is about, the Depression, men marching, marching in the rain, doughnuts, men marching, jobs, jobs! In the background, Carol, the spirit of the Depression, a blues song, no, not a blues song, but a wailing, a wailing! And this gorgeous woman singing a song that will tear their hearts out. The big parade, the big parade of tears! That's it! That's it! Work on it! Work on it!" When Brad writes the lyrics, the film can end. The end of this number shows us what is denied in the lyrics of "We're in the Money": "We've never seen a breadline, a breadline today."

Singing and dancing are the usual performance modes but not a necessary component of the genre. After all, Berkeley's girls neither danced or sang—they smiled, walked, existed. Because music is the dominant code, the performer could sing, dance, skate, swim, tumble, or have sex to its rhythms. (Pornographic films resemble the musical's relation between spectacle and narrative, a point that Linda Williams develops.) Editing, camera work, and stupendous mise-en-scènes did the rest. Hence the term *musical comedy*: when the music concludes, so does the spectacle—and the movie.

The opening and closing musical notes are re-marked by another system of mirrored, bracketing shots. Identical shots of theater stages, curtains rising, orchestras and conductors, and on-screen audiences open and close the spectacles. This theatrical iconography refers both to the origins of the genre and to the spectator in the movie theater (which often contained a proscenium stage with an insert screen). The erotic messages of the spectacles, however subdued by Hollywood convention and regulation, are celebrations of body, voice, and cinema, intensified by the interaction and duplication of visual and aural codes. Mise-en-scène, camera movement, editing, and sound rhythmically and vertically re-mark one another with a high degree of redundancy.

These bracketed and rhythmically marked spectacles, set in and apart from the overall movement of the narrative, make explicit and even exhibit certain operations that other genres work to suppress. The spectator is clearly alerted to filmic illusion, as well as to the spectator's own immobility in the dark movie theater. Spectacles can be considered as excessively pleasurable moments in musicals; ironically, the moments of greatest fantasy coincide with maximum spectator alertness. These breaks displace the temporal advance of the narrative, providing immediate, regular doses of narcissistic gratification, satiating the spectator with several "ends."

However, spectacles are ultimately contained (like the interruption of the sheriff) by the process Stephen Heath has called "narrativisation." Spectacles mirror rather than rupture, at once anticipating and delaying the resolution of the narrative. They thus function as a striptease—a metaphor that is apt for the *Gold Diggers*. (Coitus interruptus is another.) "Pettin' in the Park" is a striptease, as are the many shots of women (un)dressing. Fay Fortune is stripped of her dress, to be used as a lure for Barney: "Remember to stand in the light, Carol." Carol and Trixie strip J. Lawrence and put him to bed.

In a sense, the film is foreplay for the end, the Broadway show, with interruption narratively enacted: first the interruption of "We're in the Money"; then the delay of "Pettin'" while Brad, threatened with the responsibility for creating prostitutes, decides to enter the spectacle; the "intermission," with a shot of the playbill at the end of "Pettin'"; then the postponement of "Remember My Forgotten Man" while the marital crisis is resolved backstage. Fay continually breaks into the narrative and is kicked out by Trixie—in the apartment with the girls, in the apartment scene with Barney, in the speakeasy, and finally in the nightclub. Like her missing production number, she is a loose end, a real gold digger (and a source of female envy and competition) who threatens to unbalance the film's symmetry.

A triple seduction outlines the filmic body: of on-screen couples, of the dating couples in the audience, and of the critic by the film. Cinema traces "around bodies and sexes not boundaries not to be crossed, but perpetual spirals of pleasure."[13] These "spirals of pleasure" include film's very materials, textured figures of light and sound. Next are figurations of the human body, seduced and captured by the narrative's move to closure—the implied consummation of the couple in the brief seconds before "The End."

The dating ritual of going to the movies, cinema's second seduction, tactilely and tacitly conducted in the anonymous, discreet dark of the movie theater, replays the film's foreplay. Darkness is not only the essential condition of the film's visibility, but for Roland Barthes, "it is also the color of a very diffuse eroticism," and the movie theater "a place of disponsibiity, with the idleness of bodies that best characterizes modern eroticism."[14] Barthes further describes the movie theater as "urban darkness, a cinematographic cocoon" in which "the body's freedom luxuriates." He then extends the sexual (or sleep/dream) metaphor of moviegoing: "How many spectators slip into their seat as they slip into bed, coat and feet on the seat in front of them?" (p. 3)

The actual conditions of film exhibition portray, as I tried to show in my initial remarks, a historical rather than timeless audience, one that includes women. Going to the movies used to include live performances, prologues, orchestras. Bank nights and other giveaways (the various movies' versions of radio and late TV game shows) were instituted during the Depression, along with double and triple features. The performances included a genre mixture of cartoons, news, travelogues, shorts, and features. In the 1930s the introduction of food and drink, particularly popcorn, as well as the pleasures of air conditioning and plush decor, added to the experience. First-run theaters had an intense darkness (before recent fire codes) that required ushers, garbed in pseudomilitary uniforms and carrying flashlights, to guide us to our seats. Sumptuous movie palaces had lavish "ladies rooms" and lounges. Women went to the movies not (consciously) for punishment, not to identify with men, and not just for a single narrative but for multiple pleasures, including the luxuries of the upper class.

However, cinema's pleasure contract is negotiated prior to the movie theater. It is the result of recycled fictions, familiar conventions, activated and differentiated by advertising, gossip, the star system, and facial fashion. For the feature film, the contract has one condition: the film must narratively "make it" for us, producing a satisfying resolution, a sense of closure that ties up all the enigma—until the next time, the next movie.

To prolong this pleasure, classical narrative's absence of sexual intercourse was replaced for film theorists with terms of sexual discourse—thereby perpetuating the narrative/marital contract. This is cinema's last seduction—of the theorist by the rhymed, obsessive perfection of Hollywood's continuity style. As the bodies make it, we make it. The film bodies, at least for a few moments, "live happily ever after." Fade. The End.

Notes

1 United States Bureau of the Census, The Statistical History of the United States from Colonial Times to the Present (New York: Basic Books, 1976), 135, 164.

2 John Baxter, Hollywood in the Thirties (New York: A. S. Barnes, 1968), 50–51.

3 David Wallechinsky and Irving Wallace, The People's Almanac (New York: Doubleday, 1975), 226–27.

4 Siegfried Kracauer, "Girls and Crisis" (1931), reprinted as "The Mass Ornament" in New German Critique 5 (spring 1975); Andre Bazin, "Entomology of the Pin-Up Girl," in What is Cinema? trans. Hugh Gray (Los Angeles, Berkeley, and London: University of California Press, 1971), 2:158. Bazin differentiates the American product: "Physically this American Venus is a tall, vigorous girl whose streamlined body splendidly represents a tall race. Different from the Greek ideal, with its shorter torso and legs, she thus differs from European Venuses" ("Entomology," 158). Angela Carter in The Sadeian Woman sees this corporate analysis differently: "Her hypothetical allure and not her actual body is the commodity. She sells a perpetually unfulfilled promise. . . . The reality . . . could never live up to her publicity. So she retains her theoretical virginity even if she is raped by a thousand eyes twice nightly" (p. 67).

5 Lucy Fischer, "The Image of Woman as Image: The Optical Politics of *Dames*," *Film Quarterly* 30, 1 (fall 1976): 4.

6 Carolyn Marvin, "Dazzling the Multitude: Imagining the Electric Light as a Communication Medium," in *Mass Communication Review Yearbook*, ed. Michael Gurevitch and Mark R. Ley (Newbury Park, Calif.: Sage, 1987), 258.

7 Patricia Mellencamp, "Oedipus and the Robot in *Metropolis*," *Enclitic* 5, 1 (spring 1981): 20–44, In this sad tale I analyze Kracauer's *From Caligari to Hitler*, picking on his phallic argument describing the downfall of Germany, a series of limp-penis moments. I parallel this "patriarchal" tale to that of Fritz Lang in Paul Jensen's *The Cinema of Fritz Lang*. Although this narrative is now apparent, it was not then so easy to see Oedipal structure in films. Only after feminism figured out this narrative pattern did they become obvious. I begin by citing the parable of the scorpion and frog, as quoted in Orson Welles's *Mr. Arkadin* (1955). In *The Crying Game* (1992) this same parable is told twice, suggesting how much the story of Oedipus has been revised; the parable now functions not to explain power/ patriarchy, as it does in the Welles's film (a father–daughter film more than a father–son one), but to explain male heterosexuality/homosexuality which is *The Crying Game*'s love story. Also, rather than being invisible in movies, the penis has become an image (or a joke on late-night TV).

8 John Lahr, "Fearful Symmetry," *Harper's* (July 1977): 83. Thanks to Janet Staiger for this article.

9 I cannot relocate the anthology of 1940s fan-magazine commentary quoted here. By then Earl Carroll had a dinner theater that included performances by "his girls."

10 Sigmund Freud, "Three Essays on Sexuality," vol. 7 of *The Standard Edition of the Complete Psychological Works of Sigmund Freud* (London: Hogarth, 1959), 156.

11 Michel Foucault, *Discipline and Punish: The Birth of the Prison* (New York: Vintage Books, 1979): 164–65.

12 These few remarks are from my essay "Spectacle and Spectator: Looking Through the American Musical Comedy" (*Cine-tracts* 1, 2 (summer 1977] 27–36), which was edited by Teresa de Lauretis. She convinced me that I was smart enough to publish an essay. This essay has been reprinted in *Explorations in Film Theory*, ed. Ron Burnett (Bloomington: Indiana University Press, 1991), 3–14. I worked on twenty-five or more Hollywood musicals for this piece (including *Singin' in the Rain* and all the Astaire-and-Rogers RKO movies and the rest of the Esther Williams extravaganzas), most of which I have never written about elsewhere.

    Like Fleeber, the parodied, pompous New York University film professor in Andrew Bergman's *The Freshman* who recites dialogue in tandem with *The Godfather* during class, I sing along to musicals. Like Fleeber, I can't act or sing. (Fleeber also made his students read all his books on film.)

13 Michel Foucault, *The History of Sexuality*, vol. 1, *An Introduction*, trans. Robert Hurley (New York: Random House, 1978), 45.

14 Roland Barthes, "Upon Leaving the Movie Theater," *University Publishing* (winter 1979): 2; reprinted from *Communications*, no. 23 (1975). This is Barthes's metaphor for gay cruising. I don't know whether it works for women; I suspect not exactly. Conversely, I remember fending off roving arms that awkwardly groped in my direction. Dating and cruising are quite different seductions.

Pre-text and Text in *Gentlemen Prefer Blondes*

6

LUCIE ARBUTHNOT AND GAIL SENECA

Introduction

As feminists, we experience a constant and wearying alienation from the dominant culture. The misogyny of popular art, music, theatrical arts and film interferes with our pleasure in them. This paper discusses a departure from this familiar alienation. Howard Hawks' *Gentlemen Prefer Blondes*, a 1953 film starring Marilyn Monroe and Jane Russell as showgirls, is clearly a product of the dominant culture. Yet, we enjoy the film immensely. In this paper, we chronicle our search to understand our pleasure in this film.[1] We argue that *Gentlemen Prefer Blondes* can be read as a feminist text. We believe that it is important to recoup from male culture some of the pleasure which it has always denied us; we hope that our analysis of *Gentlemen Prefer Blondes* will suggest ways to discover feminist pleasures within films of the dominant culture, and indicate the kinds of films which might be most conducive to a feminist reading.

The logic of our argument about *Gentlemen Prefer Blondes* parallels the process we followed in trying to understand our pleasure in the film. We will briefly mention the key analytic stages of that process in this introduction, before describing each of them in some detail in the text of this paper.

First, we simply watched the film over and over to isolate what we most enjoyed about it. We realized we loved the energy that Monroe and Russell exude. Their zest and sheer presence overwhelm the film. Perhaps, we thought, we were seeing in Monroe and Russell what others have seen in such actresses as Dietrich, Garbo and Hepburn: strong, independent women, who seem to resist to some extent objectification by men. But, our pleasure in *Gentlemen Prefer Blondes* seemed to far surpass that which we found in films starring Garbo, Dietrich or Hepburn. We had found something more than the presentation of positive women who were strong enough to sometimes resist men and act for themselves.

We turned then to some recent feminist films, thinking they might suggest something about the source of women's pleasure in film, which could apply to our experience with *Gentlemen Prefer Blondes*. These films were helpful, however, only insofar as our consideration of them clarified our dissatisfaction with them. For example, feminist films in the French psychoanalytically inspired tradition (such as *Deux Fois* and *Thriller*) often present women in a manner which makes them inaccessible to male objectification. But such films focus more on denying men their cathexis with women as erotic objects than in connecting women with each other. Films such as *The Turning Point*, *Girlfriends*, and *Julia* showed friendships between women, but less openly and convincingly than *Gentlemen Prefer Blondes*. For *Gentlemen Prefer Blondes* presents women who not only resist male objectification, but who also cherish deeply their connections with each other. The friendship between two strong women, Monroe and Russell, invites the female viewer to join them, through identification, in valuing other women and ourselves.[2]

We read, then, beneath the superficial story of heterosexual romance in *Gentlemen Prefer Blondes*, a feminist text which both denies men pleasure to some degree, and more importantly, celebrates women's pleasure in each other. [. . .]

Gentlemen Prefer Blondes tells the story of two voluptuous showgirls, Marilyn Monroe and Jane Russell. It chronicles their adventures on a transatlantic sea voyage, during which they seek husbands and capture the attention of every male on board. Their quest finally culminates in a double wedding ceremony.

In our study of the film, however, we have found that this narrative of romantic adventure between the sexes is continually disrupted and undermined by other narrative and non-narrative elements in the film. This disruption is so severe and continual that we have come to regard the romantic narrative as a mere pre-text, a story which co-exists with, contradicts and disguises another, more central, text. This text consists of two major themes, neither of which fits comfortably with the pre-text of romance. The themes are the women's resistance to objectification by men, and the women's connection with each other. The following pages discuss the film's articulation of these themes, which comprise the text we read in *Gentlemen Prefer Blondes*.

1 Resistance to male objectification

The theme of resistance to male objectification is most clearly articulated on a gestural level. Even where the narrative situation seems to code Monroe and Russell for objectification by men, they resist this objectification. We read this resistance in their gestural cues or body language. Specifically, we find this resistance in their look, stance, use of space, and activity. Their costuming and Hawks' use of camera and lighting also limit their objectification.

Look

Socially it is the prerogative of men to gaze at women and the requirement of women to avert our eyes in submission. The initiation of the gaze signals superiority over the subordinate. Clearly, in *Gentlemen Prefer Blondes* men do gaze at women. Monroe and Russell are spectacles for male attention. However, Monroe and Russell refuse to signal submission by averting their eyes. Rather, they return the look. As Monroe and Russell walk through a sea of admiring spectators, they also actively search the crowd. Through their active and searching look, they appropriate the space around them, refusing to yield it to the male gaze. There are several particularly striking examples of this returned look, in which Monroe and Russell walk through a throng of gaping men but refuse to accept objectification by averting their own eyes, for example, during their initial walk through the ranks of the Olympic team on the dock, when they first enter the dining-room on board ship, and during their final walk down the aisle to the altar where they are to be married.

Stance

From the moment Russell strides onto stage in the opening number, we are cued to her resistance to male objectification. She virtually never moves in the constrained fashion of the "lady"; she strides, arms swinging at her sides, shoulders erect and head thrown back. Even when she is standing still, Russell's legs are often apart, her hands are on her hips and posture erect. Her stance speaks her strength and authority.[3]

Use of space

It is a male prerogative to encroach on women's space not only through look, but bodily as well. Women are to be looked at, moved in on, and touched by men, rather than to look, to move, and to initiate touch themselves. Female space is violable by men. In a social situation, for example, men assume the right of entry into a female conversation. Women typically do not assume the same rights with men.[4] In *Gentlemen Prefer Blondes*, however, Monroe and Russell clearly control access to their own space and also freely enter men's spaces. For example, when Monroe's fiancé, Mr. Esmond, wants to enter her dressing room in the Paris nightclub, he can do so only after Monroe and Russell consult each other:

Mr. Esmond (running after Lorelei): Lorelei! Lorelei! Wait! Look Lorelei! I've flown the entire
    Atlantic Ocean just to talk to you. And now you . . .
Lorelei: Well, you might come in for a minute, [turning to Dorothy], that's if *you* don't mind.
Dorothy: I don't mind if you don't mind. [They open the door to their dressing room, making
    him precede them.]

Similarly, when the male Olympic team is working out, Russell strides through their ranks uninvited, looking the men over, squeezing their muscles, pulling one man down into her lap by his hair. In the courtroom scene, Russell not only confidently enters male space, but transforms it into a showcase for her dancing and singing.

Activity

In all these instances—through look, stance and use of space—Monroe and Russell subvert male objectification. By becoming active themselves, they make it impossible for men to act upon them. They are actors and the initiators in their relations with men. When Russell and the detective (with whom she is allegedly in love) embrace on the moonlit deck, it is Russell who initiates the kiss. In order to retrieve an incriminating piece of film, Monroe and Russell deftly pin the detective down and pull off his pants. His helplessness is underscored when they ultimately send him off dressed only in his underwear and a frilly pink bathrobe.

It is interesting that Monroe and Russell's tight-fitting and stereotypically feminine dress does not diminish the power of their stance, their look, or their activity. Body language appears to be a more accurate index of power than clothing. Perhaps this is why, in film and in society, women can wear men's clothing without abandoning their "femininity." When Dietrich wears men's clothes, for example, she remains an object to be overpowered, because her body language signals passivity and invites seduction. Clothing cannot confer power. This is one of the reasons we find *Gentlemen Prefer Blondes* more conducive to a feminist reading than films in which Dietrich wears a tuxedo and top hat.

Costume

Costume could easily have been used in *Gentlemen Prefer Blondes* to reduce Monroe and Russell to mere objects of male sexual desire. In fact, their costuming partakes of the tension between objectification and resistance to objectification that we have described above. Their tight-fitting dresses are sometimes constraining, but they are rarely revealing. Given the mammary madness of the fifties,[5] it is striking that Hawks chose to dress Monroe and Russell in high-necked sweaters and dresses, jackets, and subdued colors. Even their most revealing costumes are cocktail dresses which neither expose nor reveal their breasts.

Camera and lighting

Hawks' use of camera and lighting add to the effects of costume in resisting male objectification. Other directors frequently photographed Monroe and Russell in profile to emphasize their body contours. Hawks rarely does this in *Gentlemen Prefer Blondes*.

Similarly, overhead lighting could have been used to emphasize their bodies, but Hawks rarely chose this effect. Their frequent costuming in black prevents any revelatory shadow play on their bodies. Hawks often shoots them in medium close-up, showing only their shoulders and faces. The use of medium close-ups in which Monroe's and Russell's zest and personality shine through is crucial in inviting us to identify with, rather than objectify, the two women.

Our discussion of body language, costume, and directorial choices illustrates our reading a feminist text in *Gentlemen Prefer Blondes*. This is not to suggest, however, that the text completely erases the pre-text. In fact, the pre-text constantly intrudes upon our reading of the film, threatening to obliterate it. A particularly blatant visual example of the pre-text is the stage set for Monroe's "Diamonds Are a Girl's Best Friend" number. Sadistic fantasy is personified in chandeliers and lamps elaborately decorated with women, all rigidly held in position with black leather halters and chains. Woman literally becomes an object. This stark explication of the pre-text, in which patriarchal relations of power between the sexes reign, ironically forms the backdrop for a song in which Monroe clarifies her preference for money over men. For us, this scene exemplifies the tension between the pre-text of male-defined hetero-sexuality and the text of female resistance to men and connection with each other.

Another example occurs in the moonlit love scene between Russell and the detective on the deck, in which Russell sustains her strong and active body language by moving toward the detective to initiate a kiss. Before she can reach his lips, however, Hawks interrupts

Russell's movement toward the detective, cutting to a shot of the detective moving to kiss Russell. What we tend to remember is the detective's successful completion of the action. The text—Russell's activity—is suppressed. Nevertheless, each time the pre-text is reimposed, new possibilities are created for fissures through which the text may emerge again. In the last scene Monroe and Russell marry, threatening to finally destroy their independence; but even here the text emerges as they turn away from their husbands at the altar to gaze lovingly at each other.

2 The women's connection to each other

Initially, we suggested that Monroe and Russell's resistance to male objectification was the primary source of our pleasure in viewing *Gentlemen Prefer Blondes*. We could think of no other film in which women so consistently subverted the objectifying male gaze. On subsequent viewings of the film, however, we realized that while we were delighted by Monroe and Russell's resistance to men, we were also deeply moved by their connection with each other. The destruction of opportunities for male objectification in this film gave us less pleasure than the construction of opportunities for our own positive identification with women in this film. As we suggested earlier, positive identification with other women is precious both because it is crucial to our own positive self-image as women,[6] and because it is suppressed both in life and in art. It is the expression and celebration of women's strength and connection with each other which so moves and pleases us in *Gentlemen Prefer Blondes*. Russell and Monroe neither accept the social powerlessness of women nor the imperative of a primary allegiance to men. Instead, they emanate strength and power and celebrate their primary allegiance to each other. The friends' feeling for each other supersedes their more superficial connections with men, which fill the narrative core of the film's pre-text. At one point, Russell threatens to sever her romantic tie with the male detective if he interferes with the perjury she is committing on Monroe's behalf. While Monroe never so explicitly chooses between her male lover and her female friend, the narrative makes such a choice unnecessary. Monroe's fiancé is drawn as a ludicrous sap whose entire worth to Monroe can be measured by his bank account. Her emotional relationship with him is sheer pretense. With Russell, in contrast, Monroe is shown to care sufficiently to give her time and energy with no hope of financial recompense.

Unlike the resistance of objectification by men, which is conveyed primarily through the text of the film, both pre-text and text collude to present a positive image of Monroe and Russell's friendship. The friendship is celebrated in the film's narrative and through its visual codes.

On the narrative level, no one can miss the centrality of the women's connection to each other as Monroe spends her time on the transatlantic voyage looking for a suitable male escort for Russell, or when Russell perjures herself in court to protect Monroe. Their lives are inextricably and lovingly intertwined. They work together, sing and dance together, travel together, and get married together. We are rarely shown one on screen without the other. They also defend each other in the face of outside critics. When the detective disparages Monroe, Russell retorts vehemently: "No one talks about Lorelei but me." Monroe is equally strident in her defense of Russell: "Dorothy's the best friend a girl ever had." And the two women continually address each other with terms of endearment: "lovey," "honey," "sister," "dear."

One of the most extraordinary and positive aspects of *Gentlemen Prefer Blondes'* depiction of the friendship between the two women is the absence of competitiveness, envy and pettiness. Commercial films rarely depict important friendships between women; when they do, the friendships are marred or rendered incredible by the film's polarization of the two women into opposite and competing camps. Consider, for example, *All About Eve*, *The Turning Point*, or *Girlfriends*. It is clear that such films portray female friends only with the specter of competition firmly implanted between them. It is also clear that this competition revolves almost exclusively around women's alliances with men. Either the friends compete for the same man or for the attentions of men in general. In a modern twist of the same theme, one friend may resent the other's freedom from men instead of seizing that freedom for herself. Or the single friend may feel herself abandoned by her married friend's frantic absorption in husband and children. In *Gentlemen Prefer Blondes*, the two friends work to form allegiances with men, but never compete for them. Rather than dividing them, their search for men unites them in a common purpose. But their friendship is not limited to that search. It includes a joyful working and leisure relationship that endures through all the disruptions on their volatile relations with men. And ultimately, even as Monroe and Russell end their search with marriage, their friendship survives. As we will describe later, their double wedding scene underscores the depth of their friendship, and the superficiality of the commitments they are making to their husbands. The power of female bonds and the threat they pose to patriarchally defined heterosexual love is clarified, not eliminated, by this wedding scene.

These narrative elements in *Gentlemen Prefer Blondes* point openly to the centrality of the women's connection to each other. But the more subtle, non-narrative clues are at least as important. These include body language (look, touch, use of space), and directorial choices, as well as audience expectations of the musical as a genre.

Look

Both on-stage, during their song and dance numbers, and off-stage, Monroe and Russell frequently gaze lovingly at each other. In "When Love Goes Wrong," they sit together at a Paris café and sing the initial portion of the song directly to each other. Even when they are with men their gaze reflects their affection for each other. For example, when Mr. Esmond and Monroe are saying goodbye in the ship stateroom, Russell looks on tenderly; as Russell and the detective strike up a romance, Monroe beams warm approval at her friend. In all the songs which they sing together their look signals their focus on each other.

Touch

Both on-stage and off, Monroe and Russell freely and affectionately touch one another. In the opening "Little Rock" number, Russell dances with her hands on Monroe's shoulders. Off-stage, their comfort with each other's bodies is unmistakable. Russell frequently punctuates their conversation with affectionate caresses, or with more forceful gestures such as shaking Monroe or pulling her by the hand. They walk, stand, and sit in close proximity, frequently shoulder to shoulder.

Use of space

We have already suggested that Monroe and Russell effectively resist male objectification by controlling access to their own space and by freely intruding on men's spaces. Their use of space also underscores their connection with each other. They frequently interrupt the other's private interactions with men, as if to say that a connection with men could never rival their connection to each other. For example, when Monroe is saying goodbye to her fiancé, Russell pushes him toward the gangplank, saying "You'd better go now." Similarly, when Monroe and Piggy are having their tête-à-tête in the ship stateroom, Russell barges in and virtually throws Piggy out.

Hawks' directorial choices

Hawks has also underscored Monroe and Russell's connectedness to each other through filmic means. The frequent use of over-the-shoulder shots or subjective shots, in which we are shown one woman from the other's point of view, visually emphasizes their involvement with each other. They are very often shown in close two-shots, with their faces filling the frame. Their connection is enhanced by the absence of others in the frame, making them our exclusive focus. One of the most striking examples of this occurs in the last frames of the film where we are watching their double wedding ceremony: after briefly showing the brides and grooms together, the camera tracks in to a two-shot of Monroe and Russell smiling at each other.

Musical as genre

One further way in which the primacy of Monroe and Russell's relationship is emphasized for the audience is its position within the movie musical genre. A typical characteristic of movie musical genre is that there are two leads, a man and a woman, who sing and dance together, and eventually become romantically involved; that they sing and dance so fluidly together is a metaphor for the perfection of their relationship. In *Gentlemen Prefer Blondes*, it is Monroe and Russell who sing—they even harmonize, adding another layer to the metaphor—and dance as a team. The men they supposedly love are never given a musical role, and therefore never convincingly share in the emotional energy between Monroe and Russell. All of that energy is reserved for the relationship between the two women. In one instance Russell even sings the part which was clearly written for a man. It is in "Bye Bye Baby," which is sung during the bon voyage party on board ship, that Russell sings:

> "Although I know that you care
> Won't you write and declare
> That though on the loose
> You are still on the square."

Monroe answers her with the following lines:

"And just to show that I care
I will write and declare
That I'm on the loose
But I'm still on the square."

Although, as we have suggested, the pre-text and the text frequently collude to affirm the primacy of the two women's connection in *Gentlemen Prefer Blondes*, there are still moments, akin to the tension we described between objectification and resistance to it, when they are in contradiction. The narrative line does purport to show Monroe in love with her millionaire fiancé and Russell in love with her detective friend; and the women do get married in the end, despite their strong friendship. But while the strong tension between the pre-text of objectification and the text of resistance to objectification never permitted either to fully obscure the other, the conflict between the pre-text of heterosexual romance is so thin that it scarcely threatens the text of female friendship. Even as they sing lyrics which suggest that heterosexual love is crucial for women, Monroe and Russell subvert the words through their more powerful actions. Here are the melancholic words to the song "When Love Goes Wrong," sung at the Paris sidewalk café:

"When love goes wrong
Nothing goes right . . .
The blues all gather 'round you
And day is dark as night
A man ain't fit to live with
And woman's a sorry sight."

They sing these words, not with melancholy, but with deep serenity, gazing at each other lovingly. Later they make a mockery of the song's sad theme by shimmying cheerfully to a jazzed up version of the same song in front of an admiring crowd. Men never convincingly appear as more important to Monroe and Russell than they are to each other.

It is the tension between male objectification of women, and women's resistance to that objectification, that opens *Gentlemen Prefer Blondes* to a feminist reading. It is the clear and celebrated connection between Marilyn Monroe and Jane Russell which, for us, transforms *Gentlemen Prefer Blondes* into a profoundly feminist text. [. . .]

Notes

1   We are using the term "pleasure" here to refer to enjoyment and delight. We are not using the word to connote a psychoanalytic framework for our analysis.
2   In this paper we assume that film viewers identify with characters on screen, and that film viewers derive pleasure from seeing characters on screen who possess traits they admire and whom they can use as positive role models. We realize that this positive identification is influenced not only by narrative elements (how a person is characterized in the film), but also by filmic elements (the use of close-ups, the amount of screen time allotted to that person, etc.). In this respect we situate ourselves more in the lineage of writers such as Philip Slater and Nancy Chodorow, and less in that of writers like Diane Waldman in

"There's More to a Positive Image than Meets the Eye," *Jump-Cut*, No. 18 (August 1978). One of us is currently carrying out empirical research on positive identification and voyeurism in female film viewers which, we feel, supports our position.

3   The Monroe character also adopts a "masculine" stride and stance, but far less consistently than the Russell character. More often, Monroe plays the "lady" to Russell's manly moves. For example, Russell opens doors for Monroe; Monroe sinks into Russell's strong frame, allowing Russell to hold her protectively.

4   T.N. Willis, Jr., "Initial Speaking Distance as a Function of the Speaker's Relationship," *Psychonomic Science*, 5 (1966), pp. 221–222.

5   Marjorie Rosen, *Popcorn Venus* (New York: Avon, 1973).

6   Nancy Chodorow, *The Reproduction of Mothering* (Berkeley: University of California Press, 1978).

7

"Feminizing" the Song-and-Dance Man

Fred Astaire and the spectacle of masculinity in the Hollywood musical

STEVEN COHAN

It's a truism of show business, which the Hollywood musical celebrates again and again, that a star performer can quite literally and quite spectacularly stop the show as proof of his or her extraordinary talent. The female performer's ability to stop the show (and the story) is a familiar enough feature of Hollywood cinema, extending from the musical genre itself to the nightclub or saloon setting of other genres, like the gangster story or the Western, which provides the star with a ready excuse to do a number. A recurring backdrop for the female star generally, Laura Mulvey has pointed out, the show setting equates femininity with spectacle; it crystallizes her position as a static icon of male desire, differentiating feminine exhibitionism and passivity from masculine voyeurism and agency. In particular, as Mulvey's own reference to Ziegfeld and Berkeley suggests, because of its reliance on spectacle the musical would appear to be the genre most responsible for reproducing this reductive binary opposition of female performer and male spectator, what with the kaleidoscopic array of chorus girls working so hard and so often to feminize spectacle for a masculine viewer on screen as well as off.[1] This division of labor, most obvious in the numerous gold diggers and sugar daddies who populate the genre from *Broadway Melody* (1929) to *Gentlemen Prefer Blondes* (1953), also makes itself felt in the narrative preoccupation, in musical after musical, with producing the ideal heterosexual couple.

However, as Steve Neale notes in passing when discussing male spectacle, the musical is 'the only genre in which the male body has been unashamedly put on display in mainstream cinema in any consistent way' (Neale 1983: 15). This Hollywood genre actually differs from others because it features men in showstopping numbers as well as women. In making such a blatant spectacle of men, the musical thus challenges the very gendered division of labor which it keeps reproducing in its generic plots. For when he stops the show (and the story) to perform a socko number and fulfill what the genre takes to be his destiny as a star, the Hollywood song-and-dance man also connotes, to use Mulvey's fine phrase, '*to-be-looked-at-ness*' (Mulvey 1975: 19). He therefore finds himself in rather problematic territory—at least as far as film theory is concerned—for the genre has placed him in the very position which the representation system of classic Hollywood cinema has traditionally designated as 'feminine.'

Such 'feminization' of male musical stars involves more than simply making them, as Neale puts it, 'objects of an explicitly erotic gaze' in a pattern just reversing the gendered terms of sexual objectification (Neale 1983: 14–15). Rather, I am arguing here through the example of Fred Astaire, something other than a conventional objectification of the male body is at stake with the spectacle of a song-and-dance man in the musical, because his 'feminization' arises from a highly self-conscious and theatrical performance that constructs his masculinity out of the show-business values of spectatorship and spectacle.[2]

The complexity of male spectacle in the Hollywood musical results from several important factors, which I shall be treating in some detail as I discuss Fred Astaire in the context of the musical genre and its production of male stardom. But let me summarize my claims at the outset. To start with, when this most exemplary of male musical performers does a star turn, even if the number means to sustain his power as dominant male in the narrative (as when he dances in order to authorize his patriarchal position as teacher, director, or lover of a younger female co-star like Cyd Charisse or Jane Powell), because he halts the linearity of the story with his musical performance, he also stops the show to insist upon his own ability to signify, to-be-looked-at-ness.' Whether relying on props and special effects or simply building off of the star's physical grace and agility, Astaire's solo numbers in particular were obviously engineered to do more than simply texture a characterization or advance a story's linear movement towards closure, since they interfere with the narrative economy of his films by foregrounding the value of his performance as spectacle. Astaire's numbers thus oftentimes exceed both linear narrativity and the heterosexual (that is, 'straight' in the cultural as well as the narrative sense) male desire that fuels it. [. . .] As a result of his clearly marked spectacular value as a musical star, I am concluding, Astaire's screen persona makes full use of all the technology the industry has to offer, paradoxically enough, in order to authenticate the ground for the audience's fascination with his male image in the so-called 'feminine' tropes of narcissism, exhibitionism, and masquerade.

In sum, to see Hollywood's song-and-dance men connoting 'to-be-looked-at-ness' does not imply as a consequence that musical spectacle automatically 'feminizes' the male star to the point of erasing his masculinity (or sexual difference) altogether. In pointing out the *comparable* spectacularity of the male and female musical star, I therefore do not mean to suggest that their treatment is even-handed and symmetrical: she is neither 'masculinized' in turn nor is her spectacular value made exactly the same as his. A pretty girl remains a melody in the musical, so the showgirl and all that she implies about female spectacle do not diminish in importance for the genre's sexual differentiation of male and female stars.[3] But what the Hollywood musical does foreground above all else when numbers interrupt the flow of narrative is the production of masculinity and femininity alike out of highly theatricalized performances of gender.

Stopping the show (and the story)

The Hollywood musical has always been seen as an expression of unbounded joy and physical liberation because the libidinal energy released in the numbers is not linear, that is, not consistent with the conservative, teleological economy of classical narrative. In *Silk Stockings* (1957), Astaire's last musical as a leading man, Cyd Charisse makes a sarcastic comment which well summarizes the uneasy relation between narrative and number. Trying to seduce her through Cole Porter's 'All of You,' Astaire (Steve Canfield) complains, 'Don't you ever let yourself go?' 'Go where?' Charisse (Ninotchka) wants to know, taking his question literally. 'I don't know,' he replies, 'Just go, go, *go!*' He lets go with a burst of dancing. 'Don't you ever feel so happy that you just want to dance all round the room?' he asks afterwards. 'Happiness is a reward of industry and labor,' she retorts. 'Dancing is a waste of time.' 'I like wasting time,' he responds, and then repeats his show of fancy footwork: 'Well?' 'You go, go, go,' Charisse concludes after watching him dance, 'but you don't get anywhere.'

Though Astaire replies, rather archly, 'You're telling *me*,' in order to place her comment back into its narrative context of seduction, Charisse's remark lingers, emblematic of what Astaire's numbers can do, do do (that is, interrupt, stall, and exceed) to the libidinal economy of linear narrative. For once he begins performing, twirling around the shiny parquet floors, his body's energy and motion redefine narrative space in completely visual terms as spectacle. His musical numbers exert a non-narrative, extradiegetic pressure—contemplation of the star performing—that remains in excess of the conservative narrative activity of the film's plot.[4]

Truth to tell, when all is said and done I do recognize that I am still talking about a Hollywood product. Most often the tension between the excesses of a film's musical numbers and its compacted narrative appears easily enough resolved in the closure; then the energy of a number does appear to have gone somewhere, namely into the linear direction of a story. Or at least this is the view of 'the ideally integrated musical,' always held up by the industry as the genre's highest aesthetic achievement, 'a musical where song, dance, and story are artfully blended to produce a combined effect' (Mueller 1984: 28). A frequently cited example of the perfect integration of narrative and number is 'Dancing in the Dark' in *The Band Wagon* (1953), where, as John Mueller has shown with his detailed analysis of the choreography, 'the change in the relationship between Astaire and [Cyd] Charisse, at once subtle and profound, is accomplished entirely in dance terms' (Mueller 1984: 35). Narratively speaking, their duet resolves the conflict in ages and musical styles which has stood in the way of their collaboration on stage, and in providing them with a basis for working together as a professional team, the number moves them on to the next segment of the narrative action, when they take the show out of town. In similar fashion, before he is through dancing to 'All of You' in *Silk Stockings*, Astaire gets 'somewhere with Charisse because he does succeed in luring her into dancing with him, however stiffly, as the music swells to a lush string arrangement of the melody. Afterwards, as she reclines contentedly on a rug, he remarks with an irony that transcends this scene—indeed, the entire picture—'so, uh, dancing is a waste of time?'

When I claim that musical numbers go, go, go without necessarily getting anywhere in the story but without being a waste of time either, I am, therefore, intentionally reading *against* the value of integration; but, at the same time, I do not mean to suggest that musical numbers bear no relation at all to their narrative context. Rather, I want to revise our understanding of the kind of pressure a number exerts on the economizing drive of the narrative frame, especially when it concerns the spectacle of a *male* star performing, since this situation also overturns the customary way in which masculinity is assumed to advance and dominate linear narrative.

In his analysis of the Hollywood musical, Rick Altman argues that a musical plot does not operate in the linear fashion one expects of other Hollywood genres but moves according to a vertical principle of formal economy. Instead of arranging its basic narrative units (scenes, settings, character traits, and most importantly, musical numbers) in simple succession, the musical plots them as a series of parallel relations.

[W]e alternate between the male focus and the female focus, working our way through a prepackaged love story whose dynamic principle remains the difference between male and female. *Each segment must be understood not in terms of the segments to which it is causally related but by comparison to the segment which it parallels.*

(Altman 1987: 20, his emphasis)

Building this dual focus around character (and a principle of comparability and simultaneity) rather than plot (and a principle of chronology and sequence), this paradigmatic structure defines sexual difference in terms of the primary opposition of masculinity and femininity, and this binary in turn generates a series of secondary opposing values (like age/youth, riches/beauty, rural/urban, nature/technology) which can be made more specific than the masculine/feminine binary to a given narrative context and as a consequence appear reconciled in the course of two hours. The harmonizing (in all senses) of those various oppositions then supplies both the cause and the effect of the heterosexual couple's successful formation as a union of complementary differences at the film's end.

Almost all Hollywood musicals follow this paradigm, which structurally organizes the numbers as well as the narrative. In *Royal Wedding* (1951) Astaire stars with Jane Powell as a brother–sister team modeled on his own act with sister Adèle in vaudeville and on Broadway. The stars perform two numbers together early in the film, one ('Ev'ry Night at Seven') which features him singing while she looks on mutely, and another ('Open Your Eyes') which reverses the labor, with Powell singing while Astaire stands by idly against the piano waiting for their waltz to begin. When it does, he dances primarily to support her—in what must be his most self-effacing musical performance since his debut opposite Joan Crawford in *Dancing Lady* in 1933. The two numbers balance each other with a display of different but complementary talents that equates the female's with singing, the male's with dancing.

The stars' solos then reinforce this homology. On board the ship taking them to London, Astaire rehearses an improvised dance with a hat rack in his sister's absence ('Sunday Jumps'), and two numbers later Powell rehearses a song in their hotel room ('The Happiest Day of My Life'). Similarly, in the second half of the film, Powell sings her declaration of love to Peter Lawford after the opening night of the show ('Too Late Now'), and moments later, Astaire articulates his feelings for Sarah Churchill by doing a spectacular dance up and down the walls and ceiling of his hotel room ('You're All the World to Me'). To underscore this dual focus, the overture playing behind the main titles is a medley of the music from these last two solos.

The final two show numbers then expand upon this dual focus to emphasize the theatricality of both the stars' performance style and their relationship in the diegesis as a heterosexual show business couple. Performed to represent the opening night of their show in London, 'How Can You Believe Me When I Said I Love You, When You Know I've Been a Liar All My Life?' casts Astaire as a gum-chewing, low-life cad and Powell, in a black wig and tight sweater, as the girl friend he has lied to, the number explicitly playing against—and so implying the similar theatricality of—their familiar screen images as debonair gentleman and blonde ingenue respectively. This is the only number in the film in which both stars sing as well as dance together, possibly because with its broad colorful strokes it aims to satirize binarized male/female roles by showing their basis in outlandish gender stereotypes. The number even ends with Powell punching out Astaire!

Their final duet together, 'I Left My Hat in Haiti,' rhymes with the opening as Astaire once again performs with a mute Powell, who doesn't appear until the second half. In contrast to that simpler first dance, which remained (by MGM standards) realistically stage-bound, this big production number—overblown, incoherent, and terrific to watch—emphasizes the value of cinema's version of theatricality. Awash with color on one of those MGM theater stages which seem to extend backwards for two city blocks, this final number fills no apparent plot function whatsoever and, indeed, goes even further to collapse whatever narrative line the verse tries to construct for itself (something about Astaire having forgotten his blue—grey fedora when leaving a one-night stand) in the interest of filling the screen with theatrical spectacle (scrims, moving stages, brightly costumed dancers, crayola-colored sets, a live monkey), which provides the background against which Astaire, in a cream-colored suit, always commands the viewer's eye.[5]

Representing sexual difference through its two stars, *Royal Wedding* operates in accordance with the dual focus of the musical genre, but upon close inspection the numbers pose something of a problem for that paradigmatic narrative structure. Many studies of the musical have explained quite well how dance functions as a metaphor for sexual differentiation, seduction, and consummation, nowhere more brilliantly, subtly, or consistently so than in Astaire's films.[6] Given the stress which the genre's dual focus places on the sexual relation of musical performers, *Royal Wedding* is an especially uncharacteristic Astaire musical since it does not have him romance his sexual partner through dance. The show numbers amplify a brother–sister relationship, placing teamwork over romance as the objective of male—female pairing. As the film ends, Alan Jay Lerner's script even implies, albeit very discreetly, that this musical teaming is indeed standing in for some other kind of sexual relation: when Astaire and Powell rush to tell their London agent that they want to get married, he exclaims, 'But I thought you two were related!' Exactly. Even though the plot recounts two romances (Astaire and Churchill, Powell and Lawford), the primary relation structuring the film—the one given musical density and specificity by the numbers—is the brother–sister act, with its stress on family sameness (and talent) over heterosexual difference (and desire). As a result of their function in elaborating upon the musical abilities, collaboration, and intimacy of the sibling team, the numbers in this film do not support either the narrative economy of conventional heterosexual romancing or the traditional sexual binary of the female as a show, the male as a spectator.[7]

Performed for an actual audience within the film, Astaire's four show numbers with Powell openly acknowledge the stars' comparable status as spectacle. During the shipboard dance to 'Open Your Eyes,' in fact, the dancers lose their balance because of the unstable movement of the ocean liner, which causes them to slip and slide across the tilting floor, even to fall into the laps of some spectators. In the context of these show numbers and their increasing appeal to spectacle over story, Astaire's two famous solos are worth a second look for the way they also focus attention on the spectacle of his body. 'Sunday Jumps' dispenses with its lyric altogether to serve as the most non-narrative of the eight numbers. Deriving its rhythm initially from a metronome, and its choreography from Astaire's spontaneous interaction with the physical objects that surround him in the ship's gym, the number turns his dancing into pure physical play. His boundless energy moves him in all directions around the room for the sheer pleasure of it and, as he gets entangled in the various machines during the middle of the dance, his chiding of his own thin and decidedly unmuscular body also implicitly makes fun of the weighty body-builders who have nothing on the physical strength necessary for his brand of light stepping. One effect of this number is that Astaire's body appears to transcend the cinematic apparatus, which seems simply to be catching him in action; in comparison, 'You're All the World to Me' foregrounds the apparent ability of his body to defy gravity through dance, the number going to the other extreme of celebrating Astaire's relation to the apparatus (emphasized all the more by the publicity explaining the technology of the dance's complicated production). If the first solo makes an audience think, 'wow, look at what he can do!' the second makes them wonder, 'wow, how did they do that?'

In keeping with Astaire's style of choreography generally, neither number concludes with the kind of bravura finish that makes the rest of the dance diminish in intensity or effect. The first solo ends with him lifting the hat rack, twirling around with it on his shoulders, then quickly pressing it up over his head and swinging it around along the floor, so that he closes with it cradled along the line of his body; then he and his 'partner' bow to the silent applause of an imaginary audience. The second number ends even more quietly: after literally dancing all around the room, he concludes by simply sitting down and contemplating Sarah Churchill's photograph (purloined from the street display of his own show), in very much the same position he was in when the number opened and then again later when he paused to look at her photo halfway through. Nor, from a formalist consideration, is either number very economically designed as a linear structure meant to reach a climax with the minimum expenditure of energy (though both are impeccably timed in terms of the dancing itself and the technological difficulties of shooting the choreography to a prerecorded track, just as the musical scoring of each is structured to advance the movement of the dance through time and to regulate its rhythm in space). In the first solo, Astaire moves around the gym at random; it is only after he fails to lift the hat rack and starts 'working out' with the equipment, though in a highly self-mocking fashion, that the number can be said to have any kind of discernible direction insofar as it finishes with a lift that he couldn't perform before. In the second number, he goes around the room twice, the first time hopping from chair to wall to ceiling, the second time jumping around more vigorously and then tap dancing on the ceiling; this repetition of his tour round the room causes the number to redouble upon itself, the second half offering a kind of encore before the number is even over.

Both numbers, finally, rely on props (the hat rack and gym equipment in one, the photograph and, much more subtly, the cinematic apparatus producing the special effect, in the other) to compensate for the female partner's absence, and the fetishizing use of these props in the dancing raises a provocative suggestion of autoeroticism consistent with Linda Williams's proposed analogy between the musical and pornography: 'To a great extent, in fact, the hard-core feature film is a kind of musical, with sexual number taking the place of musical number' (Williams 1989: 124). Specifically, she compares the solo number of a musical to a masturbation number, 'a solo song or dance of self-love and enjoyment' (p. 133). With this comparison in mind, it is important to appreciate that, far from being directed towards a slam-bang type of climax exclusively male in its libidinal orientation, Astaire's solo numbers disperse their autoerotic energy into extended foreplay—the duration of the number—so that the pleasure of the dance—not only for the performer but also, it can be assumed, for the viewer contemplating the dancer's image and identifying with the emotions and movements driving the dance—is bounded desire itself and not its consummation. That Astaire's musical numbers generally do not direct their energy towards a big, showy cumulative finish—they are actually planned out and then shot in segments so that the dancer's energy can be expended throughout the duration of the dance and not saved up for the finish—may begin to explain why they can be watched repeatedly without loss of pleasure.

'You go, go go, but don't get anywhere'

While both solo numbers in *Royal Wedding* might seem to glorify traditional—and, because of Astaire's age, patriarchal—male power as reinforcement of the binarism of the generic musical plot, the masculinity put on display is far from the phallic posturing of other types of Hollywood spectacle analyzed by Steve Neale, like the Western or gangster shoot-out. If anything, Astaire's numbers reverse the usual psychoanalytic terms for describing gender identification symbolically, since in their orchestration of the male body as a site of joy they display plenitude and not lack, presence and not absence. Rather than success-fully binding the desire of the dance to the linear trajectory of classical plot, or working out a dual heterosexual focus that reaches fulfillment in the consummation symbolized by marriage, Astaire's solo numbers in this film confirm his status for cinema as an object of vision, a male spectacle driving the musical portions to exceed its narrative containment and closure.

The disrupting effect of the numbers in *Royal Wedding* may appear more immediately striking than in most musicals because of the coincidence of its show setting with an obvious disinclination to musicalize a romance plot, but the spectacular value of Astaire's two solos and four show numbers with Powell is consistent with the dancing in his films generally, even those with Ginger Rogers or Cyd Charisse, which tend to be more successfully bound to a narrative context of male–female seduction/education. In *Top Hat* (1935), to cite the quintessential partnership of Astaire and Rogers, the dance duet to 'Isn't This a Lovely Day (To Be Caught in the Rain)?' emphasizes the equality at the heart of their joy in dancing together. The narrative motivation for the number is Rogers's fear of thunder, which, in driving her into Astaire's arms, allows her to overcome her half-hearted resistance to him. Once he begins to dance, she tries to feign lack of interest but quickly jumps in in perfect harmony to his steps. As the dance then takes its course, the two stars perfectly match their steps, timing, hand gestures, gazes so that their movement when dancing makes them comparable, not sexually differentiated, figures on screen (she is even wearing pants because she has been out riding). Then, as the dance starts to wind down and Astaire quickly spins Rogers over his feet and around his body in a very characteristic masculine ballroom dance gesture, she simply and effortlessly follows his example, and does the same to him. At the close of the dance, they shake hands and smile knowingly, as if perfectly aware that their dance has enacted a sexual ritual, choreographing their sexual relation in terms of comparability and partnership without losing its romance and erotic charge.

Most commentaries on Astaire's duets emphasize the equality of his dancing with Rogers in contrast to the sexual hierarchy that defines his pairings with younger co-stars, particularly in his last decade as a musical leading man; but such a reading of his dancing in those later films is largely influenced by the narrative contexts of the numbers. The plot of *Silk Stockings* rechannels Charisse's initial sexual indifference to Astaire ('If we are to spend the day together,' she warns, 'forget I am a woman and forget you are a man') into a passive femininity that greatly depends upon binarized sexual differentiation—beginning with her acceptance of spectacle as the proper feminine sphere, measured by her growing interest in Paris fashions—in order to demonstrate her change of commitment from communism to capitalism. 'Without love, what is a woman?' she asks him in song after her conversion, and concludes, 'For a woman to a man is just a woman, / But a man to a woman is her life.' However, 'Fated to be Mated,' the big dance number celebrating the couple in the next scene, choreographs the sexual relation quite differently on a more egalitarian ground reminiscent of the Astaire–Rogers duet to 'Isn't This a Lovely Day.'

'Fated to be Mated,' which takes place on a movie studio lot, could easily be subtitled 'Sunday Jumps Times Two.' Astaire and Charisse boisterously accommodate their dancing to the properties that fill up the space: they twirl around poles, sit on a park bench, push off pillars, swoop under parallel bars. Beginning and ending with the dancers in the same position (a medium shot of them hugging closely), this number moves serially rather than sequentially, continuously rather than cumulatively. It could conceivably go on for as long as there is music and dance space—or it could conceivably be cut down without losing its choreographic coherence.[8] Astaire and Charisse bound from one sound-stage setting to another, each locale signaling a shift in the music and, accordingly, in the tempo and style of their dancing, as the accompanying melody changes from 'Fated to be Mated' to reprises of Astaire's earlier love songs, 'Paris Loves Lovers' and 'All of You.' Now, in contrast to the staging of those other two songs (when Astaire was trying to seduce Charisse into both the benefits of capitalism for the sake of the story *and* the pleasures of dancing for the sake of the numbers), the choreography and the framing of this number treat the dancers on visibly equal terms. A great deal of side-by-side dancing keeps them together in the frame spatially, and this relation is then reinforced by the precision with which they synchronize their movement while facing the camera. As a consequence, when the many lifts, spins, and bends of this rather athletic number physically differentiate the dancers' positions, they do not connote Astaire's male superiority so much as continue to keep reconfiguring the dancers in relation to each other as two equally spectacular bodies moving through cinematic space.

In confirmation of their comparable value for the film as sources of spectacle, Charisse and Astaire do not dance together in a finale (as one might expect from the romantic plot) but individually star in big, splashy, energetic production numbers. Astaire's 'Ritz Rock and Roll,' his last big dance number at MGM, pays homage to his 'Top Hat' signature number in the film of that name and also to 'Puttin' on the Ritz' from *Blue Skies* (his premature swan song to films in 1946), and it is performed to celebrate both the opening of his new nightclub and the success of his scheming to get Charisse out of Moscow and back to Paris. All along, the plot has been working to push Astaire and Charisse into a binary sexual relation that differentiates them in terms of his masculine activity as a narrative agent and her feminine passivity as an object of spectacle; and there are indeed numbers in the film which help to achieve this stucturing of sexual difference through female spectacle (as in Charisse's 'Silk Stockings' and Janis Paige's 'Satin and Silk'), though, significantly enough, they do not occur in Astaire's presence. But if it has not been clear enough before this last number, with a shot of Charisse looking at Astaire rapturously just before he begins performing, there is no doubt at this moment that the film makes her the viewer and *him* the show. [. . .]

'So, uh, dancing's a waste of time?'

That the Hollywood musical routinely makes a spectacle of a male star, as I have been showing through my analysis of Fred Astaire, may go far in accounting for its great popularity in the late 1940s and early 1950s. Though always a significant factor in a studio's annual output since the invention of sound, the musical was most important during the ten-year period after World War II in large part because of the genre's emphasis on spectacle.[9] As Dana Polan comments, 'if musicals have seemed so typically a Hollywood art, this is not so much because they inevitably move a couple toward the finality of an ostensible productivity of an adult middle-class heterosexuality but because they propel characters toward an endless nonfinality, the spectacle as literally a showstopper' (Polan 1986: 293). More specifically, Hollywood musicals reimagined American masculinity for postwar audiences in the kind of spectacular terms that would later come to dominate a televisual popular culture, but with more mobility and flexibility.

To amplify what I mean, an understanding of the components that made up Astaire's star persona is crucial. For all his grace on the dance floor, he conformed to the marked ordinariness of almost every musical performer during the studio era. As Arlene Croce observes, 'The list of male singers and dancers who have become big stars in the movies is very largely an assortment of aging, balding, skinny, tubby, jug-eared, pug-faces and generally unprepossessing men' (Croce 1972: 8). With the exception of Gene Kelly,[10] none of the big musical stars—not Bing Crosby, Frank Sinatra, Dan Dailey, Donald O'Connor, Danny Kaye, or Fred Astaire—were likely candidates either for pin-ups or action heroes. So when musicals nevertheless made a spectacle of them, these male stars offered an alternative representation of masculinity which openly conflicted with the reductive binarism of active male/passive female that the generic romantic plots frequently promoted. The supposed evaluation of Astaire's first screen tests—'Can't act. Can't sing. Balding. Can dance a little' (Croce 1972: 14)—has continued to circulate in accounts of his career, including his AFI tribute, in order to show the myopia of studio heads, to be sure, but also, more significantly, to summarize how he revised the terms of male movie stardom by emphasizing talent over looks, dancing over action, spectacle over narrative.

This factor, I think, helps to explain the enormous attraction of both the musical genre and a middle-aged musical star like Fred Astaire for mainstream audiences during the postwar years. While Astaire may have connoted modernity and youth in his RKO films of the 1930s (where he represents the modernity of new and unpretentious popular musical sounds like jazz and swing), and tradition and maturity in the postwar era (where he now comes to represent just the opposite, the established tried-and-true show business tradition of the popular entertainer resisting the fads of postwar modernity), what authenticated his star persona on screen in either case was always spectacle, the sight of him performing as 'Fred Astaire.' Hence his star image was consistently represented by metonymies of his body, the source of his talent and charisma, throughout his career, most notably so during the 1950s when a shot of his legs (the opening of Silk Stockings), or his top hat (the opening of The Band Wagon), or even his voice singing over the titles to Funny Face), could serve instantly to signal his star identity in a film.

While those iconic signs fetishize Astaire in a way unexpected of a longstanding Hollywood leading man, they are nonetheless consistent with the means through which all of his films repeatedly authenticate his star quality as an entertainer through his spectacularity. For example, his signature style of dress—ranging from the trademark top hat and tails that became instantly identifiable with 'Fred Astaire' in the RKO series, to the baggy flannels and brightly-colored matching scarf and socks worn in the Technicolor films at Metro—insists upon the spectacle of his body in ways that go against the grain of Hollywood's typical treatment of a leading man. What's quite remarkable about Astaire's appearance in the opening of Easter Parade (1948), his comeback vehicle for MGM after a two-year retirement, is not his singing and dancing so much as the fact that, from the very first shot of the film, the vibrant colors of his costume—grey suit, pink shirt, white vest, blue carnation, black tie, white hankie, pearl tie stud, spats—turn him into a spectacle quite worthy, as the title song says in the film's finale, of the rotogravure: clearly a costume no different in purpose than the bangles and beads of a showgirl outfit, this outfit sets Astaire in an explicit relation of comparability to the women in the fashion salon ('Happy Easter'), and to the little boy in knickers with whom he competes for the purchase of a toy in the drug store immediately afterwards ('Drum Crazy'). Subsequently, when Astaire finally stands next to two of his co-stars, Ann Miller and Peter Lawford, he still stands *out* as the primary spectacle drawing the filmgoer's eye, because his costume makes a vivid contrast to the monochrome colors worn by both Lawford (dressed in shades of brown) and Miller (wearing a peach gown).

As the opening of *Easter Parade* illustrates, far from objectifying him as an erotic object in the manner of a showgirl, what the spectacle of Astaire draws attention to, in addition to the movement of his body, is the theatricality of his musical persona, which is finally what gives that body its cinematic value. Specifically, the star text of 'Fred Astaire' builds his charismatic persona out of tropes normally considered 'feminine'—*narcissism* (in his solo performances and special-effects numbers), which defines his body in terms of boundless energy and joyful motion; *exhibitionism* (in his show numbers, challenge dance duets, or those dance's performed for a bystander, sometimes for purposes of seduction), which defines his performance in terms of self-conscious spectacle and display of style; and *masquerade* (in his dandyish costuming, the levels of multiple personification required for some show numbers, the numerous plots of disguises or mistaken identities), which defines his identity in terms of theatrical play and social manners. These three elements intersect at the point of his star persona so that every characteristic of 'Fred Astaire' is an effect of their working in unison. His costuming in *Easter Parade*, for instance, has obvious implications of exhibitionism and narcissism as well as masquerade, just as his special effect number in *Royal Wedding* involves him in an exhibitionistic display of physical agility which actually serves to masquerade the technological fakery that enables him to dance on film. As a star text, all of this is to say, 'Fred Astaire' is a highly theatricalized representation of maleness on screen which oscillates between, on the one hand, a fictional character grounded in the static and reductive binarism of traditional gender roles and, on the other, a musical persona whose energy choreographs a libidinal force that revises conventional masculinity and linear desire.

Although immediately famous in the 1930s when he made the extraordinary series of dance musicals with Rogers, Astaire's star persona was most resonant for American culture after his comeback with the smash success of *Easter Parade* in 1948. For then he not only continued to defy gravity as a dancing man, with all the considerable assets of MGM and the Arthur Freed unit at his disposal to support him, but he appeared uncannily able—in the grace, ease, and energy which with he still moved on screen—to hold back the sands of time as well. This is the reason I have paid so much attention to Astaire's films from the 1950s, even though one could easily argue that his star persona was pretty much put in place during the years at RKO. Historically, though, there is a significant difference between the two stages in his career, and it is largely due to Hollywood's transformation of the Astaire–Rogers dance film into the integrated dance musical produced at MGM.

The effect of the integrated musical on the relation of narrative and number, as I mentioned earlier, is usually misunderstood or at best misrepresented, even by the people who made them, as a narrativization of song and dance. When interviewed in the late 1950s Roger Edens—song writer, vocal arranger, and associate producer for the Freed unit at Metro—

explained about the craft of integrating narrative and number: 'you have to be careful about music in films,' he said, '—so many musicals have been made in which the plot and the songs have nothing to do with each other. . . . I believe that songs in film musicals should be part of the script itself, actually sung dialogue' (Johnson 1958: 180). The actual achievement of the integrated musical, though, was not simply to use the numbers to advance the plot along, which implies a subordinate relation of the musical portions to the narrative. More specifically, as Jerome Delamater explains:

> [T]he nature of integration of the film musical lies not simply with the idea that the musical numbers and dances, in particular, should advance the plot but also suggests an integration of the entire cinematic process. The way in which the dances in a particular film are photographed, for example, suggests a kind of integration of the film making process with the dance process and that *together* they contribute to the integrity of the film. . . . Certainly part of the process of integration as [Gene] Kelly viewed it was to move easily and naturally from the regular narrative portions of the films into the numbers and back again; that requires a dancing persona, though not necessarily a character within the diegesis who is explained to be a dancer.
>
> (Delamater 1981: 98, 150)

In a truly integrated musical, even though the language of 'integration' always means to suggest the opposite practice, the extradiegetic, antirealist conventions of the numbers also purposefully shade into and influence the book portions, as when the soundtrack shifts aural registers to more closely miked sound for the dialogue before a number begins, or the music track begins to anticipate the melody of an upcoming number, or a star's movement in walking begins to take on the rhythmic dimensions of a dance. Thus whereas the numbers in 1930s musicals like the Astaire–Rogers series are by no means indifferently placed in terms of narrative development, they do differ from the story as distinctly marked moments of musical spectacle. By contrast, as I have already implied with my examples of narrative disruption and extradiegetic address, postwar musicals shift spectatorial interest from a musical film's narrativity to its continuous deployment of spectacle. This shift of interest lies behind the conventional structure of the postwar musical, one tending to build toward a big ballet (as in An American in Paris (1951)) which either interrupts the narrative with spectacle, or repeats it as dance, but rarely resolves a plot.

More to the point of what I have been arguing here, the integrated dance musical, which became synonymous with the names 'Fred Astaire and 'Gene Kelly,' also determined a revaluation of the male star and his 'dancing persona' in terms of spectacle over narrative. The Pirate (1948) in particular exemplifies this new styling of masculinity in the way it leads Judy Garland/Manuela from her infatuation with the legendary pirate Mack the Black, whose phallic masculinity is based in narrativity (the accounts of his adventures in the book she reads), to her appreciation of Serafin the Clown/Gene Kelly, whose playful and performative masculinity is based in spectacle. While a key film in any reading of Kelly, The Pirate was a historically significant film for Astaire as well because Easter Parade was intended as the follow-up Kelly–Garland teaming, and when Kelly broke his ankle, Astaire came out of retirement and into the pages of the rotogravure.[11]

When all is said and done, because of the genre's 'feminization' of the song-and-dance man through spectacle, I don't think it is simply a coincidence of film history that the integrated

Hollywood dance musical became so enormously popular for audiences and studios alike during roughly the same period as that other emblematic postwar genre, *film noir*. Though no *noir* detective ever looked so trim and dapper, or moved so swiftly and effortlessly through the city shadows, as Astaire's 'Rod Riley' in 'The Girl Hunt Ballet' that closes *The Band Wagon*, this witty and spectacular number implies some kind of an inverse relation existing between the two genres, from the number's tough-guy voice-over narration, styled parodically after Mickey Spillane, to the representation of femininity as a duality in the ballet scenario, danced with great verve by Cyd Charisse for ironic effect, since here the blonde virgin, and not the brunette spider woman, turns out to be the killer. The comparison suggested by 'The Girl Hunt Ballet' actually makes considerable sense of both genres because, like *film noir*, the integrated dance musical represented urban experience in ways highly responsive to postwar anxieties about male authority and masculinity, though to be sure, the musical went to one extreme (visual excess), and *film noir* to the other (visual spareness).[12] But each in its own way commodified the materialism of cinematic spectacle, each celebrated technological innovation, and [. . .] each featured a particular type of 'feminized' male star performance, with the song-and-dance man the counterpart of the castrated vet or rogue detective of *noir* dramas.

In contrast to the more oppressive, often hysterical, depiction of postwar America's restoration of binarized gender roles in *film noir*, the musical imagined an alternative style of masculinity, one grounded in spectacle and spectatorship, which was literally made visible and given body by Fred Astaire, and this was surely no mean accomplishment for a popular mainstream genre. But the Hollywood musical could produce this effect so easily because it was the one genre which, through its numbers, could take the performance of a star's masculinity to heart so completely, so seriously, and so openly as spectacle.

Notes

1   For further elaboration see Lucy Fischer's discussion of female spectacle in *Dames* (1934) (Fischer 1989: 132–48).

2   In my effort to move the male musical star beyond the simple reversal of male spectator/female erotic object, I should make clear that I do not mean to suggest that the sexual objectification which Neale describes does not apply in some cases (such as John Travolta, Neale's own example). Since my particular concern here is the Hollywood dance musical produced under the studio system, where someone like Fred Astaire most exemplifies the relation of the male star to spectacle, I have had to exclude from the scope of my discussion consideration of those teen music idols (Elvis Presley, Pat Boone, Cliff Richard, etc.), who came to musicals starting in the late 1950s, and whose stardom poses important questions about male spectacle in *and* out of film as conventional pin-up material.

3   Even so, some of the great female musical stars pose problems for that showgirl standard. The one who immediately comes to mind is Judy Garland. Her short-waisted body—unconventional by showgirl standards and uncontrollable, as it eventually turned out, by the studio—is a significant and transgressive element of her star image, as Richard Dyer explains (see Dyer 1986: 156–68). Too, recall the queen of spectacle at MGM, Esther Williams; when the camera lingers on the sight of her naked thighs in *Million Dollar Mermaid* (1952), the physical strength, awesome muscularity, and disciplined athleticism connoted

by her body (which in this respect is comparable to that of her co-star, Victor Mature) likewise transform the showgirl basis of her female star image into something quite different.

4 Robin Wood raises a similar argument about the numbers of *Silk Stockings*, when he states that their 'vitality . . . itself transcends their local ideological functions' (Wood 1975: 67). Significantly, though, he has very little to say about either Astaire's or Charisse's numbers, which is where the film's vitality primarily lies, as I will show later in this essay.

5 John Mueller, who reads all of Astaire's numbers through their narrative logic, thinks this is 'a garish, ghastly production number' and complains in particular about its *lack* of internal narrative coherence, concluding that 'the "Haiti" number betrays no thought processes whatever' (Mueller 1985: 329, 330). One might argue, though, that the purpose of this number, which delays the introduction of Powell for at least half its length, is to give the brother and sister one last chance to dance together, so in this respect the pattern behind the dance movement is the separation and reunion of the performing team; this may be why the fictional performers then break 'character' in their curtain call afterwards, acknowledging their mutual pleasure in the audience's applause. By contrast, they remain in low-life 'character' after the 'Liar' number on their opening night in London, possibly because for the post-performance party they plan to be each other's date and are still a team acting in perfect synchrony.

6 See, for example, the discussions of Astaire's dancing in Croce 1972, Delamater 1981, Mueller 1984 and 1985, and Mast 1987.

7 One might try to account for the casting of Astaire and Powell (in her first major adult role) as siblings not lovers by citing the age difference between them, but then wouldn't that explanation more logically result in a father–daughter team (thereby strengthening my claim)? Powell was actually the third actress cast in the role of Astaire's sister, replacing Judy Garland (this was the dismissal that ended her relation to Metro), who replaced June Allyson. The casting of Garland, who had starred opposite Astaire as a romantic lead in *Easter Parade* in 1948, and was due to play his wife in *The Barkleys of Broadway* the following year (the role went to Ginger Rogers), indicates that the age difference alone did not explain the script's focus on a sibling team. Rather, as a reference to Astaire's own professional teaming with his sister Adèle, the story situation continues the intertextual references to his star image in his MGM vehicles that began with *Easter Parade* and *The Barkleys of Broadway* and continued through *The Band Wagon*.

8 As indeed it has been cut down: the original MGM soundtrack album included an abridged version of the number, and *That's Entertainment* II showed only the last section (the part danced to 'All of You'). Furthermore, the number itself was shot in segments in an even more discontinuous way than usual, since Charisse wears a different version of her costume (one with culottes rather than a skirt) for two crucial knee spins. For the photographic illustration see Mueller 1985: 397.

9 Though today one tends to equate the musical with the blockbuster roadshow adaptation of a Broadway hit, the sheer number of ordinary musicals produced during the postwar period, especially at MGM, cannot be underestimated. In its issue of April 14, 1952, *Life* previewed several upcoming musicals in production at the Culver City studio—'glossy, brassy, cornily plotted, elaborately staged, expensively produced extravaganza'—noting that 'Hollywood, which dearly loves a cycle, is embarked on a congenial one: more producers are making more musicals and expect them to be raking in more and more

profits with them.' Two years later, *Variety* reported on June 16, 1954 that 'Metro's leadership in the musical film field continues unabated. At least one third of the company's upcoming releases are slated for the musical treatment and it appears that the number of tuners for 1954 will top the 10 (out of a total of 45) releases issued in 1953.' The musical was primarily bankable for the industry because of its capacity as 'extravaganza' to feature the spectacle of new technologies as the mainstay of its generic identity, which is also what required support from a complex studio system of artisans and technicians, so when that system collapsed, taking with it the economic support of the expensive technology necessary for the genre (like three-strip Technicolor as opposed to the cheaper and muddier Ansco and Eastman color processes), the demise of the integrated musical epitomized by MGM in particular was inevitable, as the highly reduced output of studio-produced musicals at the end of the decade evidences.

10 This is not to say that Gene Kelly is to be excluded from my general remarks about musical stars. Although more conventionally—even relentlessly—'masculine' than Astaire in his screen persona, Kelly can just as easily be examined in the same terms. For instance, a fear of losing his virility in dance seems to account for the particular inflections of Kelly's screen persona that differentiate him from Astaire: the attention to athleticism in the various set-piece ballets, to cite one characteristic, is a means of compensating for the gaze directed at his body, and yet that gaze is accentuated in some numbers by the recurring wiggle of his buttocks in tights or sailor pants. As a result, all the more conscious of his musical identity as a gender performance, Kelly goes to great extremes to disavow it, producing a more riven and less confident male screen image than Astaire's.

11 Mueller 1985 reports that the blocking of all the numbers had already been worked out with Kelly in mind, and that what Astaire primarily changed were the actual steps (p. 277).

12 Though *film noir* tends to be the genre considered most fully representative of Hollywood's postwar treatment of American male urban experience, one shouldn't forget how many musicals were similarly set in cities, or that musicals moved out of the studio to film in the streets of New York City (*On the Town*, 1949) at the same time that *noir* did. The significance of the city to musicals, Astaire's as well as Kelly's, was deeply felt by contemporary audiences, at least if Douglas Newton's appreciation of the genre in *Sight and Sound* in 1952 is any indication: 'The city is of course one of the great elements of the musical . . . and as a result the musicals are among the rare poetic works so far to accept big city life without using it simply as decorative detail or a satirical target' (Newton 1952: 36).

Bibliography

Altman, R. (1987) *The American Film Musical*, Bloomington: Indiana University Press.

Croce, A. (1972) *The Fred Astaire and Ginger Rogers Book*, New York: Galahad Books.

Delamater, J. (1981) *Dance in the Hollywood Musical*, Ann Arbor, MI: UMI Research Press.

Dyer, R. (1986) *Heavenly Bodies: Film Stars and Society*, New York: St Martin's Press.

Fischer, L. (1989) *Shot/Countershot: Film Tradition and Women's Cinema*, Princeton, NJ: Princeton University Press.

Johnson, A. (1958) 'Conversation with Roger Edens,' *Sight and Sound* 27: 179–82.

Mast, G. (1987) *Can't Help Singin': the American Musical on Stage and Screen*, Woodstock, NY: Overlook Press.

Mueller, J. (1984) 'Fred Astaire and the Integrated Musical,' *Cinema Journal* 24, 1: 28–40.

—— (1985) *Astaire Dancing: the Musical Films*, New York: Knopf.

Mulvey, L. (1975) 'Visual Pleasure and Narrative Cinema' rpt 1989, in *Visual and Other Pleasures*, Bloomington: Indiana University Press, 14–26.

Neale, S. (1983) 'Masculinity as Spectacle,' *Screen* 24, 6: 2–16.

Newton, D. (1952) 'Poetry in Fast and Musical Motion,' *Sight and Sound* 22: 36–38.

Polan. D. (1986) *Power and Paranoia: History, Narrative, and the American Cinema* 1940–1950, New York: Columbia University Press.

Williams, L. (1989) *Hard Core: Power, Pleasure, and the 'Frenzy of the Visible'*, Berkeley: University of California Press.

Wood, R. (1975) 'Art and Ideology: Notes on *Silk Stockings*' rpt 1981, in Rick Altman (ed.) *Genre: the Musical*, New York: Routledge, 57–69.

PART THREE

CAMP INTERVENTIONS

Introduction

Although the introduction to this reader comments that musicals today are viewed primarily as objects of nostalgia or discomfort, either response indicating its different value from the past as mainstream entertainment, the genre has also achieved considerable subcultural status as an object of camp, especially for gay audiences. As Paul Roen observes, "The Hollywood musical is a genre which, by definition, exudes camp." In explanation, he cites the genre's orientation toward excessive spectacle; musicals not only allow people suddenly to burst into song but they are "all awash with glitter, tinsel, and garish artifice"—and they are the place to watch two icons of gay camp at work, Judy Garland and Carmen Miranda (Roen 1994: 11–12).

What is camp? And why or how does the musical "exude" it? To start with, camp is not easy to define. More than an attraction to excessive artifice or veneration of star divas, camp marks out a rhetorical stance or posture through a combination of irony, aestheticism, theatricality, and humor (Babuscio 1984: 41). Camp, however, has a political edge, too, which can be subversive or conservative in its impact. Any understanding of camp must take into account what historically has been its target: the cultural basis of sexual and social identities in the masculine–feminine binary naturalizing heterosexuality as the single position of normality. Camp, that is, takes an ironic stance toward gender normality, parodying it through an excessively aestheticized, overly theatricalized style that inverts or disrupts the relations of form to content, surface to depth, certainly, but also of margin to center. A historical consequence of a period of sexual regulation—which, coincidentally or not, occurred at the same time as the heyday of the Hollywood musical—camp was the self-reflective style of gay men, passing as straight, who kept a "straight face" in order not to let outsiders in on the joke, yet who simultaneously winked at the initiated in shared acknowledgment of the joke. As Jack Babuscio notes, "camp resides largely in the eye of the beholder," because it "is never a thing or person *per se*, but, rather, a relationship between activities, individuals, situations, *and* gayness" (Babuscio 1984: 40–41). It follows for many that camp therefore names an act of reading culture critically. To borrow from Arbuthnot and Seneca's essay, a camp reading focuses on the incongruities, dissonances, and excesses of a text with the goal of interrupting its cultural pre-texts, beginning with the codes of heterosexuality.

As the essays in this section illustrate, the gay female icons associated with the musical, as well as the genre's affinity for spectacle, has provided a rich ground for such camp interventions.

The first piece, titled "Judy Garland and Camp" for this volume, is an excerpt from Richard Dyer's book, *Heavenly Bodies*. His chapter on Garland there offers a much lengthier explanation of why this star had a special attractiveness for gay men in the 1950s and 1960s. His entire argument is worth summarizing to provide the wider context for his more specific remarks about the camp inflection of Garland's star image, particularly as directed toward her musicals. According to Dyer, three main coordinates of the Garland image work together—on screen in her films, off screen in her concerts, but also in conjunction with the much publicized revelations about her biography—to produce its meaning for gay audiences. These are: ordinariness, androgyny, and camp.

First, the musicals construct the Garland persona as the small-town girl next door who typifies a wholesome image of "heterosexual family normality" (Dyer 1986: 159). This persona nonetheless implies "a special relationship to ordinariness" (p.156). The musicals, for instance, attribute to Garland a lack of glamour in comparison with other MGM female stars, such as Lana Turner and Hedy Lamarr, Garland's costars in *Ziegfeld Girl* (1941). Failure to be glamorous suggests the star's inability to conform to normative femininity, at least as the movies depict it, and her characters are consequently as much defined through their gender insecurity as by their normality. The musicals also build upon the intensity of Garland's singing. Whether in its vivacity or torchiness, this performance style authenticates her projection of feelings through song but in a way that exceeds "the safe, contained, small-town norms of the character," further suggesting "an emotional difference born within normality" (p.162). That Garland is readable on screen as being simultaneously ordinary and different, even more so in the light of her post-MGM biography, begins to explain her cultish appeal to gay men, because it intimates a parallel to their own location in mainstream culture: "To turn out not-ordinary after being saturated with the values of ordinariness structures Garland's career and the standard gay biography alike" (p.159).

Related to this is the second coordinate Dyer analyzes, Garland's androgyny, epitomized by the tramp costume often featured in her post-MGM concerts. The costume, taken from the "Couple of Swells" number in *Easter Parade* (1948), picks up on how the musicals often put her in men's clothes in a number or two, for instance, a clown outfit (*The Pirate* (1948)), tuxedo jacket and fedora (*Summer Stock* (1950)), baggy dress shirt and tights, or street-kid's rags (*A Star is Born* (1954)). "The tramp," Dyer explains about the importance of this signature costume, ". . . has left questions of sexuality behind in an androgyny that is not so much in-between (marked as both feminine and masculine) as without clothing," implying an escape from confining sex roles (p.177). On screen, the androgynous dimension, often underscored by the disjunction of her female characters and the show numbers which they perform in masculine costumes, adds to the Garland persona an element of theatricality which may transcend but also parodies gender. For with its overt staging of the "artificiality of naturalness and normality" (p.178), the androgyny heightens recognition of both that difference born within ordinariness and the oppressive effect of normative gender roles. Together, these two coordinates of Garland's star image help clarify how, as Dyer demonstrates in the section this volume reprints, "she is not a star turned into camp, but a star who expresses camp attitudes" (p.179). This third coordinate of the Garland image is evident in the vocal inflections and self-reflectivity of her concert performance style, to be sure, but it also informs her work at MGM, materializing most strikingly and uniformly, as Dyer shows, in *The Pirate*.

Dyer's analysis could lead one to conclude that the camp reception of Garland and her films resulted from the "special" interaction of a performer and a particular demographic segment of an audience which, during her MGM years at least, was wider and more mainstreamed. Yet as his commentary about *The Pirate* illustrates, camp attitudes can be found in the musicals themselves—in their narratives sometimes, but more often in their spectacle, in their costuming and sets, their choreography, their ideas for numbers. In Part III's second piece, "'Working Like a Homosexual': Camp Visual Codes and the Labor of Gay Subjects in the MGM Freed Unit," Matthew Tinkcom demonstrates how the camp style of the musicals manufactured by that studio's most famous and profitable production team also makes visible the otherwise invisible gay craftspeople working with Garland on films such as *The Pirate*. Tinkcom points out how generic convention, particularly the presumed subordination of number to narrative, effaces the camp sensibility underlying the spectacular production values which MGM promoted to distinguish its musicals. The camp style is therefore in the eye of the beholder insofar as it allowed the product to "pass" as wholesome entertainment, much as the studio's gay labor force passed in their daily lives, but it nevertheless builds into the films a critical stance toward the pretext of gay–straight passing, namely, the integrated form and heterosexual narratives which rendered the camp style, like the artisans, invisible to an undiscerning eye.

While the Dyer and Tinkcom pieces focus on gay camp, specifically in connection with the MGM musical, the other two essays in this section turn to musicals made by Warners and Fox. More to the point, these latter essays argue that female audiences can also recognize, get pleasure from, and find comparable significance in the genre's camp style and stars. In "Feminist Camp in *Gold Diggers of 1933*," Pamela Robertson reexamines this Berkeley musical by reading it as camp. She observes that, when the film's numbers produce their noticeable effect of dissonance between spectacle and representation, they establish for viewers the value of a camp style which extends to the plot and revises the apparent dialectical opposition of narrative and number. That is, whereas this musical's form appears to segregate the gold-digging narrative from the Berkeley numbers, the camp style forges a new and different relationship between them, one based on appropriation of the trope of the gold digger in order to parody her commodification as a prostitute. The musical's camp thus allows for a feminist perspective on both the masquerade plot and the Berkeley numbers. Viewing *Gold Diggers* as feminist camp, Robertson claims, lets women laugh at the film's parodic deployment of this trope, but also encourages them to take it seriously, which is to say, critically and historically.

Finally, in this section's fourth excerpt, "'The Lady in the Tutti-Frutti Hat': Carmen Miranda, a Spectacle of Ethnicity," Shari Roberts also discusses how spectacle in the musical can offer camp pleasures for female as well as gay audiences. Roberts does not analyze Carmen Miranda as a gay icon in the way that Dyer approaches Garland, nor does Roberts focus on camp *per se*. This essay nonetheless examines not only what, in effect, made Miranda a camp star in the 1940s, but also how her camp attitudes probably spoke more directly than one suspects to minority audiences during that era, women most of all. According to Roberts, Carmen Miranda's representation of Otherness, while regulated by her non-narrative placement in films and historically resonant with the United States' wartime national policy regarding Latin America, is laced with an awareness of self-parody which makes emphatic how her representation of gendered ethnicity is a cultural impersonation. From the Brazilian star's costumes, to her singing and dancing, to her fracturing of language, to her marginalized position in romance plots revolving around the blonde Betty Grable or Alice Faye, the outrageousness of Miranda's performance of an "othered" female identity is double-edged. The elements comprising the star as a cultural image of strange, exotic, and unassimilable female ethnicity draws from and so reinforces sexist, racist stereotypes. However, Roberts goes on to point out, the exaggerated reduction of Miranda's Otherness into a spectacular yet knowingly self-parodic style also calls into question oppressive assumptions about feminine and ethnic essence. The self-parody creates a possibility for the star's fans to negotiate or subvert the stereotypes—in other words, to see Miranda as intentionally producing her own camp reading of gender and ethnicity as cultural constructions on a par with her outlandish costuming. This dimension of Miranda's image explains why, almost as soon as she made her appearance on the New York stage and in Hollywood musicals, her figure was so easily imitatable as drag, a mainstay of camp female impersonation acts on screen (as in *Babes on Broadway* (1941)) and in all-male military shows.

Judy Garland and Camp 8

RICHARD DYER

Judy Garland is camp. Several people have tried to define both what camp is and its relationship to the situation and experience of gay men. (I do not propose to re-enter the fray of whether it is politically and culturally progressive—for, see Cohen and Dyer, 1980; against, see Britton, 1978/79.) It clearly is a defining feature of the male gay subculture. Jack Babuscio (1977) suggests that it is the fact of being able to pass for straight that has given gays the characteristically camp awareness of surfaces, of the social constructedness of sex roles (see also Russo, 1979 and Dyer, 1977). Mark Booth (1983) stresses gay men's sense of marginality which is turned into an excessive commitment to the marginal (the superficial, the trivial) in culture. Either way, camp is a characteristically gay way of handling the values, images and products of the dominant culture through irony, exaggeration, trivialisation, theatricalisation and an ambivalent making fun of and out of the serious and respectable. (See, in addition to those already cited, Sontag, 1964 and Boone, 1979, especially the latter's discussion of 'trivialisation'.)

The object of camp's making fun is often a star like Bette Davis or Shirley Bassey, and Garland can be read like that. She is imitable, her appearance and gestures copiable in drag acts (e.g. Jim Bailey, Craig Russell in *Outrageous!*); her later histrionic style can be welcomed as wonderfully over-the-top; her ordinariness in her MGM films can be seen as camp, as 'failed seriousness' (Sontag) or else the artificiality of naturalness and normality—as one writer put it:

> What I liked about this star was a sort of naive innocence, a sweetness that I believe was genuine. Now, however, I think that the gay audience—especially the sophisticated segment—would or might look upon her style as unintentional camp. This effect, of course, also has to do with the kinds of roles, as well as the movie vehicles, that she played in. Because her style, her stance, was so damned 'straight' (I use the word meaning 'serious' or 'sober'), it amounted to, as I said, that of camp or at least what appeared to be camp (Letter to author).

Even this writer doesn't say that he reads Garland like this, and I have no evidence to suggest that it is the predominant way in which Garland is camp. Anybody can be read as camp (though some lend themselves to it more readily than others), but Garland is far more inward with camp. She is not a star turned into camp, but a star who expresses camp attitudes.

In the later years this was clear, particularly in the chat at the concerts and (specially composed) verses of the songs. At Carnegie Hall, she leads into *San Francisco* with the verse:

> I never will forget
> Jeanette MacDonald
> Just to think of her
> It gives my heart a pang
> I never will forget
> How that brave Jeanette
> Just stood there
> In the ruins
> And sang
> A-a-a—and sang—

MacDonald was well established as camp queen of an already pretty camp genre, operetta. Garland extends the beat on a hum before singing her name and pauses for three waves of laughter before proceeding—for that audience, it was enough to mention MacDonald's name to get a camp response. The send-up (of MacDonald singing in the debris of an earthquake in the film *San Francisco*) that follows serves for those who haven't already got the point that MacDonald is camp.

At her last appearance at the Talk of the Town (like the Carnegie Hall concert, available on record), she introduces 'I'd Like to Hate Myself in the Morning':

> I have to do a new song. I haven't been taught a new song since Clive Brooks was a girl. (Laughter) Was he?

Here the gay connection is more direct—Brooks is not only camp because of his high, clipped upper-class English accent, but because his gender can be called into question. Her 'Was he?' presumably is a question about Brooks' sexuality, to which gay cognoscenti in the audience perhaps knew the answer.

Garland's reputation for being camp (rather than being seen as camp) was reinforced by stories that were published after her death. Her own awareness of the gay connection is made clear. Barry Conley in *Gay News* quotes (as have others) Liza Minnelli quoting her mother— " 'When I die I have visions of fags singing 'Over the Rainbow' and the flag at Fire Island being flown at half mast' " (Conley, 1972, p.11), Fire Island being a largely gay beach resort near New York. Christopher Finch (1975, pp.129–30) writes at length of her ease in the predominantly gay milieu of the Freed unit while Brad Steiger (1969, pp.103–4) talks of her frequenting gay bars in New York in the sixties. One person who wrote to me told me that her

> last professional engagement in New York City was when she took money under the table singing in a lesbian bar on East 72nd Street called 'Sisters' in about 1968–9. This $50 per session or so was paid to support her whenever she would 'wander in' and pretend to sing 'impromptu' so she could support her drug habit. Very sad but nonetheless true (Letter to author).

Although published after her death, these accounts do suggest how versed she was, or could be assumed to be, in gay culture, how inward with its procedures and cadences.

The effect of her camp is to act back on her films, in two ways. First, a repertoire of stories has built up around her own attitude to her work. The more these become part of gay fan talk, the more they will inform perception of the films. The simple sparkle of 'Who (Stole My Heart Away)?' from Till the Clouds Roll By (1946) becomes ironic when one knows Garland's apparent mirth at singing the song when she was several months pregnant. Her role as the sweet, out-of-town girl in Easter Parade may look more acerbic when informed by what Charles Walters says she said to him before shooting:

> Look sweetie, I'm no June Allyson, you know. Don't get cute with me. None of that batting-the-eyelids bit, or the fluffing the hair routine for me, buddy! (quoted in Finch, 1975, p.158).

The knife edge between camp and hurt, a key register of gay culture, is caught when one takes together her intense performance of the scene after Norman's death in A Star Is Born and her remark quoted by George Cukor, who had expressed amazement that she had reproduced such intensity over two long takes:

> Oh, that's nothing. Come over to my house any afternoon. I do it every afternoon. But I only do it once at home (ibid., p.197).

Similarly one may hear the pathos of the later performances of 'Over the Rainbow' differently when one has at the back of one's mind Garland's remark to a fan who begged her never to 'forget the rainbow'—'Why, madam . . . how could I ever forget the rainbow? I've got rainbows up my ass' (Conley, 1972, p.10—the source of the story is Liza Minnelli).

But, secondly, this bringing together of Garland's reported remarks and the films is not necessary, because there is camp in the text of the films themselves. Her films with Vincente Minnelli, especially 'The Great Lady Gives an Interview' in Ziegfeld Follies (1946) and The Pirate (1948), are rather obviously camp pieces, with their elements of theatricality, parody and obvious artifice. Garland's camp humour often has the effect of sending up the tone and conventions of her films. In Presenting Lily Mars (1943) she sings 'When I Hear Beautiful Music' in a night-club, a scene in which the character's star quality is demonstrated. It is camp in two ways. First, Garland mocks the operetta style singing of Marta Eggerth, who has sung the song earlier in the film. This is a standard camp Garland routine, used on radio broadcasts in the late thirties and forties as well as in other films—she uses excessively elaborated trills, oversweetened notes and hand-wringing, shoulder-rolling, lip-curling gestures to summon up the pretty-pretty soprano style of Jeanette MacDonald, Deanna Durbin and other such stars. Secondly, Garland's performance also sends up this standard girl-gets-big-break-in-night-club. As a waiter flashes by with a tray held aloft, Garland's eyes roll, she backs away from him, then smirks at this detail of restaurant mise-en-scène that would go by unnoticed in a more straight performance. There are several other such moments where Garland draws attention to the way the number has been set up, culminating in her stumbling over the inconveniently placed drum set, undercutting any notion of this as a straightforward moment of star quality triumphant.

In such ways Garland can seem to be reflecting back either on her own image in the film or on the vehicle in which she has been placed. As Wade Jennings (1979, p.324) puts it, there is 'lurking in her eyes and the corners of her mouth . . . [a] suppressed mirth . . . [that]

threatens to mock the silly plot and the two-dimensional character she plays'. When Dorothy emerges from the house into Oz for the first time, she says to her dog, 'Toto, I don't think we're in Kansas anymore.' It's obviously a funny line, given the shimmering Oz sets, but is it said in a knowing, camp way? Are we laughing directly at Dorothy's charming naivety, or with Garland at the over-the-top sets and Dorothy's artful gingham frock? Impossible to determine, of course, though Christopher Finch (1975, p. 85) does point out that, at 17, Garland in *The Wizard of Oz* is 'an adolescent with a grown-up's singing voice *acting* the part of a child'—the possibility of ambivalence, play, fun with the part and plot is at least there. In 1982, Rockshots, a gay greetings card company, issued a card depicting Garland as Dorothy, in gingham with Toto in a basket, in a gay bar, with her opening line in Oz as the message inside. It is not just the incongruity of juxtaposing Dorothy/Garland and men in gay macho style clothes and poses that is camp; the card has picked on Garland's irony towards Dorothy and Oz, an irony very easily transposed by gay men to their cultivation of an exaggeratedly masculine style and scene. Just as Garland in Oz can be seen as both in the magic world and yet standing outside it too, so gay culture is ambivalent about its construction of a fantasy scene that is both keenly desired and obviously a put-on.

For the most part Garland's campness might be seen as mildly sabotaging her roles and films. (Those who dislike camp feel that it is in fact deeply destructive in its insistently making fun of everything—see Britton, 1978/79.) It is seldom of a piece with the rest of the film, and only *The Pirate* seems to use Garland's campness in a sustained fashion in its play with sex roles and spectacular illusion, two of the standard pleasures musicals offer.

Sex role send-up centres on the male in *The Pirate* and Gene Kelly's role and performance as Serafin. Garland as Manuela functions in two ways in relation to this. First, she is given a string of lines to deflate his machismo, whether it be his corny chatting up of her at their first meeting or his pretending to be the pirate Macoco later in the film. In the first case she directly mocks his lines; in the second, when she has just discovered that he is not really Macoco, she wildly exaggerates the excitement of his virility while at the same time humorously hitting where it really hurts him, Serafin, by saying what a lousy actor he is (and thus calling forth a display of bruised male pride, in itself a standard moment in Gene Kelly films). Since Manuela is also a sweet, vulnerable girl, yearning for her dreams to come true (in other words, the standard Garland role), these salty quips unsettle the easy acceptance of that girlish image; and as a lot of the humour is underscored by the way Garland delivers the lines, it can seem like the performer wittily intervening to deconstruct the characters she is playing and playing opposite.

Secondly, in terms of narrative, Garland/Manuela is placed as the subject of desire; that is, the film is about her desire for a truly exciting life, and man. She constructs this desire in the image of the pirate Macoco, Mack the Black, that she has learnt from her story books. The film plays on this desire, at the same time playing with the Garland image. It turns out that, as in *The Wizard of Oz*, *Meet Me in St Louis* and so many of her films she is indeed engaged to Macoco, only neither she nor anyone else in the town knows it. The problem is that the real Macoco is nothing like the story book Mack the Black—he is the fat, fussy mayor of the town. Garland/Manuela has her heart's desire right at hand—only he doesn't look like her heart's desire at all, a point brought out later by the governor-general's rather lascivious comparison of Serafin (whom he thinks is Macoco) and the usual dull round of real pirates. When, in their betrothal scene, Macoco (alias Don Pedro) tells Garland/Manuela that he has no plans to take her travelling, that home is best, there is a reaction shot of her uttering, appalled, the word 'home', the exact reversal in tone of Dorothy/Garland's line at the end of *The Wizard of Oz* or Esther/Garland's at the end of *Meet Me in St Louis*.

The person who does look like her heart's desire, but who she knows can only play the part of it, is the actor Serafin. Through the film's complex narrative peripeteia Manuela/Garland is led to the point where she knowingly settles for the illusion of her heart's desire—she settles for Serafin.

In addition to this narrative progression, the film also suggests the degree to which Manuela's fantasies are themselves socially constructed fictions. Under hypnosis (which close-ups clearly indicate we are meant to take as having really occurred), Manuela expresses her true feelings to Serafin—but these turn out to be an amalgam of lines from earlier in the film, taken from either her story book on Macoco or from what Kelly/Serafin has said to her when he tries to chat her up. So from the book we get 'Someday he'll swoop down on me like a chicken hawk and carry me away', from Serafin's spiel 'Beneath this prim exterior there are depths of emotion, romantic longings'. Garland hardens her voice for such lines, to give them a dryly comic edge; yet her performance of going into hypnosis is soft and tremulous, her performance of the ensuing 'Mack the Black' deliriously all-out (with wildly swinging camera movements to underscore this). This kind of moving in and out of the 'emotional truth' of the character and situation allows the film, allows Garland, to point to both the vivid intensity of repressed feelings and the fact that those feelings are themselves culturally constructed, not a given authenticity.

In the second hypnosis scene, Garland/Manuela pretends to be hypnotised in order to flush out Don Pedro (whom she has only just realised is Macoco) and save Serafin (who is about to be hanged as Macoco). Again she plays out the exaggerated longing for his virility as she did before when mocking Serafin's impersonation of Macoco; here it is actually on Serafin's stage, thus doubly underlining this declaration of desire as performance. With the way it is played and cut-ins of Don Pedro getting more and more frustrated that this love is not being directed at him, the real Macoco, the whole scene works several levels of camp together. However, when Garland/Manuela then sings 'Love of My Life' to Kelly/Serafin/Macoco, although still on stage the film goes into a soft-focus close-up and standard heartfelt crooning from Garland—in other words, at the point in the film most signalled as illusion, we get the most direct expression of 'true' feeling. It is in the recognition of illusion that camp finds reality.

The treatment of men as spectacle reiterates this. It is Kelly not Garland who is the centre of the big production numbers, 'Niña' and 'The Pirate Ballet', each of them emphasising sex through costuming (tights and shorts, respectively), Kelly's movement (for instance, wiggling his bottom at the groups of women clustered about him in 'Niña', 'flexing his thighs in 'The Pirate Ballet') and camerawork (sinuous camera movement in the first, low angle, crotch centred positioning in the second), 'Niña' is not observed by Garland/Manuela, but generally in the film man/Kelly as spectacle is established as being from her point of view. (In itself quite unusual in Hollywood films—*Rebecca*, for instance, a film whose first half hour is entirely constructed around the never named female protagonist's desire for Maxim/Laurence Olivier, nonetheless entirely denies this character any point of view shots of him.) The film keeps shifting its/our perspective on how we are to take Garland/Manuela's libidinous looking. The first introduction of the fantasy of Mack the Black is through the story book pictures of him. The film starts with this, with us directly enjoying the coloured drawings of him (in which he is predominantly constructed as a figure of rape fantasy). It is only after a few pages of drawings have been turned that the camera draws back and we discover we have been entering the fantasy through Manuela's point-of-view. 'The Pirate Ballet' starts from a dissolve of her looking at Serafin in the street from her bedroom window, the implication being that the wild, exploding, sexy number that follows is how she sees him in her mind's eye. Later, when she is making fun of his assumption of Macoco's machismo, she runs her eyes up and down him saying with relish, 'Let me look my full at you'. In the second hypnosis scene, she circles Kelly/Serafin (pretending she thinks he's Macoco), gazing at him as she celebrates (sends up) his masculinity, while Don Pedro/Macoco is cut-in looking on, desiring to be looked at by Manuela as she is now looking at Serafin. The film thus fully allows Kelly as sex object, to a more sustained degree than any male star between Rudolph Valentino and John Travolta; and at the same time plays around with him as spectacle, so that he is both turn-on and send-up.

The film's resolution is the acceptance of both together, the embrace of the illusion of spectacle, and in the widest sense. Not only does Garland/Manuela settle for someone who only looks like (is the spectacle of) Mack the Black, she also opts to become a player—she will get to travel the world through the profession of pretence. Again the film gives another twist to the paradox. In the final number, 'Be a Clown', Garland/Manuela and Kelly/Serafin perform as clowns; right at the end in close-up they look at each other and burst into laughter. There is no reason why Manuela and Serafin, in love, doing a jolly number, should not as characters burst into laughter; but many have seen this as Judy Garland and Gene Kelly falling about laughing at the fun they've just been making in the film. Thus dressed as clowns on a stage in a very 'theatrical' movie-musical (in terms of performance and *mise-en-scène*), the 'real' attitude of the performers is held to come through—the reality of the pretence of illusion.

In lines and role, as well as the way Garland plays them, *The Pirate* explores a camp attitude towards life. Play on illusion and reality does not have to be seen as camp or gay. As throughout this chapter, I am neither claiming that only gay men could see it this way or that these aspects need be understood as camp or gay. What I am saying is that the particular way in which *The Pirate* plays with questions of artifice, together with the presence of Garland in it and her particular way of delivering a line as funny, make it particularly readable within the gay male subcultural discourse of camp. [. . .]

Works cited

Babuscio, Jack (1977) 'Camp and Gay Sensibility', in Richard Dyer (ed.) *Gays and Film* (London: British Film Institute) pp.40–57.

Boone, Bruce (1979) 'Gay Language as Political Praxis, the Poetry of Frank O'Hara', *Social Text*, no. 1, pp.59–92.

Booth, Mark (1983) *Camp* (London: Quartet).

Britton, Andrew (1978/79) 'For Interpretation, Against Camp', *Gay Left*, no.7, Winter 1978/79, pp.11–14.

Cohen, Derek and Dyer, Richard (1980) 'The Politics of Gay Culture', in Gay Left Collective (eds) *Homosexuality, Power and Politics* (London: Allison & Busby) pp.172–86.

Conley, Barry (1972) 'The Garland Legend: The Stars Have Lost Their Glitter', *Gay News*, no. 13, pp.10–11.

Dyer, Richard (1977) 'Its Being So Camp As Keeps Us Going', *Body Politic*, no. 36, September 1977.

Finch, Christopher (1975) *Rainbow, the Stormy Life of Judy Garland* (London: Michael Joseph).

Jennings, Wade (1979) 'Nova: Garland in A *Star is Born*', *Quarterly Review of Film Studies*, Summer 1979, pp.321–37.

Russo, Vito (1979) 'Camp', in Martin P. Levene (ed.), *Gay Men, the Sociology of Male Homosexuality* (New York: Harper & Row pp.205–10; originally published *The Advocate*, 19 May, 1976).

Sontag, Susan (1964) 'Notes on Camp', *Partisan Review*, XXXI, no.4.

Steiger, Brad (1969) *Judy Garland* (New York: Ace Books).

Wood, Robin (1976) *Personal Views* (London: Gordon Fraser).

9

"Working Like a Homosexual"

Camp visual codes and the labor of gay subjects in the MGM Freed Unit

MATTHEW TINKCOM

> Vincente [Minnelli] was not a man who was a dictator. He tried to do it in a soft and nice way. He worked in let's say . . . I don't know whether you will understand what I say . . . he worked like a homosexual. I don't mean that nastily. I have nothing against homosexuals.
> Lela Simone, production assistant at Metro-Goldwyn-Mayer[1]

Critical treatments of the relations of gays and lesbians to the production of cinema have largely taken two approaches. The first stresses the pathologizing effect of Hollywood cinema in its portrayal of gays and lesbians, with *Rope* and *Caged*, for example, offering to those in pursuit of gay-positive images particularly objectionable depictions of gay life. From this perspective, the presence of gays and lesbians producing nonhomophobic visions of gay and lesbian experience in Hollywood studios seems a remote possibility. The second approach, then, embraces gay or lesbian filmmakers outside of Hollywood, independent from Hollywood both in terms of the economic conditions under which they make movies and in terms of the array of film styles available for contemplating the role of gender and sexuality in contemporary life. The exceptions to these two approaches are notable, particularly in terms of how Hollywood can be understood as a site of production for gay and lesbian filmmakers: for example, Dorothy Arzner has rightfully taken her place as a figure of an antiauteur auteur, while George Cukor has only recently begun to be rethought as a *gay* director. In the wake of the assessment that Hollywood has traditionally been hostile to gay workers (at least at the level that their cinematic visions might reach the big screen) and that therefore it is only outside corporate studio production that gays and lesbians might make movies, we are left with a historical and theoretical vacuum when we consider that gays and lesbians have been instrumental in the productions of some kinds of Hollywood film which are not entirely antigay/lesbian.[2]

This essay attempts to rethink the situation. The essay fixes its attention upon the Freed unit of Metro-Goldwyn-Mayer during the late 1940s and attempts to dislodge the Freed films of this period from universalizing accounts of classical Hollywood cinema. The interests of my work are in accounting for the contributions of gay men, and the specific example of Vincente Minnelli, to the Freed unit and in rethinking the status of their labor as crucial to the films' hallmark style. Although I will consider Minnelli at the greatest length in terms of camp and gay-inflected production, there are numerous opportunities to discuss gay figures in the Freed unit, the most important being Roger Edens, who was responsible for the unit's daily operations and whose vocal arrangements in the American film musical are immensely important. In this respect, my essay forms an attempt to render more visible the work of gays and their sensibilities, sensibilities which I discuss in terms of camp. Further, the "gay labor" of camp is a strategic category for understanding the camp markings affected by the production of these films, and therefore gay labor, in the form of camp encodings, functioned for the studio as a way of enhancing the final product by way of "product differentiation." At stake are both a recuperative account of the contributions of men whose difference vis-à-vis sex/gender are largely ignored because of the imperatives of the closet and, equally important, the challenge to our impulses to ignore differences, whether they arise in terms of race, ethnicity, class, or gender, as such differences informed the ideological practices of Hollywood film in its larger social dimensions.

By treating the question of narrative integration in the musicals of the Freed unit, the stylistic anomalies of the Freed films which are most pronounced indicate an extra-added labor upon those texts. Keeping in mind both how camp has previously been understood as a fascination with artifice, excess, and performance and how a history of gay Hollywood lives continues to circulate anecdotally, I claim here that these features of some Freed productions (which occur most often in regard to the art-direction) provide an opportunity to see that camp is a kind of gay labor—gay in that the erotic dimensions of gay Freed workers' lives were masked by camp, and labor in that the conditions for their working were predicated on the particular economic practices of the studio in the period that I am describing. Thus, I am attempting to bring together questions of stylistic differentiation and the economic conditions for such difference to appear; by extending the idea of camp beyond its being a hallmark of consumption, I offer an analysis of where gay subjectivity appears elsewhere (and, perhaps, simultaneously) within the dynamics of capitalism, specifically as a feature of gay workers for Metro-Goldwyn-Mayer. [. . .]

Gay labor within the studio

When Lela Simone commented on Vincente Minnelli as having worked "like a homosexual," she was onto something. As a personal assistant to Freed and Roger Edens and as one of Minnelli's co-workers on the lot at Metro-Goldwyn-Mayer, Simone was in a position to recall much about the production of Freed films in the unit's heyday. Her attempts to articulate a relation between Minnelli's sexuality and the effects of his labor resonate in the way she expresses the vexations of the closet as they arise in the workplace; her words also encourage us to theorize the possibility of a capitalist enterprise accommodating marginalized sex/gender subjects because their labor could enhance a product's appeal through its differentiated style.

While recognizing that Simone's comments might appear to be mostly of biographical interest to Minnelli auteurists, I argue that there are relations between subjects and their ability to labor that mark the results of their efforts as different. In terms of the Freed unit, we need to specify how a corporate enterprise seized upon the efforts of gay men in order to enhance studio profits, and the fact that a studio was willing to employ gays means that labor is sometimes inflected by subjectivity. By this I mean that the ability to labor, what Marx refers to not as the actual output of the worker but the potential work which capital anticipates, differs for various workers. It also differs at the level of the laboring subjects' potential for making various kinds of commodities. The possibility for such differentiations is not simply coincidental to the force of capitalism as a system for the making and distribution of objects and, more to the point, value; a larger implication may be that capitalism is predicated upon difference that it can exploit.

Camp is an index of such difference, although it is a notoriously ambiguous one. As a gay sensibility, camp seldom offers itself for immediate identification as that which has been made by a gay man, and the camp commodity can bear ambiguities in such a way that, say in its potential for camp and noncamp readings alike, it heralds gay life and consciousness in its most mundane dimensions. In a sense, what camp offers to us is the commodity that "passes" through the economy much as gays themselves must pass in many of the social settings of their daily lives. Thus, what I am calling gay labor is not simply the work of gays expended on a particular commodity but the particular effort to ensure the commodity's multivalence, in that it can be consumed by gay and nongay consumers alike for retaining camp features or not. Camp figures as gay labor in its answer to the demand to pass; the difficulty of identifying gay tastes at work means that the object has served to deflect attention from those who think in camp ways as being somehow aberrant. Eve Kosofsky Sedgwick outlines the strictures of the demand to pass and the camp response:

> the typifying gesture of camp is really something amazingly simple: the moment at which a consumer of culture makes the wild surmise, "What if whoever made this was gay too?" Unlike kitsch-attribution, then, camp-recognition doesn't ask, "What debased creature could possibly be the right audience for this spectacle?" Instead, it says *what if*: What if the right audience for this were exactly me?[3]

Sedgwick's argument suggestively maintains that the question posed by the camp spectator is displaced from an interest in absolutely confirming a gay presence on the side of production to the viewers' awareness of their particular status as a camp spectator. But what if (to rejoin Sedgwick's question) camp is understood as the specific term for addressing how gay sensibilities labor in venues over which such subjects may have restricted control? The Freed unit operated within the most centrally organized and labor differentiated corporate form of filmmaking in the United States during a period marked by virulent homophobia. Yet, given the stylistic flourishes of Freed production that appeared in such a climate, the "what if" question asks how gay sensibilities could inform a film's look under such circumstances of production.

The emphasis I wish to place on the camp aspects of the Freed unit, then, stems from the articulation that Simone's comments about Minnelli make possible, between the unstable identity position of being gay, an inheritance of post-Stonewall identity politics, and the subject position of working as gay. It has been a truism of liberation politics in the past two decades that gendered identities derived from sexual activities: that one is a gay man because he maintains an erotic interest in other men. I do not want to deny this claim of identity as articulated with sexual desires and practices. I do, however, want to underscore the cultural dimensions of what being gay has meant to the work of men who have been homosexual (and whose lives may predate the political act of self-naming themselves as "gay"). Simone's claim that Minnelli "worked like a homosexual" means that labors performed by particular subjects, and not identities, can in some cases display the mark of the subject upon the product; the net effect of this claim is that some commodities are indeed, as Marx suggested, queer.

I am aligning two disparate ways of rendering the experiences of some men and women: as gendered subjects who desire others of the same sex and as workers within a capitalist enterprise. The strangeness of the juxtaposition of the terms "gay" and "worker" tells us how unaccustomed critiques of sexual politics and capitalism can be to seeing any features as common to both. The task of perceiving such "overlaps" is frustrated in light of the strategies of gays and lesbians to deflect attention from their dissident sexualities as they relate to the results of their efforts.

The primary feature of Freed productions that deflected the "what if" question posed by Sedgwick's camp spectator was the ability of gays to work in the process of creating heterosexual romance narratives, and the effects of gay participations in the creation of straight romance may be contradictory. On the one hand, they enable the dissemination of the purportedly one culturally sanctioned version of erotic and romantic bonding, a heterosexual version which customarily enforces the hidden status of gays as historical subjects and encourages their exclusion from representation. This exclusion is intensified by analyses which predict that a given film can only be read in one blindered way, that is, the romance narrative. On the other hand, the labors of such gay subjects may show up in other ways alongside narrative. These labors I am calling camp. The difference between what I am offering as camp, vis-à-vis the production of Freed musicals, and the general idea of camp as a reader's emphasis upon stylistic excess resides in the fact that, within my analysis, camp stylistics contributed to the studio's profits. Of course, the camp viewer contributes to those profits by simply buying a ticket, but camp style within Freed films circulated to noncamp audiences under the more general idea of their being "stylized" or "witty."

What then is labeled as the integration of straight romance and gay-inflected visual codes is more generally within the camp sensibility what we might call "style," or more particularly, a style of excess. Susan Sontag comments upon the impulse to call attention to the stylization of a text:

> stylization in a work of art, as distinct from style, reflects an ambivalence (affection contradicted by contempt, obsession contradicted by irony) toward the subject matter. This ambivalence is handled by maintaining, through the rhetorical overlay that is stylization, a special distance from the subject. No doubt, in a culture pledged to the utility (particularly the moral utility) of art, burdened with a useless need to fence off solemn art from arts which provide amusement, the eccentricities of stylized art supply a valid and valuable satisfaction. I have described these satisfactions in another essay, under the name of camp taste.[4]

Sontag proceeds to comment that such camp stylized art is "palpably an art of excess, lacking harmoniousness, [and] can never be of the very greatest kind," locating her own tastes for high modernism and its limited ironic vista. Sidestepping her dismissal of camp, I would suggest that the sense of integration so often attributed to Freed films achieves the very ambivalence that Sontag is describing. This occurs at the moment in which we realize earlier Freed productions to be breaking with the previous nonintegrating codes of the musical, whereby we could argue that camp stylization informs the films in their entirety and not just within the numbers. Camp style marks a critical commentary upon the narrative of heterosexual bonding. Before moving to depict Freed's gay employees as necessarily agents of transgression through their critique of heterosexual romance narratives, though, we should remember that the unit's independence stemmed, within the profit-driven logic of Hollywood film production, from its capacity to fill movie theaters. But the prestige accorded the Freed films then and now comes perhaps with the demand that we ignore the elements of camp production.

Nevertheless, despite the history-making dynamics of censorship and forgetting, recent accounts have begun to suggest that an interest in knowing the gay features of the lives of Freed employees figures in the popular rewriting of Hollywood. When we consider that commentary continues to be traded within fan culture about the erotic liaisons of key figures within the Freed unit, we are fronted with the fact that these films do circulate with varying historical accounts. Recently there has been confirmation within print media, such as when David Shipman's recent biography of Judy Garland remarks in passing that Vincente Minnelli was widely known as homosexual within the small circuit of Hollywood, and Lela Simone comments to her interviewer that Roger Edens, acknowledged by many as the figure responsible for the success of the unit's collaborative efforts, was known in the period by many to be homosexual.[5] Further speculation, unconfirmed within the popular and academic presses, circulates about many figures, some of whom are still alive and perhaps quick to summon their lawyers.

Mentioning these emerging accounts of gay life in Hollywood is not to call for an "outing" of every gay worker within the Freed unit. At the very least, this illustrates the question of whether naming particular figures as gay produces a necessarily progay history; at the worst, the claiming of particular names for a history of sexual identity disregards one vitally important feature to recall of the period of the unit's production: that the very anonymity of production, in addition to the anonymity for sexuality, that was assumed for those working within the corporate structure of MGM may have inadvertently provided the gay makers of camp Freed musicals with a venue in which to work.

If anonymity in production was a feature of the Freed unit for this particular reason, then any attempt to historicize the labor of gays will have to devise historiographical strategies of its own. Remembering Simone's caveat when commenting on Minnelli that she has nothing against homosexuals, every attempt to specify one figure as gay means that the historian might end up producing *something* for homophobic stances against the gay filmmaker. Therefore, it is less important to see current revelations about the sexuality of Hollywood figures as confirmation about what we think we know about a star or director than it is to seize upon such comments as the occasion to address the conditions under which such figures worked.

Anonymity as a feature of gay labor in the Freed setting accounts for the problems of the historian as she or he encounters the dissembling abilities of camp, most notably when many of the historian's sources are the most scorned form of historical discourses, gossip. The problem is how we acknowledge the truth-value and concurrently question the veracity of a given bit of hearsay. This is compounded by the fact that we find ourselves dealing within a subterranean history which is now almost fifty years old, and gossip has a way of accruing half-truths and misnamings to it. There is, however, a way to play to the strengths of gossip by remembering that commentary on the sexual preferences of a particular person circulates as gossip and not as monumental history, because such tale telling involves the overlapping of sexuality with production, an overlap more usually called the closet. In other instances, historians encounter similarly private and debased historical discourses; these are given the name of folklore. Like gossip, folklore accumulates truth-value to it by its circulation through more personal venues of conversation and storytelling. We should take pains, though, to distinguish the organicist strains of folklore from gossip, as the gossip surrounding gay Hollywood, current and past, is frequently antagonistic to folkloric and nostalgic versions of Hollywood history that circulate within popular venues.

The presence of gay workers and its accompanying circulation through the circuits of gossip, then, becomes a forceful way of thinking about the films made by the Freed unit because it allows subsequent viewers and historians to read the films for traces of gay sensibilities and taste while acknowledging enforced silences around sexual dissidences. But what has allowed camp features to be ignored in critical treatments of the Freed films has been the centrality of narrative as a privileged category. In seeking to classify the film musical as sharing features with all the films in the enormous construct called Hollywood Cinema, we risk losing sight of the anomalous features that may in fact distinguish one genre from another. The problem here is not only a taxonomical one but one that concerns our attempts to understand the different positions that varying genres inhabited within the complex ideological practices of cinema.

This by no means implies that we must abandon the narrative features of the Freed film musical. In fact, the first important consideration of camp within a Freed film attempted to consider the film's story as a camp romance narrative. Richard Dyer argues, in the context of reading Judy Garland's ability to make fun of her own star status, that the Minnelli-directed *The Pirate* offers differing layers of camp. While noting the "spectacular illusion" that the film plays with, containing as it does costume, disguise, and the mocking of gender performance, Dyer's reading ultimately emphasizes the camp narrative possibilities contained within the film's failed closure. We expect a union of the two main figures, Manuela and Serafin (played, respectively, by Garland and Kelly), but instead the film delivers not a marriage but another musical number ("Be a Clown"), which itself sends up the conventions of the musical by asking us to laugh with the film's stars.[6] *The Pirate* is by any measure a vivid example of camp tastes. I wonder whether its narrative anomalies are not the sole feature that should tell us about where camp production energies were more usually devoted, to the visual fireworks of the films, and not the story's ability to tamper with romantic expectations. It seems fruitful to rediscover those features of the film that are most exempt from more traditional "gay-content" analyses which revolve around the narrative at the expense of the remarkable visual feasts to be witnessed in the films.

Camp style and the problem of integration

The comments of film-goers who attended previews of *The Pirate* confirm that the studio knew that the film tended to emphasize its own spectacular art direction while sometimes disregarding streamlined storyline and clear characterization. There seems little doubt that, in some measure, this seeming imbalance in the films offered by the unit were known to those at MGM who took an interest in seeing the studio's profits enhanced: the studio circulated audience responses to producers and directors within days after an audience in Pasadena had passed judgement on the film. In the preview cards, where anonymous viewers offered praise and disparagement, a repeated emphasis on the art direction arises: "[the] sets detracted from the people and the music was too loud," "not realistic enough," "entirely too surrealistic," "the beautiful background settings were exceptional," "plot rather thin," "truly one of the most exciting pictures from every standpoint, directions, artwork, color, dancing, scoring," "beautiful coloring," "slightly fantastic plot not developed in as natural and realistic [a way] as it could have been," and perhaps the most telling, "Minnelli back to the small minority who really appreciate him."[7]

The above comments would suggest that these viewers had screened a film by Dalí or Buñuel, not the product of MGM after twenty years of corporate film-production experience. Nor would these responses make sense when we account for the fact that the Freed unit recruited some of the most renowned writing talent of the period for its films and devoted attention to the writing and revision of its script properties during preproduction and production.

Indeed, given these audience responses, I would argue that historically contemporaneous viewers perceived these films as residing within the tensions between story and spectacle. We risk losing sight of this when we emphasize the former as part of the impulse to subsume Hollywood musicals to the larger "ultragenre" of Hollywood narrative cinema. Thus, from Rick Altman's account of the Hollywood film musical, I would particularly reiterate his suggestion that genre, as both historical and theoretical category, is repressive. By this it seems that the aspects of production that pertain to a given genre, in this case the Hollywood musical, not only dictate what will be included within a specific film's making but also by implication delimit what cannot be included in its critical treatment. As Altman puts it: "genres are not the democratically elected representatives of a group of like-minded texts. They are autocratic monarchs dictating a single standard of allegiance for all subjects. In short, genres are not neutral categories, as structuralist critics have too often implied; rather they are ideological constructs masquerading as neutral categories."[8] Altman quite rightly, to my reading, argues that the various features of a generic text which different critical projects value, often in wildly fluctuating ways, are not mere coincidences. Critics notice different features of a text for their particular interests: thus musicals can be read as ideological practice, "mere" entertainment, a vestige of folk culture, and so on. The argument for a particular reading relies upon the priority of one set of traits over another, and no critical project is exempt from having its hierarchy. Musicals have largely been understood as primarily narrative films at the expense of other features.

There is little doubt that the relation of story to number counts for much in the meanings attributed to film musicals, and the plotline that structures many musicals is that of straight romance and marriage. The world in which a man and a woman meet and find initial attraction, in which their union is frustrated, and where ultimately the prohibitions to heterosexual bonding are overcome through the mediation of the song and dance number is typically the world of the musical. But there is more to the making of musicals beyond the plotline and its ancillary subplots, all of which are said to be brought to happy closure at the film's completion.

For one thing, song and dance occur in the space of spectacle, and this space seems in excess of the realist codes which lend credibility to the space of the more humdrum story. Perhaps the most dazzling examples of the differences between the codes of narrative and number are those of the Busby Berkeley backstage musicals made at Warner Bros. in the 1930s.[9] For the Freed unit in the fifties, the spectacular number became the benchmark of the prestigious films that MGM was known for making; the large amounts of time, labor, and investment of the studio in the Freed unit stemmed from the requirements of staging such sequences. Here I would draw out the differences in readings that emphasize one aspect, narrative, over another, spectacle.

What seem to have been the memorable features of Freed unit musicals for contemporaneous viewers were their dazzling sets, costumes, use of color (in terms of film stock, set painting, and lighting) and choreography. These specific elements of film production are perhaps most likely what the various viewers' cards cited above are locating as the Freed unit's distinguishing style, or, to remember the viewer who commented on the "small minority" who might be interested in Minnelli films, that this style was idiosyncratic enough to have both fans and detractors. This style distinguished the unit's films from those of its rivals, even those appearing from other Metro production units making musicals.[10]

Minnelli's work habit of plotting a film's numbers by creating a series of paper dolls and scaled-down sound stages in which to place these figures suggests that his first impulses were to conceive of a film through its mise-en-scène rather than its storyline. As James Naremore argues, "within the limits of the system, Minnelli was able to say a good deal about sets and costumes (departments that could be intractable), and he usually influenced the overall visual conception of his films."[11] Minnelli himself described his move from Broadway productions: "when I arrived in Hollywood, I didn't look down on musicals as so many people who were doing them did, treating them as a romp, a slapstick, nothing to be taken seriously."[12] The seriousness of the labor which Minnelli expended upon Freed films suggests that camp manifests itself in what has more commonly been described as the high degree of visual stylistic integration within Freed productions; that is, camp becomes an important way for thinking about Minnelli's efforts inasmuch as it shaped his work on the films' visual style.

The argument regarding integration as a hallmark of Freed production maintains that the movement from narrative to number was refined beyond that of the previous Hollywood product. By this it seems that the number, and its potential for appearing discordant with the codes of narrative realism, was written and choreographed in such a way as to appear as natural and spontaneous; that is, the numbers seem less bracketed from the narrative. When, for example, Fred Astaire dances the "Will You Marry Me?" number in *Yolanda and the Thief* (1945) the motivation for this dream sequence dance is his uneasy conscience over taking advantage of the wealthy Yolanda, the prey for his con-games with whom he is simultaneously falling in love. The dream seems more explicable within the story because it has motivation both in terms of the narrative and in terms of Astaire's character.

I would emphasize the potential for reading integration, as part of Minnelli's stylistics, as the camp emphasis upon the performative aspects of everyday life. If the musical number implicates its performers as mystifying the conditions of mundane life, in which it is impossible to break into song and dance with full orchestral backing, a camp emphasis on performance also points in the opposite direction, implicating everyday life as performative, not least of which when it comes to thinking about gender. When the number becomes elegantly situated within its narrative constraints as less abruptly breaking with the realist narrative codes which mask the number *as* number, then I would argue that it is possible to read the narrative, too, as also baring its performative aspects. Ed Lowry addresses this dual tendency of integration as creating both heightened realism and emphatic performance by claiming that in Minnelli's films there is a constant tension between his awareness that the Hollywood musical is artificial and false, and his contradictory delight in being able to create that artificiality so well—a conflict which manifests itself in his unpretentious attitude that his "art" is just a job (beautifully expressed in *The Bandwagon*, a film which forwards a professional ethos on a par with the best of Howard Hawks) and an opposing desire to create in a purely stylized and transcendent form (as in the elongated ballets of his musicals), of which the dream in *Yolanda* is said to be the first in film.[13]

Couched not only in the terms under which the Hollywood musical seems "artificial and false" because of its extranarrative codes but also in the sense in which a camp sensibility can point to the limits of romance narrative for addressing all viewers, the contradiction which Lowry describes is not simply one of stylistics but also of the challenge posed by camp as it encounters the realist tradition in which heterosexual romance is depicted. In order to privilege heterosexual realism, then, we are called upon to see the films as integrated. Describing the films' style as integrated, though, bolsters a reading that neglects the differences of camp commodity production that Freed films so vividly display.

Further, the opening to *Yolanda and the Thief* provides a moment in which to note the juxtaposition of several different surfaces which are gathered together in what can only through analytic gymnastics be seen as part of a tradition of Hollywood realism. The opening titles place colorful hand-lettering upon a brightly painted primitivist landscape, what we will subsequently learn is the utopia of Patria, where the film is set. As the film commences, the camera then moves us into a foreground of the painting, which becomes a backdrop for a country schoolroom which is set upon a grassy bluff where the benevolent (and oddly German-accented) schoolmaster instructs his pupils, mostly by commanding them to sing the national song, coyly named "This Is a Day for Love." Passing shepherds in the background then usher the camera into a sunny exterior backlot and the convent in which Yolanda has been raised, and finally into another sound-stage interior of the convent. The entire sequence is held together through the musical sound-bridges of the song, which is passed from the pupils to the shepherds and finally to the schoolgirls, who reiterate it as they bathe.

The initial set of images offered in the film, then, gather together a remarkable number of different kinds of filmmaking: wildly "unrealistic" backdrops, extravagant MGM-style exteriors, and elegantly stylized interiors, playing out a fantasy of the then-current vogue for all things seemingly "south of the border." We might describe the composition of these multiple diegetic spaces as contributing to an ultimate realism of the film. The fact that the "This Is a Day for Love" number so handily binds together, for the sake of moving the narrative from Patria's bucolic beauty to the convent where we find Yolanda, such disparate kinds of film media can be read as in some sense being driven by the story. But questions of narrative economy aside, we have to accept the fantastic opening images of *Yolanda and the Thief* as a gesture forcing us to accept the film's aesthetic anomalies as in excess of the movie's story. As Lowry suggests, "the landscape which we knew could not be real is still no more real, but has been established as the 'reality' of the world depicted in *Yolanda and the Thief*.[14] However, the "unreality" which the film demands we respect as the place in which the narrative will unfold also seems then to implicate the narrative itself.

The narrative of *Yolanda*, in brief, offers a romance between a naive and wealthy young woman, Yolanda Aquaviva (Lucille Bremer), who is tricked by a con man, Johnny Riggs (Fred Astaire), into believing that he is her guardian angel. Johnny plays upon Yolanda's gullibility in order to convince her to confer her power of attorney on him, but just as he is ready to depart with the goods, he finds himself romantically and erotically drawn to her. His attraction to her surprises Johnny, because he ostensibly does not expect to find Yolanda a figure of erotic contemplation, and his jaded sensibilities lose out to his romantic impulses. But moments of camp playfulness in the film offer another reading of Johnny's surprise at discovering himself in a seduction beyond his overarching greed and cynicism, for there are strong possibilities for seeing him as gay.

In the "Will You Marry Me?" number, for example, he wrestles with the trauma of potentially being trapped in a marriage to Yolanda for her money. This dream sequence ballet opens with Astaire dressed in a remarkable dandy outfit, a pair of off-white satin pajamas with Byzantine silk-cord closures on the shirt.[15] Becoming restless in his bed, Johnny dresses and walks through the streets of Patria's unnamed capital, where he moves into increasingly surreal landscapes in which various women trap him in symmetrical dance steps: washerwomen unfold furls of different-colored fabric in stark geometric patterns that form a prison out of which he cannot escape, Yolanda appears throwing off a series of veils trimmed in coins, and sirens in short dresses and high heels entice him with a cask into which Yolanda has dispensed her gold. The number effectively links Johnny's fear of marriage with his greed, or, more properly according to the dream-logic of the "Will You Marry Me?" sequence, his greed is the film's alibi for not stating more directly his desire not to bond with a woman, no matter what her beauty or wealth. I would argue that the film temporarily addresses the question of whether Johnny will accede to the demands of marriage through the camp art direction's treatment of him as gay.

Steven Cohan's discussion of Fred Astaire's performances illustrates even better what I am talking about, for Cohan insists that Astaire's virtuoso dances served to feminize him, inasmuch as they rendered him a spectacle to be enjoyed beyond the narrative. As Cohan writes, "Astaire's numbers oftentimes exceed both linear narrativity and the heterosexual (that is 'straight' in the cultural as well as narrative sense) male desire that fuels it."[16] Cohan argues, though, that it is not simply a feminine man (in this case, Astaire) who appears within the dance number, and that the narrative must "retrieve" him in order to reintegrate him into the straight story, but that performance disrupts the narrative by momentarily disregarding the force of the story for the power of the spectacular dance routine.[17] Likewise, I would argue that the backdrops and costumes perform a similar function but that we tend not to notice their potential to antagonize narrative because, of course, most often the disjunctive features of the mise-en-scène to which I am pointing are maintained in the film's movement back to the storyline.

Against the more usual tendency to argue that the innovation of Freed productions was the high degree of integration of number into narrative, I would suggest that what I am calling the visual excesses of the film's numbers cannot be cleaved from other moments in *Yolanda and the Thief*. The problem with the ways that integration has been understood is that it commonly serves as a rhetorical strategy that precludes reading *against* the narrative force of such films in favor of a consideration of their spectacular numbers. If the strength of Freed numbers, and the camp proclivities heralded in their look, is understood as only lending credence to the film's closure around marriage, the possibility for interpreting the camp signs of the film are foreclosed.

Thus, a moment ripe with camp play can be easily ignored because it contributes little to understanding the relations between the film's visual style and the tensions around whether

Johnny and Yolanda will bond. In an early encounter between the two, Yolanda is summoned from her mansion (where she is bathing in a glass-lined tub fed by baroque marble waterfalls) to meet with Johnny, whom she assumes to be her angelic overseer. In preparation for this meeting, Johnny and his sidekick, Victor Trout (Frank Morgan), rearrange the furnishings of the hotel lobby in order to backlight him on a gilt throne in front of a baroque mural of clouds and cherubim. Yolanda, sporting a kind of mantilla which is meant to affirm her piety and naïveté, has an initial vision of him as he feyly holds his hand out and jadedly stares to the heavens. Read as part of a seduction, it would be difficult to see Johnny as an affected aesthete and Yolanda as a schoolgirl unfamiliar with the effete posturings of a gay man. In another sequence of the film's conclusion, Johnny seems bewildered to discover himself married to Yolanda and is further confused when Yolanda's real guardian angel, Mr. Candle (Leon Ames), appears as a wandering tourist who gives them a photo. As Johnny contemplates the picture, a divinely offered snapshot into their future where he and Yolanda are surrounded by their children, he blanches, perhaps not only because of the paranormal dimensions of the picture, but because of the familial setting in which he never expected to find himself and whose dangers were so vividly enacted in the "Will You Marry Me?" number. Johnny's aversion to marriage, then, and the sense of entrapment from which he awakens (and which concludes the number) foreshadows the conclusion of the film, for the number is more than a recapitulation of the plot as it has unfolded up until the number is staged, but Johnny's shock is anticipated through the camp mise-en-scène of the crucial "Will You Marry Me?" number.

Another Freed film that allows us to see the secondary importance of narrative as a vehicle for the staging of number is the 1944 production, The Ziegfeld Follies. That film offers a series of numbers which are ostensibly the enactment of a live performance of Ziegfeld's Broadway spectacle. Seemingly returning to the backstage musical, the film consists entirely of comedic skits and musical numbers strung together with only the intermittent page of a playbill to announce the name of the number and its performers; no storyline serves as a hammock to hold the separate pieces together, other than a wish by the angelic Flo Ziegfeld (now ensconced in a pink luxury suite in heaven) to see who might appear on his stage in the year 1944.[18]

Ziegfeld Follies could be said to be a film that is all number and no narrative, visual and musical styles are indeed varied and remarkable. An opportunity for different talents to appear in a Hollywood production that might otherwise never find a place within narrative, Follies showcases Lena Horne and Fanny Brice, stage stars too "ethnic" for the middle-brow WASP depictions sought by Metro. Without recourse to (or constriction by) a story, the film provided the opportunity to see African-American "exoticism" and Yiddish comic play largely unavailable in a Hollywood vehicle.[19]

Ethnicity, though, is not the only trace of difference which informs Ziegfeld Follies. The camp play of Minnelli's direction appears in one of his most elegant and mocking numbers, "The Great Lady Has 'an Interview.'" The Great Lady numbers involve Judy Garland sending up the star-images of dramatic actresses of the period, Greer Garson the most notable target for Garland's breathless pomposity.[20] The Great Lady announces her boredom at appearing in the demanding roles which have garnered her attention, and the press corps that surrounds her provide the musical troupe through which she can then springboard into a song, "Madame Crematon." The song provides the opportunity for the fictitious actress to perform the light comedy which she wants to do but which her star persona prohibits her from doing.

Two elements of the Great Lady sequence offer clues to the camp sensibility that underpins the number. First, the dance troupe/press corps appears as a gay entourage which has descended upon the star's house as a contingent of adoring fans eager for a glimpse of her. Dancing in through the entrance door under the disapproving eye of her butler, they link arms and merrily kick-step their way into the receiving room. The dance ensemble depicts an important relation of gays to the figure of Judy Garland, because the young men in this number seem to adore her as fans but not necessarily as straight men interested in making a sexual score. Dressed identically in dark suits and neat ties, they dance with themselves as much as they do with Garland; in fact, given her initial hauteur, it is their ease with one another which displaces attention from the star back to themselves and in which she can relax. Garland becomes, through her release into comic play in a nonseductive situation, a star capable of bonding with her "camp followers," depicted in this scene by the male chorus.[21]

Second, the art direction of the star's home is executed in a style which is paradoxically spare and yet overwrought. On a lush background of walls treated in mocha-colored silk hangs an oversized baroque mirror, under which a white art moderne table sits with a craggy floral arrangement of seemingly prehistoric orchids. The effect is one of refined vulgarity; expensive materials and extreme lines offer the camp attention to the ways that high and low distinctions of taste can be blurred for comic effect.

In most cases the dance cast and set decoration could easily become elements of a secondary order, after the purportedly overarching and determining structure of the plot. But *Ziegfeld Follies* offers no plot, and thus, I would argue, the dancing and sets are what the number "means," in contrast to any feature of a story that might be played out. Liberated from the constraints of cause/effect relations, even from the idea of events themselves, *Follies* plunges into the camp pleasures of texture, masquerade, and performance. [. . .]

Notes

I wish to thank the Lambda Foundation of Pittsburgh for their generous support for my work on this subject in the form of a research and development grant that allowed me to travel to Los Angeles. I am also indebted to Ned Comstock at the University of Southern California and Barbara Hall at the Academy of Motion Picture Arts and Sciences Margaret Herrick Library, both of whom were instrumental in the research for this essay.

1 Interviews with Lela Simone conducted by Rudy Behlmer for the Academy of Motion Picture Arts and Sciences Oral History Project. These conversations took place by phone over a period of several months during 1990–91 and were taped by Behlmer and transcribed by Barbara Hall, the Academy's oral historian.

2 See Judith Mayne, *Directed by Dorothy Arzner* (Bloomington: Indian University Press, 1994), for a theoretical treatment of lesbian auteurism and Patrick McGilligan, *George Cukor: A Double Life* (New York: St. Martin's Press, 1991), for a more popular account of a gay male director's work within studio production. We should note that important work in the field of queer studies has emphasized the processes of reception by gays and lesbians; the emphasis in Mayne and McGilligan is on the dynamics of production and the role that gays have played within that domain of commodity culture. Further, despite our best intentions, we might remember that, as Marx argues, every moment of production is simultaneously

one of consumption, and attempts to exclude one from the other are frequently simplifi-cations of the workings of commodity circulation. I argue, indeed, that the importing of a camp sensibility by gay workers to Hollywood figures as one of those nexus moments of which Marx speaks. See Karl Marx, "Production Is at the Same Time Also Consumption," in The Grundisse, trans. David McLellan (New York: Harper and Row, 1961), 23.

3 Eve Kosofsky Sedgwick, The Epistemology of the Closet (Berkeley: University of California Press, 1990), 154.

4 Susan Sontag, "On Style," in A Susan Sontag Reader (New York: Viking, 1983), 141.

5 David Shipman, Judy Garland (London: Fourth Estate, 1992). Shipman comments in the introduction: "the most contentious matters in most biographies are the sexual ones, and I can only say that of all the people I spoke to who knew Garland and Vincente Minnelli only one did not take it for granted that I already knew of Minnelli's homosexuality" (xi).

6 Richard Dyer, Heavenly Bodies: Film Stars and Society (New York: St. Martin's Press, 1986), 185–86.

7 Audience preview cards from screening held at Academy Theater in Pasadena. California, 10 October 1947. Although these cards record the number of viewers whose opinions were solicited (in this case, 150) they do not convey whether this is the entire audience nor the conditions under which audience responses were solicited, such as whether there were two screenings, trailers, cartoons, and so on. In most cases the responses were typed in all capital letters and mimeographed for studio executives. Audience preview cards in the Arthur Freed files on The Pirate at the University of Southern California Metro-Goldwyn-Mayer archives.

8 Rick Altman, The American Film Musical (Bloomington: Indiana University Press, 1987), 5.

9 In his account of the films of Busby Berkeley, Martin Rubin argues that the narrative/number tension cannot be resolved, even through what seems a high degree of inte-gration, inasmuch as the tension defines the musical form. Rubin comments that "nonintegration—a built-in and formalized resistance to the ultimate homogeneity or hierarchy of discourse—is essential to the musical genre, which is based precisely on a shifting and volatile dialectic between integrative and nonintegrative elements. Viewed in this way, the history of the musical becomes not so much a relentless, uni-directional drive toward effacing the last stubborn remnants of nonintegration, but a succession of different ways of articulating the tension between integrative (largely narrative) and nonintegrative (chiefly spectacle) elements." See Martin Rubin, Showstoppers: Busby Berkeley and the Tradition of the Spectacle (New York: Columbia University Press, 1993), 12.

10 It is striking that the MPAA censoring of the Freed productions occurred in terms of innuendo around the heterosexual narrative while the camp visual codes went unnoticed. The MPAA files on Freed films reveal the gaze of the Breen office to have been keen to the games that Cole Porter, Betty Comden, and Adolph Green played with their song lyrics and scripts around male–female bonding. In excess of what MPAA readers could detect as licentious were the visual codes of art direction, where at the level of content there seems little room to note the presence of gay production. In this context, Minnelli's history in Hollywood is striking, given his reputation as a director who devoted much of his energy to art direction and the mise-en-scène. See MPAA files on The Pirate at the Margaret Herrick Library.

11 James Naremore, The Films of Vincent Minnelli (Cambridge: Cambridge University Press, 1993), 28.

12 *Film Quarterly* 12, no. 2 (winter 1958): 21.

13 Ed Lowry, *Cinema Texas Program Notes: Yolanda and the Thief* 12, no. 4 (1977): 64.

14 Ibid., 64.

15 Interestingly, this ensemble was noted within popular critical appraisal of the film's fashions: "Astaire's most attractive outfit was a pair of eggshell pajamas with oversized collar and huge frogs," claims the reviewer in a column titled "New Astaire Film Introduces Unusual Styles by Yolanda." Unfortunately, the source for the article, other than a by-line for a Harriet Wilbur, is not included in Freed's files, although the notation that the clipping comes from "Irene Scrapbook" suggests that *Yolanda and the Thief*'s costumer is the source for circulating the review within the studio.

16 Steven Cohan, "'Feminizing' the Song-and-Dance Man," in *Screening the Male: Exploring Masculinities in Hollywood Cinema*, ed. Steven Cohan and Ina Rae Hark (New York: Routledge, 1993), 47.

17 The problem of how we describe Astaire's apparent femininity, what might more usually be termed effeminacy, within the heterosexual narrative stems from the codes of effeminacy as being connotative, and not denotative, of male homosexuality. Like camp, effeminacy serves as a baffle or barrier to locating any "real" or "actual" homosexual while also offering to others within gay subcultures the opportunity to wonder about a "fellow traveler." See Alan Sinfield, *The Wilde Century: Effeminacy, Oscar Wilde and the Queer Moment* (New York: Columbia University Press, 1994), for a discussion of the history whereby the connotative codes of effeminacy came to signify gayness in urban subcultures.

18 According to Hugh Fordin, *Ziegfeld Follies* was conceived at the onset as a showcase for Metro talent and a commemorative film for the studio's twentieth anniversary in 1944. Delays in the production and the deletion and addition of various numbers held up the film's release until 1946. Hugh Fordin, *The Movies' Greatest Musicals: Produced in Hollywood USA by the Freed Unit* (New York: Frederick Ungar, 1975).

19 The emergence of marginal identities and sensibilities within the wartime revue musical can be witnessed elsewhere in *Star Spangled Rhythm* (1942) and *Stage Door Canteen* (1943).

20 Garson's position as a target for Minnelli's mockery was no accident: the number was originally conceived as a way for audiences to see the star of numerous somber biopics and melodramas as having a lighter, playful side. When courted to do the number by Freed and Minnelli, Garson displayed a marked humorlessness and abruptly refused. It was then offered to Garland, who apparently took relish in lampooning her primary rival as the studio's most important female star. See Hugh Fordin's account of the production of *Ziegfeld Follies*.

21 Garland's relation to gays would continue until her death. Although the work of documenting and analyzing gay fan relations to Garland has shed light on the fascination of gay fans with the Garland star persona, little work has been devoted to the depiction of her with the boys in the chorus. For example, one of her signature numbers, "Get Happy," from *Summer Stock*, dresses her in suit jacket and fedora, hair tugged cleanly up into a butch chignon. There she temporarily becomes one of the "boys in the band," while simultaneously maintaining herself as a figure of feminine seduction for the audience through the emphasis on her high heels and bared legs.

Feminist Camp in
Gold Diggers of 1933

10

PAMELA ROBERTSON

Busby Berkeley's camp aesthetic

Although the camp sensibility can be productively traced throughout the genre of the Hollywood musical, the musicals Berkeley worked on are the most stylized and extravagant in the canon. Further, because Berkeley's numbers equate entertainment so outrageously with feminine spectacle, his choreographic style has provoked other feminist analyses. Berkeley contributed four numbers to *Gold Diggers of 1933* besides "We're in the Money." The other three numbers, "Pettin' in the Park," "Shadow Waltz," and "Forgotten Man" (to which I will return below), represent Barney's second successful show. In brief, "Pettin' in the Park" and "Shadow Waltz," both featuring Dick Powell and Ruby Keeler, are songs of love and romance visually expressed through trademark Berkeley feminine spectacle. "Forgotten Man," a call to remember the poverty-stricken "forgotten men" of the First World War, features Joan Blondell as a prostitute and substitutes a bevy of not-so-beautiful men (the Bonus Marchers) for feminine spectacle.

Throughout his career, Berkeley's signature style adheres to the philosophy of the title song of *Dames* (1934): "What do you go for? Go see the show for? / Tell the truth—you go to see those beautiful dames." The chief structuring elements of the Berkeley aesthetic are so identifiable that Berkeley has earned a place in the slang lexicon: "busby berkeley: A very elaborate musical number; any bevy of beautiful girls; a spectacular."[1] The typical Berkeley number showcases scores of beautiful white women who form intricate, fairly abstract patterns, who do not necessarily dance but walk and smile, and/or are mechanically transported; it kaleidoscopes female forms in ever changing cinematic designs.

Berkeley was assigned most often to a film as the choreographer/director of dance sequences, while another director was assigned to the narrative sequences. In many Berkeley films, the numbers seem like separable, isolated units, bearing little obvious relation to the rest of the film. In and of themselves, Berkeley's numbers produce a camp effect that renders the live Ziegfeld tradition outmoded. After an establishing shot that places the number on a live stage, Berkeley abandons all pretense to theatrical verisimilitude and instead offers a "stage" spectacle available only to a film audience.

Consider, for example, the second number of *Gold Diggers of 1933*, "Pettin' in the Park." The first chorus begins with a medium shot of Ruby Keeler and Dick Powell on a park bench singing to each other. Close-ups of the couple follow. Then, as they rise to leave the bench, the camera tracks to a close-up of a box of animal crackers on the bench. A drawing of two chimps on the box dissolves into an image of live-action chimps in a zoo cage.

In the second chorus, panning the park zoo, we see numerous couples each "pettin'" in the park and a "baby" (midget Billy Barty) in a carriage. A cut removes us to another area of the park where a policewoman (Aline MacMahon) shows Ruby Keeler the entrance to a roller-skating service "For Little Girls Who Need an Escort." First, loads of women in matching costumes skate out of the entrance. Then, a large number of policemen on skates join Ruby Keeler to escort her home. The baby/midget intervenes, shooting a spitball at the police, and a chase ensues. Snow begins to fall, and the camera cuts to a row of girls with huge "snowballs."

The third chorus begins with a pan left in close shots of the girls' faces, then the camera cuts to an overhead shot as the girls form abstract, quasi-organic patterns with the lines of their bodies and the spherical snowballs. Cutting from the overhead shot to a medium shot, we see the baby/midget exit the circle of women. He rolls a snowball to the camera. A match cut shows a rubber beach ball rolling back from the camera to the baby/midget, who is suddenly dressed in summer play clothes. He runs back into the park, now filled with couples lounging on the grass. The camera tracks forward showing numerous panty shots of the women in revealing costumes and poses. It begins to rain and the women run for cover behind a sheer backlit screen. As we see their presumably nude silhouettes in the background, the baby/midget, dressed in a rain hat and slicker, looks for a way to raise the curtain as Dick Powell, similarly attired, watches. When the baby/midget raises the curtain, the women appear in metallic swimsuits. Ruby Keeler joins Dick Powell on a bench where he discovers to his chagrin that the swimsuit is really made of tin. The baby/midget supplies a can opener and the curtain falls.

This typical Berkeley number exemplifies the way in which Berkeley used the camera and editing to divorce objects and images from clear referents in time and space. In most backstage musicals, a filmed version of a live stage show might use close-ups, tracks, and pans to assure the film spectator of the "best seat in the house" and to bridge the distance between spectator and spectacle created by the proscenium arch. At the same time, shots of the theatrical audience would be used to establish continuity between theater seats and movie-theater seats and to create an identification between the internal audience and the film audience.[2] Berkeley's extraordinarily fluid camera movements, dissolves, and match cuts dismiss the fiction of theatrical space and live performance altogether. Yet the numbers still open and close with establishing shots of the theater audience, who presumably provide a relay for our look. However, after watching a Berkeley number, a dizzying enough experience for a film spectator, the follow-up shot of a theater audience politely and appreciatively clapping comes like a jolt, reminding us of how far removed we are from them. It is impossible to imagine what show they have seen. Without the benefit of extremely rapid set changes, a theater with rotating overhead seats, and an audience willing to take miraculous leaps of faith, the notion that a Berkeley number could ever be a live performance falls apart.

For Berkeley, aesthetic effect was more important than adherence to backstage convention. When Zanuck first saw Berkeley in the rafters of a Goldwyn soundstage, he said, "You can't take an audience up there." "I know," Berkeley replied, "but I'd like to. It's awfully pretty from up here."[3] In emphasizing cinematic technique, rather than live performance, Berkeley's numbers remove the show from the fictional theater space and jettison it to the film studio's back lot, optical lab, and editing room. In addition to displacing the theatrical spectator, Berkeley effaces the myth of live entertainment, denying both the labor and the appeal of song and dance. Instead, he offers a purely cinematic vision of entertainment in which the camera itself dances and the spectator identifies with its movements, rather than with characters who sing and dance.

The camp effect of Berkeley's numbers depends not on the viewer appreciating the beautiful effects of artifice and style but on the viewer perceiving the dissonance between the purported object represented—a live musical number—and the mode of representation, which gleefully abandons verisimilitude. Rather than being moved by the aesthetic or utopian effect of song and dance, the film spectator's experience is one of sheer astonishment—at the product qua produced, as the fact that Berkeley transforms live action into such amazing and impossible abstractions.

Berkeley's camp effect consists in part in this assertion of the primacy of extravagant style over the demands of plot, of the pleasure principle over reality, cinematic effect over backstage convention. To abstract the camp effect of the numbers from their narrative motivation, however, endlessly reproduces the camp effect. Such a reading obscures the representational aspects of the spectacle (the numbers rely, after all, on the spectacle of female bodies) and reasserts the primacy of style over content without examining what work this camp style does in the narrative. Although Berkeley operated with some degree of independence from the directors of the narrative sequences, the numbers he choreographed were still conceived as part of specific films and were exhibited to audiences as parts of a whole.

Narrative versus number in Berkeley musicals

Berkeley's three 1933 films—*42nd Street* (dir. Bacon), *Footlight Parade* (dir. Bacon), *Gold Diggers of 1933* (dir. LeRoy)—are the first and probably the best in Berkeley's Warner Brothers period; and they are the three most obviously conceived as a unit.[4] These films take the Depression as their subject matter and depict the success of the show as an economic necessity for the hundreds of performers and technicians involved. The stylistic disparity between Berkeley's numbers and the rest of the diegesis in these films exaggerates the apparent frivolity and meaninglessness of Berkeley's numbers.

The backstage musical notably has two diegetic levels, apparent in the contrast between the backstage plot and the show-within-the-show. These separate diegetic levels are created in order to be overcome and united; the success of the romantic plot and the success of the show are made mutually dependent; the world offstage and the world onstage are synthesized in the end through the union of the romantic couple. Berkeley musicals, however, resist this synthesis. As Jane Feuer observes, "Busby Berkeley musicals rope off the show as a separate universe, a world of cinematic excess and voyeuristic pleasure in sharp contrast to the low-budget verisimilitude of the backstage sequences. . . . The Berkeley number epitomizes the show as secondary diegesis."[5] The backstage pattern limits the extreme stylization of the Berkeley number to the secondary diegesis of the show, but the degree to which the excess and camp of the secondary diegesis are ultimately contained by and synthesized with the primary diegesis is unclear.

According to Arthur Hove, the narrative sequences root Berkeley's numbers in reality and offset the camp effect: "Berkeley's numbers provide an augmentation that certainly makes

[*Gold Diggers of 1933*] more appealing. Without the story, however, the musical numbers would be meaningless fragments, a visual tutti-frutti with no reason for being other than to show off the director's imagination and skill."[6] Rather than seeing a close interaction between narrative and musical sequences, Hove posits a content/style split between story and numbers. According to Hove, the Depression is not the primary focus of the show-within-the-film: "Pettin' in the Park" and "Shadow Waltz" are "puff pieces that have no bite whatsoever" and "Forgotten Man" is an incongruous footnote. Hove views the numbers and their "tutti-frutti" excess as contained by the narrative, the emphasis of which is on romance.[7] Mast, by contrast, foregrounds the manner in which stylistic excess undermines narrative concerns. Mass asserts that the "paradoxical effect today of many Berkeley numbers" consists of "laughter at the monstrous audacity of his not seeing anything about a social situation except an opportunity for decorative design; wonder at his energetic execution of that design and absolute commitment to its visual execution."[8] Mast and Hove view the disjunction between narrative and number from different angles, but both highlight the threat Berkeley's numbers pose to narrative coherence. Reflecting the sense that Berkeley's numbers fail to fit easily into narrative sequences, Sontag places Berkeley in the category of "unintentional" camp, as an example of something that aims to be dead serious but fails. For Mast and Hove, the seeming naïveté of Berkeley's 1930s numbers consists in the irony and incongruity of inserting the excessive kaleidoscopic spectacle of female bodies into progressive narratives of the Depression.

Disregarding the camp effect of Berkeley's numbers, Mark Roth has analyzed Berkeley's Warner Brothers numbers as not incongruent but complementary to the primary diegesis. *42nd Street*, *Footlight Parade*, and *Gold Diggers of 1933* were made at the most Democratic, pro-Roosevelt studio in the same year that FDR and the New Deal were inaugurated. Roth parallels the strong directors of the show-within-the-film featured in *42nd Street* and *Footlight Parade* (Warner Baxter and James Cagney, respectively) and the new strong leadership in the country. He argues that Berkeley's numbers in these films, in downplaying the role of individual stars in favor of blocks of figures moving in tandem, symbolize the spirit of cooperation and community characteristic of the early stages of Roosevelt's presidency. Connoting the New Deal spirit, these films transform the ideal of individual success into an ideal of success through collective effort under the leadership of a strong male director. Roth thus offers a Great Man theory that posits a New Deal symbolism in all three of Berkeley's 1933 films, but he largely ignores the role feminine spectacle plays in Berkeley's aesthetic, and he cannot account for the relationship between the primary and secondary level of diegesis in *Gold Diggers of 1933*. "*Gold Diggers of 1933* is a good film," Roth concedes, "but is weakened by the lack of a strong male lead (such as Baxter or Cagney)."[9] Roth discounts the role of the actual leads in *Gold Diggers of 1933* to make his point, yet the strong female presence in *Gold Diggers of 1933* offers a potentially more complex view of the Depression than either *42nd Street* or *Footlight Parade*, one related not so much to New Deal solutions but to the economic problems facing working women in the Depression.

Richard Dyer, in line with Hove and Mast, notes a shift in *Gold Diggers of 1933* between the narrative "realist" aesthetic—which reinforces the film's "realistic" emphasis on the Depression, poverty, the quest for capital, gold digging, and prostitution—and the "non-real," nonrepresentational numbers. The numbers express a utopian sensibility, offering abundant spectacle in place of poverty and energy in place of Depression-induced dispiritedness. Dyer argues that the spectacular mode of presentation undercuts the palliative effect of the numbers by denying it the validity of "realism." Instead of ultimately undermining the narrative, however, the nonrepresentational level "reprises the lessons of the narrative—above all, that women's only capital is their bodies as objects."[10] For Dyer, neither the narrative nor the numbers, though rooted in the Depression, are specifically about 1930s New Deal economics but are more generally about women's role in the sexual economy.

Dyer's analysis incorporates many of the conclusions drawn by Lucy Fischer's discussion of the "optical politics" of *Dames* and Paula Rabinowitz's investigation of commodity fetishism in *Gold Diggers of 1933*.[11] Fischer interprets Berkeley's "plastic abstractions" as "the essence of image itself—a vision of female stereotypes in their purest, most distillable form." Noting that "stereotype" denotes on one level "having no individuality," Fischer asserts that the Berkeley showgirl loses her individuality because each girl's physical appearance is so similar (Berkeley described his "girls" as matched pearls on a string) and because their identities are consumed in the creation of an overall abstract design. The women, passive and objectified, function as fetishized objects, while the men take the role of voyeur.

Rabinowitz plays on both the Freudian and Marxist meanings of fetish in her discussion of *Gold Diggers of 1933*. Berkeley's abstractions of the female form signify both the Freudian fetish, the substitution of an object for the phallus, and the Marxist model of commodity fetishism, a process of reification and alienation engendered by capitalist relations. Their individuality abstracted into an assembly line-like production, the women in the Berkeley musical function as both fetishized image and fetishized commodity. "We're in the Money," which visually links female sexuality and money, establishes the dual commodification of women and money. With the film's conflation of female performance, gold digging and prostitution, *Gold Diggers of 1933* asserts that a woman's only resource is her body—which can be used legitimately, on stage or film, or illegitimately, as a sellable commodity. Rabinowitz argues that by refuting the cinematic conventions of the narrative (Dyer's "realist" aesthetic) the musical structure overpowers the narrative structure. The numbers represent an alienated use of female imagery as fetish that effectively controls and neutralizes the strength of the female protagonists in the plot.

Departing somewhat from these critical models, Patricia Mellencamp emphasizes the role of the female protagonists in *Gold Diggers of 1933* and characterizes the disjunction between narrative and number not as a content/style split, but as a representation of an apportionment of female and male spectatorial address:

> With the crucial qualification that Berkeley's spectacles are addressed to the male spectator, literally coded as voyeur or fetishist, LeRoy's narrative demonstrates the pleasure of female friendship—the solidarity between Trixie, Carol, and Polly—and is propelled by fast-talking, inventive women (who are transformed into identical, anonymous, Freudian symbols in the spectacles that stop the advance of the story) who are infinitely more interesting, idiosyncratic, and clever than the wimpy men.[12]

With its emphasis on female leads in the primary diegesis and its reliance on feminine spectacle in the secondary diegesis, *Gold Diggers of 1933* belies theories that presume an organizing male spectatorial address in all classical Hollywood films. Instead, according to Mellencamp, it "suggests an address and appeal to women—who are let in on the joke" as the primary level of the diegesis while it still conforms to a Mulveyian model (the spectator as masculine voyeur and fetishist) in the spectacles that temporarily halt narrative progress.

Although Mellencamp raises interesting questions about textual address, she eventually abandons the promise of a dual feminine/masculine address and warns that the pleasure this film offers to the female spectator is compromised by the musical numbers, which use women as commodities, and by the final unions of the romantic couples, which separate the women from each other and contain them in a patriarchal institution. Ultimately, like Dyer and Rabinowitz, Mellencamp claims that the film's sexual economy reasserts masculine authority: "Knowledge, which the women have about men, is not power; money is."[13] The female spectator's pleasure is thus coded in hindsight as masochistic, a quality Mellencamp aligns with masculine sadism and fetishism.[14] This claim confirms a Mulveyian view of the female spectator's position. While the male spectator comfortably assumes the role of voyeur and sadist, the female spectator shifts from an empowered, knowledgeable spectator position to a masochistic transvestite identification with the masculine point of view. Her knowledge, and the appeal to her knowingness, are undermined and turned against her.

I would suggest, however, that the tension between narrative and number that Mellencamp describes might work in the opposite direction: in other words, that the textual address to women as the narrative level may undermine the film's spectacles and its ending. According to Mellencamp, the female spectator identifies with the gold diggers who know "about men." But the gold diggers also know about money, about power, and about the relation between sexuality and economics—the same knowledge and relationships represented by the fetishistic coin-costumes in "We're in the Money." If the female spectator is "let in on the joke," and the joke is on the men in the film, why must we assume that she stops laughing when confronted with feminine spectacle or the resolution of a romance plot? The knowledge that the female spectator gains about men, money, power, and economics in the primary diegesis provides her with a means to read the spectacles from a feminist camp perspective, one which enables her to recognize herself in the fetishized images but from which she is able to knowingly distance herself.

Mellencamp, Fischer, and Rabinowitz predicate their assessment of Berkeley's sexual politics on the assumption that Berkeley's numbers are unequivocally addressed to a masculine spectator and that they wholeheartedly support the patriarchal ideology that they, undoubtedly, portray. They attribute fetishism solely to men—even when, as Fischer argues, a Berkeley number like "The Girl at the Ironing Board" in *Dames* ascribes this classically male fantasy to the behavior of a female protagonist. (Here, Joan Blondell, playing a laundress, attaches herself fetishistically to men's underwear as a substitute for the "normal" sexual object.) This assumption also ignores female spectators whose same-sex desire might locate a lesbian erotic in the numbers. A number like the title song of *Dames* (which features images of women two by two in bed, exercising in sexy pajamas, and bathing together before turning into black-and-white abstractions) seems equally available to be read as lesbian imagery as well as in terms of the girl–girl eroticism favored in straight male pornography.[15] Even if we assume a masculine address, we need to understand these and other potentially oppositional ways in which female spectators might be able to negotiate their experience of these texts.

At face value, Dyer too represents the numbers in fairly dogmatic terms, as "lessons" taught to gullible (female) spectators. But Dyer acknowledges that contradictions inhere in the numbers themselves—contradictions between the materialist abundance of the spectacle and its association with the immaterial (magic, the imaginary) and between the creative energy of the dances and their mindless automatism. These contradictions are intrinsic to Berkeley's elevation of a mode of cinematic entertainment over "realistic" live entertainment.

To return to Mast's description of the musical's "alternative vision," which both disguises social critique and allows its implications to be read, these tensions may reflect a dual view of the palliative effect of numbers, one which simultaneously proffers relief while mocking its own offer, recognizing the absurdity of substituting feminine spectacle for material aid. In representing a two-sided view of entertainment's ameliorative possibilities, the numbers in *Gold Diggers of 1933* also offer a two-sided view of women, which both supports and critiques the notion that women's only capital is their bodies. This two-sided view inheres both in the camp spectacle of the numbers and in the activity of the gold diggers, who jokingly and knowingly manipulate their commodity status and further promulgate their commodification.

These contradictions at the representational level in both the narrative and numbers of *Gold Diggers of 1933* furnish the female spectator with sufficient material to enable her to read the film through a double vision: not as a transvestite who identifies with male voyeurs but as a camp spectator who simultaneously identifies with and laughs at her image. While the Berkeley numbers in *Gold Diggers of 1933* are certainly part of the film's camp effect, to discern what makes the film *feminist* camp—as distinct from other, even campier Berkeley—requires that we situate the camp effect of the musical numbers in the film in their narrative context and analyze how the camp masquerade of the gold diggers in the narrative recodes the camp effect of the numbers—an effect that taken out of context could be read as antifeminist—from a feminist perspective. At the same time, I suggest that we can read "spectacular elements" in the narrative itself, elements that work against closure and lend the film to a feminist camp reading.

Narrative spectacle and feminine vision

Fischer's claim that the women are rendered passive objects by the active and voyeuristic male gaze depends on the presence of a diegetic male figure of identification. According to Fischer, this diegetic male functions as bearer of the look and organizer of the vision, and he stands in for Berkeley. In *Dames's* "I Only Have Eyes for You," for instance, Dick Powell's fantasmatic imagination "produces" hundreds of Ruby Keelers. Similarly, in *Footlight Parade*, James Cagney plays a Berkeley-like figure who produces gimmicky and spectacular live musical prologues to cinema attractions. In the film's most outrageous moment, his bizarre gaze lights on a group of black children playing by an open fire hydrant and "sees" a Berkeley spectacle: "Say, that's what that wood nymph needs—a large waterfall splashing on beautiful white bodies." The policeman standing nearby confirms the patriarchal authority of this extraordinary—and racist—vision when he tells Cagney, 'I've got ideas, too, Mr. Kent." *42nd Street* aligns the male gaze so closely with the director (Warner Baxter) that he seemingly exudes the spectacle from his own body—his spent body virtually expires once the show ends.

In *Gold Diggers of 1933*, however, as Mark Roth suggests, it is difficult to pinpoint a diegetic male character—among those Mellencamp characterizes as the "wimpy men"—who functions as the bearer of the look. Brad provides the cash and writes the songs for the show and, as in Powell's other films with Ruby Keeler, he sings the opening chorus of two numbers with Keeler. "Pettin' in the Park" and "Shadow Waltz" potentially do represent his fantasy. "Pettin' in the Park," as I mentioned earlier, ends with Powell opening Keeler's metallic chastity suit; and in "Shadow Waltz," he intones "Let me dream a song that / I can bring to you" and "dreams" a song rife with Freudian symbols in which women play neon violins and form a highly sexualized violin-and-bow shaped pattern. Nevertheless, the narrative minimizes the degree to which a spectator could be said to identify with Brad or attribute authority to him. In *Dames*, Powell directs and produces the show, as Cagney and Baxter do in *Footlight Parade* and *42nd Street*. Powell's Brad, though, is hardly in charge. He obtains the money from inherited, not earned wealth. When he expresses his desire to marry Polly, he loses control over that money to his brother, over whom the women take charge. Even within the numbers, the only one of the three leads whom he manipulates is Polly, who plays the ingenue in relation to the other two women as well as filling that role in the show-within-the-film. Carol does not appear in either "Pettin' in the Park" or "Shadow Waltz" and Trixie only appears in "Pettin' in the Park," where, dressed in a policeman's uniform, she represents a counter authority figure.

As director of the show, Barney presents the next logical choice of a male figure for voyeuristic or sadistic identification. Barney's "vision," however, extends primarily to the "Forgotten Man" number:

> That's just what this show's about—the Depression—men marching—marching in the rain—marching—marching—doughnuts and crullers—jobs—jobs—marching— marching—marching in the rain—and in the background will be Carol—spirit of the Depression—a blue song—no, not a blue song—but a wailing—and this woman—this gorgeous woman—singing this number that tears your heart out—the big parade—the big parade of tears.

Barney envisions not a female spectacle but "men marching." The "gorgeous woman" will be "in the background" and not passive or mute but "wailing" and tearing "your heart out." His vision reverses the structure of most Berkeley numbers: it delegates men to the role of mass spectacle and grants a woman both voice and empowered vision; the forgotten men will be produced and thus remembered by Carol's "wailing" song.

Moreover, unlike the directors played by Cagney and Baxter, Barney disappears for the better part of the film. For a backstage musical, *Gold Diggers of 1933* devotes very little screen time to rehearsals. Aside from the dress rehearsal for "We're in the Money," we get only one brief glimpse of a rehearsal—for "Pettin' in the Park." This scene establishes Brad's superiority to the juvenile lead; Barney figures only in the background. And, while *Footlight Parade*, *42nd Street*, and *Dames* each concludes with the show's opening night, focusing all narrative energy on producing the show, *Gold Diggers of 1933* uses opening night to propel the second half of the narrative, the gold-digging scheme, in which Carol and Trixie function as our main points of identification, the principal organizers of our vision.

The show produced through the collaboration of Barney and Brad frames and complements the narrative but does not determine it. Rather than taking place backstage, the primary plot of *Gold Diggers of 1933* unfolds offstage in the everyday world of the showgirls. This plot effects a synthesis with the secondary level of the diegesis, not by making the show serve narrative demands, but by incorporating thematic and symbolic concerns of the show into the narrative in a production staged by the women protagonists themselves. Apparently bored by Barney's vision of "men marching" and by Brad's drippy songs. Trixie asks Barney if this show will have any comedy, her speciality. He responds, "Plenty. . . . The gay side, the hard-boiled side, the cynical and funny side of the Depression. . . . Be the best thing you ever did, Trixie." Aside from "Forgotten Man," which could be called cynical, the numbers we see bear little relation to Barney's promise of showing the many sides of the Depression. In the show-within-the-show that we see, Trixie's only role is a silent bit as a policewoman in "Pettin' in the Park." Trixie does, however, perform her comic specialty in the film. She produces this comic, multifaceted show "backstage," as it were, in producing the show of gold-digging show girls for Lawrence and Faneuil.

In acting out the stereotype of the gold digger, Trixie and Carol (and Polly, to a degree) make a spectacle of themselves. This spectacle, unlike the musical numbers, features active and controlling women who manipulate passive men. In pretending to be gold diggers, the women play upon the trope of female commodification and undermine the viewer's belief in that trope by suggesting that it is only an act. At the same time, the show they produce, like the show Barney produces, has the Depression as its primary subject matter, and the narrative acknowledges the limitations women face in the economic sphere, limitations that make their act a necessity. We need, therefore, to understand the particular historical circumstances that gave rise to the stereotype of the gold digger and how that stereotype reflects and represses economic and social conditions related specifically to the Depression.

The stereotype of the gold digger

The gold digger first entered the American lexicon with the production of Avery Hopwood's play *The Gold Diggers* in 1919. Warners had filmed two versions of the play before 1933: a silent version in 1923 and a talking version, *Gold Diggers of Broadway*, in 1929. Encouraged by the success of the latter, Warners revived the play yet again in *Gold Diggers of 1933*.[16] In a different arena, the literary prototype of the gold digger, Lorelei Lee, was born in 1925 with the publication of Anita Loos's *Gentlemen Prefer Blondes: The Illuminating Diary of a Professional Lady*. The stereotype of the gold digger was thus produced and popularized on the heels of the Progressive Era, a time of extraordinary reform ferment and activism targeting a variety of social ills, notably prostitution.

During the first two decades of the twentieth century, Progressive Era reform set in motion the most intensive antiprostitution campaign ever waged in America. Antiprostitution movements addressed social and psychological anxieties related to the changes that were corrupting and invading American society—particularly commercialization, urbanization, and industrialization.[17] The prostitute symbolized the failure of women to gain access to the material benefits of industrial society due to low wages and a sexual double standard in the workplace. Antiprostitution reform movements linked prostitution to the second-class status of women and, therefore, created a forum for addressing women's economic and political inequality. Ultimately, however, the focus on prostitution deflected these broader concerns, as reformers focused more on eradicating prostitution rather than the unequal conditions that fostered prostitution.

In the 1920s, as the image of the "new woman" and the flapper entered the public imagination, antiprostitution reform discourse moved away from policies embracing economic, social, and political issues. Instead, the discussion narrowed and shifted almost exclusively to the character of the prostitute—her inherited traits, criminal tendencies, and psychological disorders—so as to define her sexuality and social position as deviant.[18] Reformers divided prostitutes into two very different stereotypes: the innocent victim, on one hand, and the sinister polluter, on the other. The stereotype of the innocent victim responded to behaviorist theories of the Progressive Era. The innocent victim was pictured as an all-American girl—young, rural, and white—whose innocence, ignorance, and poverty had been manipulated by urban male pimps or white-slave traders; potentially, if not actually, a lady, she was coerced or tricked into vice by external forces.[19] The sinister polluter, by contrast, was typically portrayed as a naturally depraved lower-class non-white or immigrant who craved excitement and material goods. She was pictured as a polluter both literally, spreading venereal disease, and figuratively, as a corrupter of morals.[20] While targeting the failure of industrial society to meet women's changing needs, antiprostitution movements contradictorily blamed women's new position in industrialized America for altering the essential nature of "good" women and for rewarding "bad" women.

The stereotype of the gold digger was established just as the stereotype of the prostitute underwent this transformation. If the prostitute represented the new woman's leaning toward deviant sexuality and criminal tendencies, the newly minted stereotype of the gold digger represented her greed and amorality. Dictionaries define the gold digger as "a girl or woman who attaches herself to a man merely for gain"; "a young woman who accepts a man's attention for the sake of his gifts"; "a woman who uses her charms and favors to get money, presents, etc. from wealthy men."[21]

When antiprostitution discourse abandoned Progressive Era arguments about women's rights and the effects of commercialization, industrialization, and urbanization, the behaviorist explanation formerly allocated to the innocent victim was, in a sense, transferred to the gold digger. But instead of being seen as motivated by low wages, the gold digger's actions were attributed to an excessive desire for material goods and leisure suited to the giddy prosperity of the 1920s. The stereotype of the gold digger serves to empty Progressive Era antiprostitution discourse of its content. The concept of gold digging still raises questions related to the effects of commercialization, industrialization, and urbanization on sex roles and sexual behavior. But, because the gold digger's actions are attributed to greed and not need, her image is divorced from the broader issue of women's inequality that had previously grounded feminist concern over the cultural emphasis on material acquisition and commercialized leisure. [. . .] [M]elodramatic treatments of the fallen-women theme in the 1930s and 1940s virtually equate the gold digger, the prostitute, and the kept woman. Generally, though, the gold digger serves as a comic and cynical counterpart to the prostitute.

Not coincidentally, the comic gold digger generally appears on the cultural scene in times of perceived prosperity. Born in the Roaring Twenties, she was revitalized in the 1950s in films like Howard Hawks's *Gentlemen Prefer Blondes* and Jean Negulesco's *How to Marry a Millionaire* (both starring Marilyn Monroe), and she reappeared in the Reagan era as the quintessential "material girl," Madonna. In times of prosperity, the figure of the gold digger parodically mimics the culture's emphasis on consumption and deflects feminist issues related to women's work and equal rights by suggesting that women desire to achieve the material benefits of industrial society but not to labor in the workforce for them. In the comic variant, the figure of the gold digger aestheticizes and makes a joke of prostitution; she parodically appropriates the behavior of the prostitute for camp effect.

The comic gold digger would seem to be an outmoded stereotype in the 1930s insofar as her excessive greed can no longer be imagined or justified in a time of real economic worry.[22] *Gold Diggers of 1933*, however, inserts the comic gold digger into a narrative of the Depression. During the Depression, a new round of federal and state laws forced thousands of women out of the workforce and new federal wage codes institutionalized lower pay rates for women. The film responds to these changes, linking gold digging not to the greedy acquisitiveness of prosperous times but to the economic concerns of women trying to survive in the Depression. It revitalizes Progressive Era critiques of unfair labor practices and women's low wages. To achieve this end, *Gold Diggers of 1933* anachronistically inserts various tropes of Progressive Era antiprostitution discourse into the diegesis.

Gold digging and the masquerade

In enacting the stereotype of the comic gold digger the film plays upon the outdated stereotypes of the sinister polluter and innocent victim. Lawrence and Faneuil invoke the image of the sinister polluter in characterizing the gold-digging showgirl as a "parasite." Lawrence believes he can outmaneuver the women, getting Carol (whom he mistakes for Polly) to transfer her affections to him, thereby proving that she is a gold digger. But he confesses that he is "afraid"—"Polly" (Carol) "fascinates" him and presents a danger to which he may "succumb." Trixie and Carol play on this image to parody the stereotype of the gold digger, exaggerating the gold digger's traits for comic effect, hyperbolizing the gold digger's masquerade, theatricalizing it to create an ironic distance from it. They exaggerate their desire for material goods—Trixie, for instance, catches sight of Faneuil's lighter and exclaims "GOLD!"—and force the men to buy them hats, corsages, furs, and a slew of other goods. They mimic the stereotype of the "bad" woman. In order to discuss how much money "Polly" (Carol) will take to leave Brad alone, they go to a speakeasy, where they drink lots of champagne and Trixie fondles Faneuil's knee. At a nightclub, Carol snuggles provocatively with Lawrence on the dance floor: "You think it's vulgar, don't you, dancing this way?" In the final act of their masquerade, the women act out a scenario of actual prostitution: when Lawrence passes out drunk in the girls' apartment, Trixie convinces him that he slept with Carol and demands $10,000 payment for services rendered.

While Trixie and Carol mimic the behavior of the sinister polluter. Polly plays upon the trope of the innocent victim, revealing the element of masquerade in her seemingly genuine status as the ingenue of the trio. Lawrence links acting as a profession to prostitution when he states that Polly is unlike the "cheap" and "vulgar" women of the theater and that she is the woman his brother should be interested in: "How did a girl like you—? What are you doing in the theater?" Polly tells Lawrence that she is an orphan, whose father was an official in the government and whose mother was an invalid: "I had to find something to do—earn money— and all I could find was—[shrugs]. You see?" Trixie, Carol, and Brad watch and listen to Polly's discussion with Lawrence from a balcony above, providing an audience for this staged spectacle. In comic asides, Trixie deciphers the codes of Polly's masquerade: "Her father was a letter carrier!"; "Her mother could have licked John L. Sullivan." Polly has previously been delegated to the role of ingenue in relation to the other two women in the film, as well as in the musical numbers of the show. Here, in parodying her status as ingenue, she suggests that all stereotypes, even her goody-two-shoes persona, are masquerade, performance.

Instead of viewing women as fitting into one of two categories, wholly good or wholly bad, *Gold Diggers of 1933* represents a range of types and gradations between these two poles. It is not the case that the film denies that gold diggers exist—Fay Fortune is, after all, a "true" gold digger. Rather, it blurs the distinction between gold diggers and other women, between authenticity and masquerade. By contrast, the final shooting script reinforces these distinctions. According to the final script, Trixie cannot continue with the hustle and confesses her genuine love for Faneuil, just as Carol confesses hers for Lawrence and Polly truly loves Brad. In the film's final cut, however, Trixie's motivation in marrying Faneuil is left ambiguous. She may truly love him or she may just decide to fully enact the role of the gold digger and take Faneuil for his wealth. In another vein, even as Carol admits to being in love with Lawrence, she plays the sinister polluter to his corruptible heart. She describes herself as "cheap and vulgar." "Everytime you say cheap and vulgar," Lawrence proclaims. "I'm going to kiss you." The film depicts a range of heterosexual relations—young, innocent love (Polly and Brad), mature, sexual, sophisticated love (Carol and Lawrence), and older, asexual, cynical love (Trixie and Faneuil)—each of which is brought about through the masquerade and none of which is without an element of masquerade, no matter how genuine the love that informs it. In theatricalizing the masquerade's construction of gender identities, the women protagonists force the recognition of these heterosexual relations as culturally constructed.

Gold Diggers of 1933, therefore, deepens and confirms the psychoanalytic view that genuine womanliness and the masquerade are "the same thing," points on a continuum. However, the film also reveals the class bias inherent to the notion of masquerade by associating the masquerade with working-women's survival strategies. Riviere models her original conception of female masquerade on her observation of certain intellectual women who have gained a measure of power in the intellectual sphere and then have put on a "mask of womanliness" to placate men who resent their power. Although Riviere claims that all women participate in the masquerade, she conceives of the masquerade as primarily a gesture of disavowal, denying and abrogating "masculine" power and knowledge. In a patriarchal and oppressive society, however, most women do not have such privileged access to masculine power. Feminists have primarily used Riviere's notion of the masquerade to support theories related to the constructedness of gender identities; we need, however, to reconsider what relation, if any, the everyday masquerade has to female empowerment.

If, as I claim, female masquerade is a camp strategy, it also partakes of the pathos of camp and reflects the fact that camp is a product of oppression. As Richard Dyer argues, gay men developed an eye and ear for surfaces because they had to be skilled at disguise to adapt to society's conventions: "We couldn't afford to stand out in any way, for it might give the game away about our gayness."[23] Gold Diggers of 1933 reverses the order of Riviere's examples and suggests that women can use masquerade not only to disavow masculine power but also to gain strategic access to power and privilege typically denied them as women. This masquerade merges the thin theatricality of performance with the deeper drama of the lived. Here, the person who has real needs and desires consciously takes on a persona to realize those needs and desires. Her masquerade entails a camp recognition of herself as a stereotype and her manipulation of that stereotype for her own ends. She not only camps, creating an artificial masquerade, but perceives herself as camp, as enacting the serious joke that is her life. The women protagonists in the film theatricalize the masquerade, both to create an ironic distance from oppressive stereotypes (exacting revenge on Lawrence and Faneuil), and to use those stereotypes to their advantage (becoming effective and successful gold diggers who, in fact, use feminine charms to marry three rich men).

The masquerade in Gold Diggers of 1933 represents a working-class women's strategy of survival and not simply a placating gesture to patriarchal authority. The film evokes the threat of prostitution at both levels of the diegesis to make clear that the choice for working women in the Depression is not a choice between masculine power and feminine disavowal but between unsuccessful and successful masquerade, between prostitution and gold digging. [. . .]

Notes

1 *American Thesaurus of Slang* (New York: Thomas Crowell) 580, subheading 594.b.
2 Jane Feuer, *The Hollywood Musical*, 2d ed. (Bloomington: University of Indiana Press, 1993), 26ff.
3 Bob Pike and Dave Martin, *The Genius of Busby Berkeley* (Reseda, California: Creative Film Society Books, 1973), 33.
4 Gerald Mast, *Can't Help Singin': The American Musical on Stage and Screen* (New York: Overlook Press, 1987), 123.
5 Feuer 69. See also Rick Altman, *The American Film Musical* (Bloomington: Indiana University Press, 1989), 200–71. Rather than a narrative/number split, Altman emphasizes four "sites" in the backstage musical: city and theater, stage and backstage.
6 Arthur Hove, "Introduction: In Search of Happiness," in *Gold Diggers of 1933*, ed. Arthur Hove (Madison: University of Wisconsin Press, 1980), 19.
7 Ibid. 27–30.
8 Mast 120.
9 See Mark Roth, "Some Warners Musicals and the Spirit of the New Deal," in *Genre: The Musical—A Reader*, ed. Rick Altman (New York: Routledge & Kegan Paul, 1986), 41–56.
10 Richard Dyer, "Entertainment and Utopia," in Altman 186.
11 Lucy Fischer, "The Image of Woman as Image: The Optical Politics of *Dames*," in Altman 70–84; Paula Rabinowitz, "Commodity Fetishism: Women in *Gold Diggers of 1933*," *Film Reader* 5 (1982): 141–49.
12 Patricia Mellencamp, "The Sexual Economics of *Gold Diggers of 1933*," in *Close Viewings: An Anthology of New Film Criticism*, ed. Peter Lehman (Tallahassee: Florida State University Press, 1990), 181.
13 Ibid.
14 Mellencamp clearly distinguishes her use of masochism from recent feminist rewritings that claim masochism *for* feminism as a female spectatorial mechanism. Gaylyn Studlar, for instance, defines masochism as a mother-centered, pre-Oedipal phenomenon and argues for the importance of a "masochistic aesthetic" in film. See Gaylyn Studlar, *In the Realm of Pleasure: Von Sternberg, Dietrich, and the Masochistic Aesthetic* (Chicago: University of Illinois Press, 1988). A principal text on the theory of masochism is that of Gilles Deleuze, *Sacher-Masoch: An Interpretation*, trans. Jean McNeil (London: Faber and Faber, 1971).
15 On this point, see Alexander Doty, *Making Things Perfectly Queer: Interpreting Mass Culture* (Minneapolis: University of Minnesota Press, 1993), 13–14.
16 Although the success of this film motivated Warners to produce variations on the theme in *Gold Diggers of 1935*, *Gold Diggers of 1937*, and *Gold Diggers in Paris* (1938), none of these films were as successful as the 1929 and 1933 versions, and they do not feature true gold diggers so much as attach the term generally to chorus girls, much as Dean Martin did in his TV variety show.
17 For histories of antiprostitution reform movements in the Progressive Era, see Mark Thomas Connelly, *The Response to Prostitution in the Progressive Era* (Chapel Hill: University of North Carolina Press, 1980); Ruth Rosen, *The Lost Sisterhood: Prostitution in America, 1900–1918*

(Baltimore: The Johns Hopkins University Press, 1982); and Barbara Meil Hobson, *Uneasy Virtue: The Politics of Prostitution and the American Reform Tradition* (New York: Basic Books, 1987; Chicago: University of Chicago Press, 1990).

18 Hobson 183ff.

19 Numerous films capitalized on the white slavery panic, notably *The White Slave* (dir. Miles Brothers, 1907), *Traffic in Souls* (dir. Tucker, 1913), *The Inside of the White Slave Traffic* (dir. Beal, 1913), *The House of Bondage* (dir. Kingsley, 1914), and *Intolerance* (dir. Griffith, 1916). See Kay Sloan, *The Loud Silents: Origins of the Social Problem Film* (Chicago: University of Illinois Press, 1988), 80–86; Kevin Brownlow, *Behind the Mask of Innocence—Sex, Violence, Prejudice, Crime: Films of Social Conscience and the Silent Era* (Berkeley: University of California Press, 1990), 70–85; and Miriam Hansen, *Babel and Babylon: Spectatorship in American Silent Film* (Cambridge: Harvard University Press, 1991), 221–25.

20 Rosen 47–48.

21 Definitions from *Oxford English Dictionary*, *Thesaurus of Slang*, *Dictionary of Slang*. See also Kathy Peiss's discussion of "treating" in "Charity Girls' and City Pleasures: Historical Notes on Working-Class Sexuality, 1880–1920," in *Powers of Desire: The Politics of Sexuality*, ed. Ann Snitow, Christine Stansell, and Sharon Thompson (New York: Monthly Review Press, 1983), 74–87.

22 According to Lea Jacobs, 1930s comic gold-digger films were considered "sex pictures" like melodramas of the fallen woman. The tendency in these pictures to glamorize the heroine and to associate the scenario of class rise with female sexuality was considered to be especially repugnant by the industry censors. See Lea Jacobs, *The Wages of Sin: Censorship and the Fallen Woman Film, 1928–1942* (Madison: University of Wisconsin Press, 1991), 66–67. While censors criticized Mae West's "sex pictures," her gold digger is [. . .] anachronistically inserted into an 1890s setting.

23 Richard Dyer, "It's Being So Camp as Keeps Us Going" (1976), reprinted in Dyer, *Only Entertainment* (New York: Routledge, 1992), 144.

"The Lady in the Tutti-Frutti Hat" 11

Carmen Miranda, a spectacle of ethnicity

SHARI ROBERTS

While films starring Carmen Miranda are racist and reductive, Miranda herself appeals to modern audiences largely because she seems so excessive and outrageous, so clearly entertaining, so beautifully camp, especially when seen outside of her historical context. For her contemporary audiences, Miranda perhaps provided a more complex pleasure as fans appreciated her outrageous performances within their problematic film settings and alongside the tensions of home-front America. Feminist theorists have asked whether it is possible to represent women in a nonsexist way. I could ask whether it is possible to represent ethnicities in a nonracist way. Although some film anthologies have noted supposed progress in Hollywood studios' portrayal of Latinos due to their Good Neighbor implementation, by trading negative "lazy greaseball" stereotypes for positive "happy children" stereotypes, the Fox Latin America musicals clearly did not come close to escaping racist representation.[1] Given that Carmen Miranda's star matrix referred so obviously to the world war and to the United States' ongoing struggles with Latin America, one might ask how contemporary audiences achieved pleasure through her texts at all? Certain elements of Miranda's star text were emphasized and repeated in her films and extrafilmic publicity material, and the same elements were noted (with pleasure) by fans and reviewers. These elements centered on her look, especially her bright, multi-textured outfits, and on her voice—that is, her singing voice as pure sound as opposed to any message she communicated.

All of Miranda's films during wartime were in Technicolor, which emphasized her vivid, brightly colored outfits, like those of "native" Latina girls, suggesting to some "the brash colors of tropical birds."[2] Not unusual with stereotypes of foreign women, the popular press described Miranda in terms of the physical, of the body—as wild, savage, and primitive, like an exotic animal, "enveloped in beads, swaying and wriggling, chattering macawlike . . ., skewering the audience with a merry, mischievous eye."[3] *Motion Picture* compared her to "a princess out of an Aztec frieze with a panther's grace, the plumage of a bird of paradise and the wiles of Eve and Lileth combined." Beyond the usual savage and bestial qualities, this fanzine suggests that the fall of man might also be attributable to Miranda.[4]

But what audiences loved most about Carmen Miranda was her extreme Otherness, especially the difference enunciated by her Other language; what they loved was that they could not understand her. As one *Collier's* review reads, "The songs were not listed in the program and nobody . . . had the faintest notion of what they were about. Precisely four words were intelligible, . . . which she repeated several times, . . . 'the Souse American Way.' These didn't mean much, either, but they implied that the South American way was very excellent indeed. . . . Nothing, though, could have been of less importance than her language."[5] *Life* magazine comments that "partly because there is no clue to their meaning except the gay rollings of Carmen Miranda's insinuating eyes, these songs, and Miranda herself, are the outstanding hit of the show."[6] Any language she might employ consists of those "universal" languages of the body. Miranda's songs are often nonsensical plays of sounds, words that do not signify in any language, such as "Chica Chica Boom Chick" or "I-Yi-Yi-Yi." Reviewers, confronted with Miranda's lack of words, are contaminated: unable to control her spectacle with their words, the medium that they normally control, they lose voice. Common tropes include expressing an inability to describe her performance and, alternately, imitating Miranda's comic speech patterns. One *Motion Picture* writer says Miranda "seengs song from Brazeel and her body sings with her. . . . If you've seen her, words are an anti-climax. If you haven't, keed! What you've missed!"[7]

Latina actresses in Hollywood films generally fit neatly within one of two stereotypes of the foreign Other: the exotic sex object (such as Delores Del Rio, the "female Valentino") or the ignorant comic actress (such as Lupe Velez, the "Mexican Spitfire"). Miranda is unique in that she initially straddled both categories: she was perceived by contemporary audiences as simultaneously sexy *and* comic, a vamp and a joke. The split created a tension between her hypersexualized *visual* presence available through performance as spectacle, foregrounding her body, and her comic *oral* presence available through interviews, foregrounding her words, her "paprika English."[8]

Reviews of her first shows describe her as overwhelmingly sexy and sexual:

> What it is that Carmen has is difficult to describe; so difficult, in fact, that dramatic critics have grown neurotic in their attempts to get it into words that would make sense and at the same time not brand them as mad sex fiends. Nevertheless, it must be attempted again. First, there is the impact of Carmen's costumes, . . . always covering her thoroughly with the exception of a space between the seventh rib and a point at about the waist-line. This expanse is known as the Torrid Zone. It does not move, but gives off invisible emanations of Roentgen rays. [Her songs'] words are absolutely unintelligible to a North American . . . , but what the listener hears—or hopes he is hearing—is unmistakable.[9]

Naming Miranda's mid-section the "Torrid Zone" conflates Latin Americans, or at least this Latin American woman, with her country, equating her "equator" with that of the planet's, the "torrid zone" of South America, where it's hotter than the rest of planet and where the natives are stereotypically wilder, sexier, and more naked than other people. Another reporter refers to numerous contemporary articles which pointed directly, if euphemistically, to Miranda's sex appeal by commenting, "Call it 'oomph,' 'yumph,' or go 'way back to Elinor Glyn and call it 'it.' That's Miranda."[10]

At the same time, in the popular press, Miranda's foreign accent is emphasized by comic malapropisms and mispronunciations of English, suggesting that foreigners are incapable of good English and, by extension, promoting a "primitive," ignorant stereotype. The topics of Miranda's speech reported most often are "primal" subjects, topics related to primal needs and basic subsistence, such as money, food, or sex: "'I say monee, monee, monee,' she told an amazed group on the boat before a single question had been asked. 'I say twenty words of English. I say yes and no. I say hot dog! I say turkey sandwich and I say grapefruit. . . . I know tomato juice, apple pie and thank you,' she says brightly. 'De American mens is like potatoes.'"[11] A *Newsweek* reviewer condescendingly and bizarrely describes her as "a Brazilian chanteuse . . . who with eyes dreamily closed and doubtless thinking of Dinty Moore's juicy hamburgers sings the softly romantic and insinuating songs of Rio."[12] In trying to peek "inside" Miranda, this critic cannot imagine a subjectivity behind her ethnic, feminine mask, except for this stereotype of raw, yet consumer-oriented, primal drives.

Only later, after her two U.S. stage shows and her first Hollywood movie, when she was incorporated into plots and made to speak her comic, pidgin English in the films (tempering her performative spectacle with narrative), does Miranda become *merely* comic, the nonsexual camp female grotesque, as she is remembered by today's fans. Miranda is presented in these later (still wartime) films simply as a grotesque comedienne, and her grotesqueness is emphasized both visually and orally. Visually, her costumes become distanced from her original explicitly Bahian costume: she wears a candy-cane costume in *Greenwich Village* (1944), and a battery-operated lighthouse costume in *Doll Face* (1945–46). Orally, she mixes Portuguese with comic malapropisms and mispronunciations of English, saying, for example, that she wears "lip-steak." In the only film in which she was given the romantic lead, *Copacabana* (1947), Miranda plays a dual role that enacts her typical position, fluctuating between a dark-haired, comic personality and that of a blonde, star-quality, glamorous, and refined *chanteuse*. The discarding of half of her original star appeal was due perhaps to audiences' inability to accept her contradictory, or double, image. One reason why Miranda's feminine star text failed to sustain the sexual/comic split past her first, nonintegrated shows in the United States is that a sexually attractive foreign Other would compete with the feminine WASP norm posited by the studio in the figure of Betty Grable and the other Fox blondes. U.S.–Latin American harmony could be suggested by a marriage of North and South Americans, but only if the U.S. feminine star was presented as the single acceptable object of desire. The war film's job was not only to entertain the "boys" on the front but also to reinforce their ties to home; encouragement to look at foreign feminine Others as sexually desirable would be counterproductive to the studio's mission. Therefore, Miranda's inclusion in the plots necessitated a simultaneous segregation from the cross-national couple.

In addition, Miranda's star text has been the object of a continued love–hate relationship between the United States and Brazil, a symbol alternately accepted and rejected as a part of Brazilian national identity. Miranda's image influenced the formation of Brazil's multiracial self-identity as it was reconceptualized in the 1930s, inclusive of the large, disempowered African-Brazilian population, which asserted its presence partially through the acceptance of the music and dance traditions of samba. *Samba* and *candomblé*, music and religion, together constitute an integral part of black Brazilian culture. After the abolition of slavery in 1888 and the lifting of the ban against African religion and its music and rituals, newly freed black slaves established *favelas*, the destitute hillside African-Brazilian communities of Rio, and there developed the original samba *de morro*. Etymologically, "samba" stems perhaps from the Angola word *semba*, or prayer, and also *umbigada*, a euphemism for the touching of the genitals during the dance. With the introduction of the radio in Brazil in the 1920s, the samba proved profitable for record companies and quickly spread as a form of popular music throughout Brazil.[13] The original samba *de morro* evolved into the mellower samba popularized by singers such as Miranda from the 1930s forward.

The *candomblé* temples of Rio were established by women, freed slaves from Bahia, the sixteenth-century capital of Brazil. These women, Bahians, were stereotyped within Brazil as women with shawls, turbans, and flirtatious ways. In addition, "Their special relationship with the old continent was . . . recognized. . . . They knew the religion, they had 'samba in the foot,' they had survived, and they kept the culture going."[14] To masquerade as a Bahian for Carnival was initially a tradition not only for women, but also for men. Miranda adopted this Bahian costume, which signified African religion, music, and tradition to Brazilians, as her trademark outfit, and it came to mean Brazil to North Americans via Fox's Bombshell. Thus Miranda's influence on Brazil's self-image affects U.S. perceptions of Brazil. In an interview, Miranda discussed the origin of her costume, which at least in 1941 was still available to fans not only as Brazilian but as African-Brazilian:

> Her costumes were inspired by those of the Negroes in Bahia. Like any creator she takes good ideas where she finds them and gives them new life. . . . In Bahia, the Negro girls walk to market, wide skirts flaring. . . . Carmen explains, 'An' wone boy, born in Bahia, make song in Brazeel about theez Bahiana dress. An' I say, I will put theez dress an' seeng theez song. You can't put theez dress, they say, because theez dress only Negroes put. Bah!' She gave it the brush-off. 'I put, but in gold an' silk an' velvet, an' I seeng in Rio. One week before Shubert see me in Casino, I put this Bahiana dress.'[15]

Miranda's words foreground her authorship of her Brazilian star image, enacted seriously, in the manner of a carnival masquerade costume. In addition, Miranda imagines an anthropo-morphized Brazil telling her, "You can't put theez dress . . . because theez dress only Negroes put," thereby highlighting the way Brazil has traditionally denied its own black population and traditions.

Contemporary accounts of Miranda's much-publicized return "home" to Brazil in 1940 reveal the split between Brazilian and U.S. perceptions of the star. Brazilian news reports describe the reception of her performance as extremely negative, the crowd booing and whistling. Reviewers claimed Miranda had lost her voice, had changed her style and her soul: Miranda had become Americanized.[16] With typical savvy, Miranda incorporated this negative reaction into subsequent Rio performances by adding new songs such as "Disseram Que Voltei Americanisada" ("They Say I Came Back Americanized") and "Voltei P'ro Morro" ("I'm Back in the Morro"), thereby salvaging the remainder of her Brazilian tour. In the United States, however, where Miranda has come to represent Brazil/Latin America, most articles reported an unmitigated success for Miranda: the "South American Bombshell" returned to loving crowds, making Brazil and Brazilian people complicit with how North America imagined and distorted South America. For instance, a *New York Times* article reports that Miranda's arrival caused "one of the city's greatest ovations," adding the curious detail that most of the people in this fantasy crowd were women.[17]

While Miranda played a role in shaping a Brazilian national identity, she also affected U.S. wartime national identity negatively by aiding in popular conceptions of the United States and its role in international politics and its relationship to other countries. Miranda's star text, concomitant with the fad of samba in the United States, influenced the way Brazilian culture came to be understood and identified in the states. For instance, Orson Welles, in his "Hello Americans" broadcast, conflates Brazil with its musical tradition: "The music . . . is rich, deep, Brazilian. It comes rolling down to Rio from the hills, throbs in the streets, everybody dances to it. It's called samba. If you scramble the two words 'music' and 'Brazil' and then unscramble them again you end up with the word 'samba.' Also if you scramble a moderate number of Brazilians together and then unscramble them, you find out they've been dancing the samba. . . . Brazilian babies can beat out a samba rhythm before they can talk, and dance to samba before they can walk."[18] A reporter explains, in an article titled "Miss Miranda and the Samba Here for Good," that "the samba is a native Brazilian dance, introduced here by Miss Miranda. It is more than likely that the whole hemisphere will twirl to its rhythm."[19]

Miranda's star image later became a symbol for Tropicalism, the third phase of Cinema Novo, which parodied myths that represented Brazil as a tropical paradise, as in *The Heirs* (1969).[20] In 1968 Caetano Veloso, one of the movement's pop artists, wrote the song "Tropicalia," a manifesto for Tropicalism which ended with the words "Viva Carmen Miranda-da-da-da-da." Veloso explains, in a recent *New York Times* article, that "Tropicalismo appropriated [Miranda] as one of its principal signs, capitalizing on the discomfort that her name and the evocation of her gestures could create."[21] That Miranda's image still holds great emotional power for Brazil and still influences Brazilian self-perception and Brazilian identity was demonstrated recently in New York at a well-meant, although dramatically unsuccessful, attempt to free Miranda as a Brazilian artist from her Hollywood stereotyping.[22] (This failed resuscitation was performed by Arto Lindsay and other Brazilian performance artists, along with Laurie Anderson and Miranda's aging sister Aurora Miranda.)

On the one hand, Carmen Miranda's star matrix reinforces typical negative stereotypes of ethnic women by enacting a nurturing earth-mother cliché. By taking as her costume enormous flowers, fruits, and vegetables intermixed with exaggerated traditional Brazilian dress, Miranda becomes the image of an overflowing cornucopia of South American products, ripe, ready, and eager for picking by North American consumers. In addition, Miranda's comic element relies on the "primitive" qualities emphasized in her persona: her inability to speak (in English); her ignorance, stemming from language and cultural barriers; and her secondary status and inferiority. All of these exaggerated qualities contribute to negative conceptions both of "foreign" Others and of women. On the other hand, Miranda's appeal resides in the parody of these stereotypes. Because Miranda so exaggerates signifiers of ethnicity and femininity, her star text suggests that they exist only as surface, that they do not refer, and in this way Miranda can become sheer spectacle. For instance, the joy reviewers articulate about Miranda's lack of English stems partly from the illusion of masculine and American superiority but also from an enthusiasm for a freedom within or without language, the freedom allowed by songs when the listener has "no clue to their meaning"—the freedom experienced through the recognition of the artifice, as opposed to the essence, of social definitions of ethnicity and femininity.[23]

Carmen Miranda is exemplary as a musical star famous *as* spectacle, as excess, as parody or masquerade. Many recent feminist theorists have looked to fantasy scenarios, in particular to theories of spectatorial masquerade, as a way to enact or perform femininity and thereby throw into question concepts of feminine essence, opening alternative viewing options for female spectators.[24] Studies on masquerade attack the idea that an essential feminine exists prior to the concept of "woman" as constituted in any age. Masquerade mimics a socially constructed identity in order to conceal, but at the same time to indicate, the absence that exists behind the mask and ultimately to discover the lack of any "natural" gender identity. Similarly, ethnic masquerade works to undermine the concept of ethnic essence. An exploration of notions of the feminine and ethnic minorities in society at a very specific, complex, historical moment can reveal possibilities for the use of masquerade by female spectators amid other marginalized spectators in wartime society.

Miranda performs a femininity so exaggerated that it becomes comical, undercutting any threat that her female sexuality might pose but also calling into question society's assumptions about feminine essence. Additionally, while Hollywood representations of different ethnicities often draw on, emphasize. and contribute to stereotypical ethnic clichés and myths, Miranda's ethnic persona nears hysteria with its exaggeration. Miranda's costumes lampoon both feminine fashion and traditional and stereotypical Latin dress—stacks of accessories, shoes so high they impede walking, and cornucopia hats. Miranda's outfits suggest female sexuality in excess, revealing and accentuating her sexually invested body parts—the navel, breasts, and legs. Busby Berkeley's number "The Lady in the Tutti-Frutti Hat" in *The Gang's All Here* lampoons *both* U.S.–Latin American trade relations and notions of feminine sexuality through the casting of Miranda as the overseer of countless enormous, swaying phallic bananas buoyed up by lines of chorus girls who dance above other girls who have oversized strawberries between their legs. A *New York Times* reviewer notes that these "dance spectacles seem to stem straight from Freud and, if interpreted, might bring a rosy blush to several cheeks in the Hays office."[25] The "Tutti-Frutti Hat" number was censored in Brazil.[26] Miranda's sexual excess extended beyond her film roles, most notably during a widely circulated 1941 scandal caused by a low-angle photo of Miranda dancing with Cesar Romero in which she is clearly naked beneath her swirling skirts. In response to the scandal, Miranda reportedly said, "Why should I be so foolish to dance weethout de pants?"[27]

At this point we may ask how can a racist and sexist stereotype be positive? And why would we want to pursue such a stereotype, why would we want to spend the time, energy, and perhaps misdirected pleasure on understanding this text? I believe that Miranda's appeal and fame resided in fans' perception of her as a producer of her star text, as in control of her own self-parody. Miranda's contemporary audience accepted and enjoyed her as a caricature, as a parody of herself, as a demonstration of masquerade. For instance, in 1943, after only four years in Hollywood, Busby Berkeley showcased Miranda in "The Lady in the Tutti-Frutti Hat." Miranda stands in front of a forced-perspective set painting, creating the illusion of an impossibly enormous banana hat and enunciating the ultimate, classic image of herself as parody. Further evidence of fan perception of Miranda as parodic text lies in the frequency with which she was and continues to be imitated by both women and men in drag, from Mickey Rooney in *Babes on Broadway* (1941) to Bugs Bunny in *What's Cookin', Doc* (1944) to Ted Danson in *Three Men and a Little Lady* (1990). She was the female character most impersonated by both gay and straight GIs, so that in 1944 a *Theatre Arts* writer reported that "cries of anguish can still be heard from harried Special Services officers who were tired of 'impersonations of Carmen Miranda.'"[28]

Unlike other entertainers who simply become the objects of parody, Miranda was presented in the discourse of the time as both subject and object of self-parody. To begin with, Miranda was known as the author of her own costume and her own image. The Bahian costume was not designed for her by Broadway or Hollywood designers. She first adopted it for her last Brazilian film, *Banana de Terra* (1938), in which she impersonates a Bahian woman for a performance of a song written by a Bahian composer, Dorival Caymmi. Articles and publicity commonly report that Miranda designed her own costumes and "turbans" and insisted on bringing her own musical accompaniment, the Bando da Lua, with her from Brazil.[29] Imogene Coca's popular parody of Miranda's "Sous-American Way" in the *Straw Hat Revue* was presented by the producers of Miranda's first U.S. theater show, *The Streets of Paris*, at the same time that Miranda appeared in this show. While flamboyant performers are commonly burlesqued, Miranda is perceived in contemporary articles as having a hand not only in the production of this parody but also in the manufacture of her own image. In this instance, the popular press publicized the fact that Coca learned to parody Miranda from Miranda herself: Coca told the papers that "she burlesqued herself for my benefit more than I'd ever dare."[30]

For all of her reported naive, cutely stupid remarks concerning "American mens" and other aspects of U.S. culture, Miranda occasionally reveals a more perceptive self behind her "primitive Other" persona. For instance, in 1939 she expresses irritation at North Americans' refusal to understand other cultures and our negative stereotyping of foreign Others: "I met an American girl in a doctor's office here and she say, 'Ees thees how a Brazilian womans look?' . . . as if I am supposed to have feathers in my hair like Indians. And she ask if in Brazil they have electric lights yet. HAH! . . . North Americans do not want to learn about other countries, especially their language. Yanquis expect us to learn their language instead."[31] Miranda demonstrates a sophisticated recognition of the profitability of her artificial persona in the following interview, in which she shows more insight into the appeal of her supposedly fragile grasp of (English) language than do her previously quoted U.S. reviewers: "She said that [her singing 'con movimientos'] was creation. . . . 'I feel like an artist,' she said. 'In Brazil I do the same thing. I sing in the same songs. But everybody knows what I sing. They comprehend the language. Nobody here knows what I sing. All they can do is understand from my tone. From my movement. It is a maravilla.'"[32] Miranda understood the advantage of her own ethnic masquerade. Miranda reveals in an interview that she is aware that, in Hollywood, a foreign "accent is an asset."[33] As a 1939 *Collier's* article on Miranda notes, "an actress or singer who murders English gets a lot more headlines than one who talks as though she had been brought up in Boston."[34]

At the World's Fair in 1939 Miranda won a Charlie McCarthy doll, a replica of Edgar Bergen's popular wooden alter ego. She expressed her delight in *controlling* her dummy, of playing Bergen to an image, a persona, detachable in the real perhaps but ultimately inescapable and integral to his popularity: "'He is home, this Charlie,' she said. 'I push a button. I make him talk. He talks what I say. He is the artificial man, I can control him.'"[35] Miranda's supposedly ingenuous remarks about a doll won at a fair suggest self-knowledge on her part and an understanding of the way her self-created image has a life of its own in the popular imagination of the U.S. public. A further provocative revelation of agency behind the star persona comes at the end of a typical article on Miranda's life-style, in which the female journalist metaphorically steps back from her own reporting to question the recognized artifice of the Miranda façade. "There was a glint in her eye—I looked at her publicity man. . . . Carmen, are you kidding?" I find it significant that the only reporter to attribute to Carmen an awareness of the artificiality of her star image is a woman.

The press often reported Miranda's desire to appeal to a female audience, as in an article titled "No 'Men Only' for This Carmen": "She isn't happy unless she can please the wives and sweethearts, too."[36] In another article titled "Ladies Invited," Miranda is linked explicitly with female fans' role in the war effort.[37] Women readers are urged to "keep your hands soft," as Miranda does, in order to achieve hands as beautiful and expressive as are hers. The beauty tips, presented as direct advice from Miranda to female readers, are connected to the war effort since women's hands are needed to make "sweaters, or socks, or scarfs" for the army and bandages for the Red Cross, for which they may be rewarded with "a salute from the army

. . . a bow from the Red Cross," and if lucky, "an engagement ring from you-know-who." Also, Miranda's costumes popularized a South American fashion trend for women's hats and shoes.[38] And consumers were urged, in a full-page 1939 advertisement that featured a glamour photo of Miranda, to "Do as Miss Carmen Miranda does, learn your foreign language at the Barbizon School of Languages, for better accent."[39] Miranda fans who perceived themselves as "foreign," and in this way identified with her, also imitated her. Fans encouraged to mimic Miranda through consumerism also recognized that a feminine or ethnic image bought, to wear or discard at will, was no more essential to their identity than any other beauty product. By applying cosmetics, donning hats, altering accents, fans physically perform the Miranda masquerade, highlighting for themselves the artificiality of the stereotypes that interpellate them in their everyday life.

This masquerade performed by consuming fans was also perhaps enacted during individual film-viewing experiences. By looking closely at a single film sequence, we can explore the insinuation of self-authorship in Miranda's film presence, to examine further the way she was understood by fans. The opening sequence of Down Argentine Way, in which Miranda sings "Sous American Way," provides a clear example of her appeal—her control over her own joke, her self-parody. Here in her first Hollywood performance, completely unintegrated with the film, Miranda appears in an excerptable clip which in fact works as a prologue for the film proper. She sings only in Portuguese and has no dialogue or interaction with the other film characters. The mainstream 1940 U.S. viewer must read her body . . . the "universal" language of her gestures and music—because she does not speak (English); she seems to be denied subjectivity. Miranda clearly knows how to "read" herself, however. She understands both her own body, along with the viewer, as well as her words; she is, moreover, in on the joke. Miranda's aural and visual presentation of herself as out-of-control excess is in fact a demonstration of her hypercontrol over her own voice and image. The knowingness she expresses in this clip indicates her own subjectivity, insinuating that she knows a secret to which the viewer will never have access.

Because Miranda controlled her own image, some fans were able to understand her stereotypical persona as manipulated by the star herself in a kind of masquerade and were thereby, through interpretation and fantasy, able to identify with her as one way to negotiate or cope with their own minority status in society. I want to clarify that I am neither trying to develop a theoretical move to excuse any negative stereotypes nor suggesting that any star can be understood to be performing a masquerade. For instance, this kind of relationship would be more difficult to imagine between a similarly racially stereotyped secondary star, such as Stepin Fetchit, and her fans. While Stepin Fetchit was, like Miranda, in control of his image, exploiting his character as a lazy, shuffling "coon," a "natural-born" comedian, in order to get film roles,[40] it is important that he was not seen by fans as in control of his own stereotype. Miranda could emerge from behind her character, using her own name and speaking in her first language of Portuguese instead of pidgin English,[41] but Stepin Fetchit was always Stepin Fetchit both on screen and stage and off. Fans would not know that his real name was Lincoln Perry nor that he could speak in a different manner or with different words than those used by his stammering, slow-witted character. No distance existed between the character and the star that would allow for masquerade. In addition, while Miranda's wink at the camera indicates understanding of the play and control of the show, Stepin Fetchit's performance remains consistently caught in the confines of a regressive racial stereotype, which would offer little appeal of identification for viewers. In more direct comparison to Miranda, none of the contemporary Latin American copycats, such as Lina Romay or Maria Montez, were able either to escape their stereotypes or to achieve control over their image. Importantly, none of these B-movie Miranda mimics ever neared her fame or her lasting power, indicating, perhaps, Hollywood fans' disinterest in the simpler stereotype.

In conclusion, while Miranda's parodic text works undeniably to reinforce regressive stereotypes of Latin Americans and of women, and to support racist and sexist conceptions of the dominant ideology, her text at the same time reveals them as stereotypes, allowing for negotiated or subversive readings by fans. For instance, the gay servicemen who turned Miranda into an immediate camp icon recognized her parody of gender roles and were able to use her text in impersonations at camp shows as an allowable expression of their subjectivity. Miranda's text could, in this way, be used to speak for particular marginalized minority audiences, including ethnic and female viewers.

By foregrounding excessiveness, Miranda's text addresses two of the most consistent marginalizations in the studio system and in wartime, as well as in our current society. Her star text speaks to the erasure of women—specifically women's sexuality—and of ethnic minorities. For a secondary star of forty-five years ago to be remembered so vividly seems quite unusual, but Miranda's is a still-current image for audiences. That the very elements of her persona that threaten to disturb the Hollywood studio system are precisely those for which she was and is still famous suggests that this disruptiveness is what has sustained her fame so vividly and for so long. What appealed to and continues to attract fans of Miranda is the double masquerade which insists on questioning both feminine essence and foreign stereotyping, and so offers resistant, alternative viewing options.

Notes

Unless noted, all articles for this essay were obtained from primary sources at the Billy Rose Theater Collection in New York, the University of Chicago Library and Inter-Library Loan Department (thank you Diane and Sandy), the Chicago Public Library, the Museum of Modern Art in New York, the Library of Congress, and the Museum of Television and Radio in New York. Thanks to Miriam Hansen. Corey Creekmur, Bill Brown, Bill Veeder, and Jonathan Rosenbaum for all their help.

1 See, for instance, Allen L. Woll, The Hollywood Musical Goes to War (Chicago: Nelson-Hall, 1983), 120.
2 Current Biography (1941): 586.
3 "New Shows in Manhattan," Time, 3 July 1939, 42.
4 Ida Zeitlin, "Sous American Sizzler," Motion Picture, September 1941, from the Billy Rose Collection.
5 Henry F. Pringle, "Rolling Up From Rio," Collier's, 12 August 1939, 23.
6 "Broadway Likes Miranda's Piquant Portuguese Songs," Life, 17 July 1939, 34.
7 Zeitlin, "Sous American Sizzler."
8 Miranda uses "paprika English," according to Louise Levitas in "Carmen Gets Unneeded Vocabulary," PM, 7 September 1941, 55.
9 Robert Sullivan, "Carmen Miranda Loves America and Vice Versa," Sun News, 23 November 1941, from the Billy Rose Collection.

10 "Carmen, Rio Style: This One Has a Last Name (It's Miranda) and She's the Good Neighbor Policy Itself," *Boston Evening Transcript*, 3 June 1939, from the Billy Rose Collection. Glyn was the popular Jazz Age novelist and screen writer who coined the term "it," which became Clara Bow's tag name.

11 Although many articles refer to this Miranda speech, this quote is from Pringle, "Rolling Up," 31.

12 George Jean Nathan, "The Streets of Toujours," *Newsweek*, 3 July 1939, 28.

13 See Alma Guillermoprieto, *Samba* (New York: Random House, 1990), 8–9, 52–53 and Martha Gil-Montero, *Brazilian Bombshell: The Biography of Carmen Miranda* (New York: Donald I. Fine, 1989), 24–26.

14 Guillermoprieto, *Samba*, 52.

15 Zeitlin, "Sous American Sizzler."

16 Gil-Montero, *Brazilian Bombshell*, 106–107.

17 "Rio Hails Carmen Miranda," *New York Times*, 11 July 1941, from the Billy Rose Collection.

18 "Hello Americans," tape recording available at the Museum of Television and Radio in New York.

19 "Miss Miranda and the Samba Here for Good," *New York Herald Tribune*, 9 March 1941, sec. 6, 4.

20 See Randal Johnson and Robert Stam, eds., *Brazilian Cinema* (New Jersey: Associated University Presses, 1982), 38–39.

21 Caetano Veloso, "Caricature and Conqueror, Pride and Shame," *New York Times*, 20 October 1991, sec. H, 34.

22 I saw this performance at the Brooklyn Academy of Music, 25 October 1991. Also see Julian Dibbell, "Notes on Carmen," *Village Voice*, 29 October 1991, 43, 45 [preview of the BAM *Carmen Miranda* performance].

23 Julia Kristeva's concept of the "semiotic" and chora, that which "does not yet refer . . . or no longer refers . . . to a signified object," that which is "anterior to naming," is helpful here, although her inability to imagine a disengagement from the symbolic without a simultaneous essentializing of the feminine is problematic. See Julia Kristeva, "From One Identity to Another," in *Desire in Language*, ed. Leon S. Roudiez, trans. Thomas Gora, Alice Jardine, and Leon S. Roudiez (New York, Columbia University Press, 1980), 133.

24 See Joan Riviere, "Womanliness as Masquerade," in (1929) *Formations of Fantasy*, ed. Victor Burgin, James Donald, and Cora Kaplan (New York: Routledge, 1989), 35–44. For the introduction of the concept into film studies, see Mary Anne Doane, "Film and the Masquerade: Theorizing the Female Spectator," *Screen* 23 nos. 3–4 (September/October 1982): 74–87; "Masquerade Reconsidered: Further Thoughts on the Female Spectator," *Discourse* 11, no. 1 (1988–89): 42–54; and Claire Johnston, "Femininity and the Masquerade: Anne of the Indies," in *Psychoanalysis and Cinema*, ed. E. Ann Kaplan (New York: Routledge, 1990), 64–72. See also Stephen Heath, "Joan Riviere and the Masquerade," in *Formations of Fantasy*, 45–61.

25 "At the Roxy," *New York Times*, 23 December 1943.

26 See Tony Thomas and Jim Terry, *The Busby Berkeley Book* (New York: New York Graphic Society, 1973), 152–54.

27 See, for instance, "Springtime in the Rockies," *Time*, 9 November 1942, 96; for photo, see Kenneth Anger, *Hollywood Babylon* II (New York: Dutton, 1984), 275.

28 Allan Bérube, *Coming Out under Fire: The History of Gay Men and Women in World War Two* (New York: Free Press, 1990; New York: Penguin, 1991), 89.

29 See, for instance, Sullivan, "Carmen Miranda Loves America"; Constance Palmer, "Not Half as Wild as You Think," *Silver Screen*, May 1947, 51; "Brazil's Carmen Miranda," 10.

30 "Miranda Will See Herself Burlesqued," *New York Herald Tribune*, 22 October 1939, from the Billy Rose Collection.

31 Candide, "Only Human," *Daily Mirror* (New York), 26 May 1939, from the Billy Rose Collection.

32 "Gestures Put It Over for Miranda," *New York World Telegram*, 8 July 1939, from the Billy Rose Collection.

33 Hyman Goldberg, "Miranda Clings to Souse American Accent—Brazilian Singer Fights Off Learning English," *New York Post*, 8 September 1941, from the Billy Rose Collection.

34 Pringle, "Rolling Up," 31.

35 "Gestures Put It Over for Miranda."

36 Sue Chambers, "No 'Men Only' for This Carmen," *The Milwaukee Journal-Screen and Radio*, 13 February 1944, from the Billy Rose Collection.

37 Gloria Mack, "Ladies Invited," *Photoplay*, January 1942, 84.

38 See, for instance, "Up From Rio" in "The Talk of the Town," *The New Yorker*, 28 October 1939, 15.

39 From the Billy Rose Collection.

40 See, for instance, correspondence from Stepin Fetchit to John Ford at the Lilly Library at the University of Indiana in Bloomington.

41 Press articles identified her as Carmen Miranda or, occasionally, as Maria da Cunha, as in "Springtime in the Rockies," *Time*, 9 November 1942, 96.

PART FOUR

RACIAL DISPLACEMENTS

Introduction

When, as invariably happens in Fox musicals, the Latina ethnicity of Carmen Miranda heightens the whiteness and Americanness of her blonde female costars, the visible contrast points out a cultural blindspot of the Hollywood musical overall, namely, the relative absence of non-white entertainers in proportion to their contributions to and influence on the entertainment industries, despite their marginalization by a segregated society. This absence structures how musicals represent the genealogy of American entertainment. Taken as a whole, the genre recounts a history of twentieth-century popular music—set in the eras of vaudeville, supper club and nightclub revues, the Ziegfeld Follies, Broadway, and the movies—which is noticeably white, even when the music refers to sources in ragtime, jazz, or the blues, or the tap dancing derives from leading African-American talents, such as Bill Robinson. Studios featured black entertainers in musicals at times but as specialty acts; brought in to perform a supplementary number, they were otherwise segregated from the rest of the film.

The career of Lena Horne at MGM is exemplary if also unique in comparison with other black performers. Put under contract with some fanfare as the first African-American to receive a full star build-up by the studio, Horne appeared as characters in two of the rare all-black musicals produced by the majors, *Cabin in the Sky* (1943) at MGM and *Stormy Weather* (1943) opposite Robinson at Fox. In addition, she played Julie in the condensed version of *Show Boat* that opens MGM's *Till the Clouds Roll By* (1946). In her other appearances in MGM fare throughout the 1940s, however, she appeared only to perform an inserted solo, usually as the entertainment watched by the fictional characters, played by white star leads, when they go to a nightclub or theater.

The essays in this section examine the whiteness of the Hollywood musical, exploring how the genre manifests the displacement of race in its representations of entertainment. In "Dancin' in the Rain," Carol J. Clover reappraises *Singin' in the Rain*, arguing that its thematic concern with giving credit where credit is due, which focuses on white women's singing voices, masks a much wider anxiety about the indebtedness of white male dancers, not to say the Hollywood musical at large, to a tradition of black men dancing, which the genre has effectively effaced from the screen. Looking closely at this film's text to find traces of the cultural history informing it, Clover attends to slippages and half-references which she reads as symptomatic glimpses of this unacknowledged tradition, notably in the famous title number.

Singin' in the Rain recounts the inaugural moment of the musical and the talkies alike, and Clover also pursues the significance of the visual image that crystallized this moment: Al Jolson singing in blackface in *The Jazz Singer*. Blackface, a staple of musicals throughout the 1930s and 1940s, originated in the nineteenth-century minstrel show, a revue format in which entertainers applied burnt cork to their faces and performed songs in a racially exaggerated style. For the twentieth-century film musical, the convention of white performers appearing in blackface in show numbers had a complex cultural significance. The racism of blackface caricatures of African-Americanness is undeniable; so is the backhanded recognition of black entertainers through citation of a tradition associated with them but which in fact marks their absence on screen. But the genre's deployment of blackface as the emblem of an entertainment past—nineteenth-century minstrelsy, valued as distinctly American, not European—further complicates the convention's racialized meanings.

Historically, what blackface represented in the twentieth century as a supposed tried-and-true show biz convention was different from what it represented in the nineteenth, when, as some scholars have claimed, it challenged white genteel entertainment and liberated performers from fixed, classed norms of masculinity and male sexuality. In his book *Blackface, White Noise*, Michael Rogin argues that in the early twentieth century blackface performance on stage allowed for the national incorporation of immigrant ethnic groups into the melting pot at the expense of racial minorities; this was especially the case for Jewish singers like Jolson, who assimilated through his stage stardom. "As disguise," Rogin comments about the relation of racism and Jewish assimilation in *The Jazz Singer*, "blackface capitalizes on identity as sameness; under burnt cork, the Jew could be a gentile. As expression, blackface creates individual identity as difference from one's origins" (Rogin 1996: 102). "New Deal Blackface," the excerpt from Rogin's book reprinted in this volume, examines blackface musicals from the 1930s and 1940s, analyzing the implications of this cultural trope of "American entertainment" as it marked a homogenized national identity without origins.

Blackface was by and large masculine in its performance and its connotations. In the section's final essay, "Beautiful White Bodies," Linda Mizejewski first looks at female blackface—more specifically, the "café au lait" lighter variant given respectability in the Ziegfeld revues and reproduced in a Busby Berkeley number from *Ziegfeld Girl* starring Judy Garland—pointing out that it destabilizes the essential whiteness of the showgirl featured in Berkeley musicals. The credo of the Ziegfeld Follies was "Glorifying the American Girl," and this motif supplied an implicit framework for viewing, as well as publicizing, what Berkeley did with the women in his production numbers, too. The blackface number as performed by Garland, Mizejewski argues, begins to expose how the "Glorified Girl," that culturally accepted ideal of desirable, heterosexual femininity, was premised on unacknowledged racial difference which, in turn, equated desire with whiteness in order to embody but also commodify female sexuality in the showgirl. Mizejewski then turns to *Gold Diggers of 1933* to demonstrate how this film's "slippages of difference," as she terms it, interrogate the constitution of "glorified" white femininity. In the critical attention it has received, *Gold Diggers* has exemplified for all four of these sections the rich complexity that follows from close scrutiny of the genre. Mizejewski's concluding reexamination of *Gold Diggers* therefore marks a fitting close to this volume, too.

Dancin' in the Rain

12

CAROL J. CLOVER

More than forty years after its release, *Singin' in the Rain* (1952) remains America's favorite object lesson on giving credit where credit is due. At stake is the talent of Kathy Selden (Debbie Reynolds), who, in the transition from silent movies to talkies, serves as a voice double for the famous Lina Lamont (Jean Hagen). Like John Gilbert, the silent actor on whom her character is based,[1] Lina has a voice that falls fatally short in the new technology of sound. Kathy is willing enough to "give" her voice when Cosmo Brown (Donald O'Connor) suggests it, but Don Lockwood (Gene Kelly) objects: "I couldn't let you do it, Kathy." "Why not?" she asks. "Because you wouldn't be *seen*. You'd be throwing away your own career." Kathy's selflessness prevails at first, but when Lina later learns that Kathy will be getting "full screen credit" for the talking and singing in the film-within-the-film ("You mean it's going to say up on the screen that I don't talk and sing for my*self*?"), she uses her financial importance to the studio to extort a promise that Kathy's voice will remain unacknowledged. If that were not enough, Lina tells R. F. Simpson, the producer, that she wants the arrangement extended indefinitely: "If [Kathy's] done such a grand job doubling for my voice, don't you think she oughtta go on doing *just that*? And nothing *else*." Simpson is appalled: "Lina, you're out of your mind. . . . Lina, I wouldn't do that to her in a million years. Why, you'd be taking her career away from her. People just don't *do* things like that!"

He *does* do it, of course. Money talks, in this film, and as the star property of Monumental Pictures Lina gets her way, at least in the short run. But the injustice will be dramatically redressed in the final scene, when the curtain behind the lip-synching Lina is jerked away and the true talent—Kathy at the microphone—is now, at last, *seen*. Lest the audience miss the point, Don calls it out: "Ladies and gentlemen . . . *that's* the girl whose voice you heard and loved tonight! She's the *real* star of the picture: Kathy Selden!" The film's final shot shows a billboard on which Don Lockwood's name and picture are paired not with Lina Lamont's, as before, but with Kathy Selden's. Not only has Kathy's talent been publicly credited, but Kathy herself has been lodged in the "firmament" that Lina cannot even pronounce.[2]

The concern with doubling precedes Kathy's appearance in the film, for, as the opening sequences tell us, Don Lockwood began his own film career as a stunt man. Indeed, in much the same way that the story of Kathy claims to present the originary moment of voice doubling, the story of young Don claims to present the originary moment of body doubling. The main actor in a western is knocked out in a saloon brawl, and Don proposes to the frantic filmmakers that he stand in. So his career goes for a while, hidden under a bushel basket, until he too gets his break and appears as his own body and under his own name. Once again, the wrong is righted and is thus not so much a wrong as a kind of benign apprenticeship in the show business life cycle, in which giving your talent away in the beginning is a kind of investment in the future. In the end, your talent will be joined to your person and you will be *seen*. Credit is given where it's due—just not right away.

The great irony here is that *Singin' in the Rain* itself enacts the kind of talent "relocations" it claims to deplore and correct. It is a well-known fact about the film that every song in it but two had a prior life in some other venue (the plot was famously invented to accommodate the pre-existing songs of Nacio Herb Brown and Arthur Freed) and that one of the two original works, "Make 'Em Laugh," was so shamelessly similar to Cole Porter's "Be a Clown!" from *The Pirate* that it amounted to "a stolen song," as Stanley Donen called it (quoted in *WE*, p. 359).[3] Certain elements of the plot itself, including the shift-to-sound framework, are suspiciously reminiscent of *You're My Everything*, a Dan Dailey vehicle from 1949. Credit became an issue in another way when, in a letter to the studio executive in charge of advertising, producer Freed objected to the absence of a credit to his contribution as lyricist and Brown's as composer. "I do not care how much you reduce my credit as the producer," he wrote, "but as an artist I rebel against not receiving proper credit as a lyricist. . . . I know . . . your new duties . . . have made you a little ruthless in giving anybody else credit."[4] Nor did the film feel constrained by its subject matter in the practice of dubbing. Kelly postdubbed the tap sounds for Debbie Reynolds's dance in the "Good Morning" number,[5] and, more to the point, in the scenes in which Kathy Selden is shown dubbing Lina's speaking lines, the real voice is that of the actress playing Lina, Jean Hagen, merely speaking in her normal tones.[6] What's more, of the songs in the movie-within-the movie (*The Dancing Cavalier*) that seem to its audience to be sung by Lina Lamont and that are presented to us, the audience of *Singin' in the Rain*, as sung by Kathy Selden/Debbie Reynolds, one, "Would You?" is in reality sung by a certain Betty Noyes or Royce (different sources give different names), a woman neither *seen* in *Singin' in the Rain* nor mentioned in the credits.[7] If Noyes/Royce eventually came into her own, it must have been in a small way; she does not figure in any of the standard Hollywood handbooks, and it seems a fair guess that she never made it to a billboard, either. On behalf of Betty Noyes/Royce, it seems, no Simpson moralized about giving credit where credit is due. Maybe the split between a movie's story and its production practices is so complete that it didn't occur to anyone that there was something funny about not crediting Noyes's/Royce's voice in a film that is precisely about the crediting of voices in film. Or maybe it did occur to someone but didn't seem funny or problematic enough to override whatever real-life protocol governs who gets and who doesn't get screen credits. In any case, Betty Noyes/Royce ended up without one, thus leaving her singing voice on permanent deposit in the account of Debbie Reynolds.

So wide is the gap between what *Singin' in the Rain* says and what it does that one is tempted to see a relation between the two—to see the moralizing surface story of *Singin'* as a guilty disavowal of the practices that went into its own making. Certainly the film itself invites a reflexive reading: the final movie in the sequence of movies it is about, the one the others lead up to and the one advertised on the climactic billboard, is *Singin' in the Rain*. Of course this narrow, in-house reading cannot explain the film's enormous popularity with four decades of viewers who know nothing of the backstage circumstances of its production. But if we proceed from the assumption that what may seem to be local anxieties are often universal ones in neighborhood drag, we might look again at the gap between *Singin' in the*

Rain's theory and its practice and ask what the larger resonances are. That is the point of departure of this essay, in which I argue that *Singin' in the Rain*'s morality tale of stolen talent restored is driven by a nervousness about just the opposite, about stolen talent *unrestored*, and that one reason for its abiding popularity is the way it redresses our underlying fear that the talent or art we most enjoy in movies like *Singin' in the Rain* is art we somehow "know" to be uncredited and unseen. The question is what talent and who it belongs to.

The obvious point to be made about *Singin' in the Rain* is that its soul lies not in stunt acts, or spoken voices, or songs, or even the singing claimed by the title, but in dancing. The showstopping musical numbers, the ones that stick with us, are those in which Kelly and O'Connor, singly or together, burst into tap-based dance—above all, Cosmo's solo "Make 'Em Laugh" (a gymnastic tour de force of pratfalls, one-legged hopping, body-spinning on the floor, running up walls and backflipping down, and so on), the Cosmo/Don duet "Moses" (which turns an elocution lesson into a "spontaneous, anarchic dance routine"),[8] and, of course, the "Singin' in the Rain" sequence itself, which is to the genre of the musical what the shower sequence of *Psycho* is to the genre of horror. Most of the other dance numbers in *Singin' in the Rain* are of the production-number sort: costumes, ballroom- and balletlike choreography and movement, linear narrative, and controlled affect—the "elegant style," as the commentaries call it.[9] The three Kelly/O'Connor dances, on the other hand, are muscular, apparently impromptu, unrestrained, exuberant, largely tap-based routines in which the interest lies to a considerable extent in the athletic feats of the (male) body: how fast the feet, sinuous the twists, high the jumps. Kelly had a political agenda here, one that he would spell out three years later in a television show he did for Alistair Cooke called *Dancing: A Man's Game*, in which he showed how the moves of male dance matched the moves of male sport (baseball, football, boxing, and basketball) in hope of dispelling the "stigma of effeminacy that has always clung to the art of the dance" (*GK*, p. 261).[10] ("For Kelly," Peter Wollen sums it up, "obsessed with the validity of male dance, the presence of the body was all-important, a male body that is acceptably exhibitionist in its athleticism.")[11] It is in any case Kelly who insisted on adding into the lyrics of the title song the word "dancin'." Where the Freed–Brown original has "I'm singin', just singin', in the rain,"[12] Kelly puts, "I'm singin', and dancin', in the rain," and, to the policeman, as an explanation for his behavior, "I'm dancin', and singin', in the rain." A small but telling adjustment, it acknowledges that the title does not do justice to which art is really at stake.[13]

Although there are no body doubles here (Kelly and O'Connor are after all really doing their own dancing),[14] I want to suggest that the film nonetheless worries rather openly about the "authorship" of certain of the moves they perform, that it is haunted by an anxiety of influence of a peculiarly American sort. Of course, to echo another formulation, popular culture *is* because it borrows; by definition it trades in a marketplace of endlessly circulating moves, riffs, bits of sound and image—a process that has always stood apart from high-culture notions of authorship and attribution and one that continues to confound copyright law.[15] "Shuck," dancer Eddie Rector said, "if you could copyright a step, nobody could lift a foot" (quoted in *JD*, p. 338). Still, even within the world and terms of popular culture's processes, there are rules of thumb, general understandings about when a move is sustained and close enough to a distinctive "original" to be attributable and, in such a case, what sort of attribution paid the debt. It is said that the "unwritten law" of the Hoofers Club was "Thou Shalt Not Copy Another's Steps—Exactly" (*JD*, p. 338). How exactly turned on the context: the same reflex might be regarded as an homage in a noncommercial performance, but as plunder in venues where there was money to be made. Marshall and Jean Stearns write that inside the Hoofers Club "you could imitate anybody inside the club, and it was taken as a compliment," but "you must not do so professionally, that is in public and for pay" (*JD*, p. 338).[16] It is worth remembering here that the English word *guilt* is related to the German *Geld* and originally denoted a concrete debt of money or property. Also worth keeping in mind is *Singin' in the Rain's* preoccupation with literal money: how much the studio stands to lose if the borrowing is revealed and the donor seen. For all his pieties about proper credit, Simpson never strays from the bottom line.

That *Singin' in the Rain* is not uninterested in progenitors is clear from the extended preface to the Broadway number, which takes us from the burlesque stage to vaudeville to the Ziegfeld Follies to the musical of the film's present, all clearly seen and clearly labelled under the urgent lyric "gotta dance." This spelling out of genealogical "credit" reminds us of the film's larger concern with individual credit, which in turn invites us to ponder the completeness of this particular evolutionary account. Which in *its* turn leads us to the thought that, although this may be a correct enumeration of the institutional categories that precede the cinematic dance musical, it is history with something missing. The omission is all the more striking in light of what some might consider outright "quotations" from the routines of, for example, Bojangles Robinson, John Bubbles, the Berry and Nicholas Brothers (especially backflips off the wall),[17] Peg Leg Bates (one-legged dancing), and other tap artists of the forties. Surely these performers were more immediate models for Kelly and O'Connor in *Singin'* than were athletes Bob Cousy, Johnny Unitas, Mickey Mantle, and Sugar Ray Robinson, whose moves Kelly claimed to be the essence of dance,[18] or for that matter than were Martha Graham and other modern dancers, whom Kelly cited as inspirational, but whose actual influence on his work was minimal.[19] But my point here is not to argue that *Singin' in the Rain* is built of thefts, much less to identify the sources or insist on "ownership." Nor is it to suggest that this musical is unusually derivative or derivative in unusual ways. It is to suggest that, for whatever reason, *Singin' in the Rain* is itself worried about something along these lines—if not about whether the screen credit "Musical Numbers Staged and Directed by Gene Kelly and Stanley Donen" really meets the terms of its own moralizing about giving credit where credit is due, then more generally about the possibility that too many of the unseen artists whose moves have been put to such brilliant and lucrative use in the "white dancer's field" of the film musical are black.[20]

The moment to be reckoned with in *Singin' in the Rain's* consciously unconscious relation to African-American dance comes midway in the film, when Don and Cosmo present to the producer their idea of remaking *The Duelling Cavalier*, which has flunked miserably as a simple sound film, as a musical. Studio director Simpson loves the idea, but then halts.

Simpson: The title. The title's not right. We need a *musical* title. Cosmo?
Cosmo [thinks for a moment, then comes up with an idea]: Hey! *The Duelling Mammy*!
[All three pause.]
Cosmo: No. [Pause.] I've got it! [Pause.] No. [Pause. Then, triumphantly]: *The Dancing Cavalier*!

Duelling cavalier—duelling mammy—dancing cavalier. "Dancing" is the word the sequence aims toward, the word that will solve the problem of the musical ("We need a *musical* title"), but it can only be suggested by and arrived at through a reference to "mammy"—a reference that in a split second puts African-Americans into the picture and acknowledges that the artistic bridge between a brittle eighteenth-century melodrama and a vibrant twentieth-century musical is a racial one. But blackness is no sooner admitted than it is denied, for the next full sentence erases the one before it. Not immediately, but after a teasing sequence of pauses and false starts that has the character of a set of inarticulate permutations—the in-betweens of morphing, as it were. We can only speculate on what thoughts are suppressed by the "no's" that lie between "duelling mammy" and "dancing cavalier," but insofar as they get us from female to male in a context of blackness and dance, one of them surely adumbrates a dancing black man, invisible in the given story, but a logical step in the sequence. In any event, the scene ends jubilantly, with Cosmo dancing the Charleston,[21] and that is the last we hear of the bridge term that got our movie men from a white loser to a white winner. The question is why it is there at all.

This is not the first occurrence of "the word Al Jolson had made famous" in *Singin' in the Rain*.[22] "Mammy" is also spoken, or rather sung, by Cosmo in a direct imitation of Jolson's voice in *The Jazz Singer*—an imitation that lasts no longer than the word itself, but one that captures Jolson's unmistakable voice catch. *Singin' in the Rain* is of course set in 1927, and in it *The Jazz Singer* is mentioned repeatedly as the competition, the new Hollywood benchmark, the watershed between past and future. Indeed, insofar as *Singin' in the Rain* claims to show the originary moment not just of the sound movie but of dubbing and the musical, it presents itself as *The Jazz Singer*'s imaginary contemporary. The films are ideologically connected, as well, both effecting the transition from a root-bound, European past (Jewish family and religious ritual in *The Jazz Singer*; eighteenth-century formulaic melodrama in *Singin' in the Rain*) to a free, American present defined by the music and dance of the jazz age—the "heart" story of the Hollywood musical (*HM*, p. 57). But where, however ambivalently, *The Jazz Singer* acknowledges the blackness of that enterprise and indeed shows us in detail the act of blackface that Jakie Rabinowitz must perform in order to belong to and profit from it, *Singin' in the Rain* skips the blacks and blackface part or reduces them to references so fleeting as to be almost invisible and almost inaudible.[23]

It is perhaps inevitable that in the single scene in which black people appear in *Singin' in the Rain* they are not black. I refer to the moment that Don, heading to the movie set of *The Duelling Cavalier*, crosses the set of another movie, some jungle picture with a bunch of cannibals in tribal regalia.[24] As he walks by, he greets a particularly garish fellow in body paint, mask, and headdress: "Hiya, Maxie." "Oh, hi, Don," the fellow responds and briefly joins him in conversation. The joke is that the savage is not a savage and probably not even black. But it goes further than that. What the cannibals are *doing* when we first see them is dancing—a wild, primitive dance. The point is that if one of them is a white guy named Maxie, so might they all be—a bunch of white guys in blacked faces and bodies performing allegedly African dance. ("More steam in the kettle! More action, boys! A little more rhythm, boys!" the scene director calls out.) Lest we miss the connection, Cosmo at this moment rushes up to Don and announces that he's just read in *Variety* of a new talking picture called *The Jazz Singer*, an all-time hit in the first week. ("All-time flop into the second," counters another cannibal, clearly visible as a white man in blackface.)

What is so striking about these moments is not just that they are the only bits of blackness in an otherwise white film and not even that the blackness in question is arrived at through an act of blackface.[25] It is that they are so uncalled for. *The Jazz Singer* references may be justifiable in a plot about the shift to sound, but Cosmo's imitation of Jolson's blackface "Mammy," the "Duelling Mammy" title, and the dancing cannibals are downright gratuitous.

So gratuitous that they want consideration as a system of symptoms, the kind of symptom that, in the postmodern critical scheme, is readable as a sign of repressed anxieties that underwrite the text but are denied by it. More particularly, I would suggest that these symptoms look for all the world like the complements of the paradoxical process Freud called *Verneinung*, negation, whereby the effort to "forget" necessarily calls up the very "memories" it means to put down.[26] The moments I have just enumerated in *Singin' in the Rain* seem to me just such "memories" in the framework of "forgetting." Glancingly but unmistakably, they suggest that *Singin' in the Rain*'s concern with miscredit has a racial underside—that its real subject is not white women's singing voices, but black men's dancing bodies.

It could be argued that black men's dancing bodies haunt even the film's title number.[27] The venue, at least, of the "Singin' in the Rain" sequence and the figure of the policeman conjure up the "school of the street" in which black tappers learned their trade in the shadow of the law. One tapper, LaVaughn Robinson, tells how dancers ranked corners and competed to get the best one and how, when a policeman was spotted, they quickly stopped and went back to their work shining shoes.[28] To judge from the number of film-musical street scenes that play out some version of the scenario, it was a well-known one among people who made (and danced in) movies in that era and presumably to some degree among audiences as well. One such movie sequence has a black tap dancer doing a street dance with a number of happy people looking on, a group that includes, in a spectacular example of pop-culture *Verneinung*, a couple of smiling, clapping white policemen (see *T*, p. 131). "Singin' in the Rain"'s policeman is also benign, but he at least has a monitory effect on the dancer he catches in the act, an effect that hints at some other story behind this one, some other dancer and some other policeman behind these. If we in the nineties do not know the racial resonances of the trope of the street-dance-interrupted-by-policeman, Kelly and his colleagues surely did. Perhaps he even got a kick out of responding to Jolson's performance in blackface with a performance of his own in black space. In any event, the setting of what has been called "the single most memorable dance number on film" is yet another racial gesture, one that puts Kelly where a black man used to be.

There is in itself nothing startling about *Singin' in the Rain*'s happy use of African-American dance styles (and setting, in the case of Kelly's solo dance). In this respect, the movie becomes part of the very history it gestures toward in the "hiya, Maxie" scene and *The Jazz Singer* references. These moments point to the immensely popular tradition, on stage and film, of the performance, by whites in blackface and often in venues that did not admit African-American performers, of music and dance deeply indebted to those performers. The film musical in particular drew heavily and variously on black art and talent. Only in the "Negro musical" was that talent front and center. The more common pattern was to put it off to the side (for example, the use of the Nicholas Brothers as Gene Kelly "flanks" in a number in *The Pirate*) or behind the scenes (for example, teachers like Herbie Harper and Buddy Bradley) or out of "creditable" range altogether (as in the case of those artists whose influence is palpable but altogether indirect).[29] The indirect influence of African-Americans was nowhere more obviously admitted than in blackface numbers like those of the Jolson films, and numbers like Fred Astaire's "Bojangles dance" in *Swing Time* (1936).[30] For a variety of reasons, the Negro musical faded, and in the forties, in the wake of "post-World War II embarrassment about racial subordination and stereotyping" as well as in the wake of a deal the Hollywood studios struck with the NAACP on hiring and representational practices, and with the beginnings of the movement for civil rights, blackface came to an end.[31] Traditional blackface, in any case.

Blackface "more broadly understood"—whites simply imitating blacks, without the cork—throve as vigorously as before, notably in the phenomenon of covering in the music business.[32] Although it could "no longer root itself in open blackface display," Michael Rogin writes, "the theft of black music and performance styles energized 1950s popular culture"—a theft helped along, one might add, by the very sound technologies that *Singin' in the Rain* claims to expose.[33] It could be argued that there was a perverse honesty to traditional blackface. In its own way, *The Jazz Singer*'s blackface act does point to where credit might be due. Not so *Singin' in the Rain*, whose art, dancing, is surely as "energized" by African-American forms as *The Jazz Singer*'s singing is.[34] But keeping with its investment in the form of blackface "more broadly understood" that will characterize the coming generation of popular culture, *Singin'* keeps its energy source firmly covered.

Kelly and O'Connor were hardly unaware of their own relation to African-American dance. Both acknowledged their indebtedness to black performers and their pride at being accepted and appreciated by them. As Fred Kelly tells it, a high point in the Kelly Brothers' early career was their acceptance into and success in an all-black show, a job for which they applied under false pretenses. When the time came to audition, "We just marched right backstage and asked for the manager. I remember this enormous black man came out, and that he was sporting a Derby hat. He looked down on us and asked, 'You're The Kelly Brothers?' " The manager called for Cab Calloway to break off rehearsal and come over: " 'Cab . . . meet The Kelly Brothers!' Cab walked in, took one look at us, looked at his manager, and in a real Amos and Andy put-on said, 'Somebody done make a *big* mistake!' " But of course all turns out well. "Gene and I danced the thing, and as soon as it was over, they all stood up and clapped and cheered. That was really something. The guys we were nuts about were applauding us!" (quoted in *T*, pp 177–78). Similarly, O'Connor:

> I knew Bill [Bojangles Robinson] very well. He was a wonderful guy and great to me as a kid. When I was fourteen, my family would work a lot at the Apollo Theater on One hundred twenty-fifth Street in New York. I met Bill up there a couple of times, and we'd go around to different night clubs. White guys, well, they weren't permitted in. With Bill I got in all the time. Everybody got to know me, and they nicknamed me King. They started calling, "Where's the King, where's the King." And after a while I was known as the "King of Harlem." [Quoted in *T*, p. 149][35]

One could hardly ask for a plainer expression of the speakers' desire to be as good as black: white men can *too* dance.[36] But what I want to draw attention to in these two accounts is the ironic fact that, whether true or imagined and however mixed with other feelings, they contemplate scenarios in which credit is given where it is due, even across nervous racial lines. At least as these white dancers tell it, blacks give their stages over to them, applaud them, call them "king."[37] It is a favor that *Singin' in the Rain* does not return.

But it is also a favor that it cannot forget. Fred Astaire once said of his style of dance, "I don't know how it all started, and I don't want to know. . . . I just dance."[38] It's a funny sentence, the second clause unbalancing the first, suggesting that he *does* know (certainly his Bojangles dance in *Swing Time* "knows") or knows more than he would like but doesn't want to deal with the implications of that knowledge and so willfully denies it: I don't want to know, I just do it. So *Singin' in the Rain*, which on one hand denies, by whiting out, knowledge of black dance, but which on the other hand, as if enacting the second clause of Astaire's sentence, undercuts that denial and in so doing obliquely admits not only that it *does* know but that it feels guilty about it. No matter how energetically *Singin'* directs our attention to singing and whites, it keeps sending sideways glances to dancing and blacks.[39] Take those sideways glances (*The Duelling Mammy*, Jolson citations, dancing savages, Kelly's insertion of the word "dancin'" in the title song, street-and-policeman dance setting), put them next to the film's story of money and credit, consider both of these in the context of the lead dancers' charged relation to the black performers in their past, and you arrive at the anxiety that I am arguing both underwrote the production and to some extent drove and may still drive the reception of the most famous musical of all time. What *Singin' in the Rain* doesn't-but-does know is that the real art of the film musical is dance, that a crucial talent source for that art is African-American performance, and that, relative to its contribution, this talent source is undercredited and underpaid. It is admitting, in effect, that although there may be no fixed line between homage and theft in the world of the film musical, there are roughly zones, and even white people know what they are.[40]

Recent studies have questioned the conventional view of the cultural appropriations of early nineteenth-century blackface minstrelsy (1843 to the 1860s) as vicious theft, pure and simple. Directing our attention to the "slips, silences, and (in)admissions" that attend the various texts around and about minstrelsy, Eric Lott proposes that the act of blackface was, in the white racial unconscious, a far more complicated affair than the standard account would have it, one haunted by desire (toward black men) and guilt.[41] Although there are traces of desire in the Kelly–O'Connor anecdotes of their early experience among African-American performers and arguably in Kelly's style of dance as well (or at least in his obsession with dance as masculine display, a "man's game"),[42] it is the guilt theme that bears most heavily on *Singin' in the Rain*. Lott notices in the early accounts of "meetings between racial representatives" (encounters in which whites expropriated the clothes, songs, dances, language, gestures of African-Americans) repeated references to ownership, payment, exchange value, cultural capital—to business transactions, in short. Insofar as they suggest that "all accounts have been paid in full," such references to transactions, however denigrating, and true or not, disclose "white guilt or anxiety around minstrelsy as a figure for the plundering of black culture," one stemming from the "slavery's unremunerated labor" ("LT," pp. 41, 42, 41).

Slavery may have been remote to audiences in 1952, but the plundering of black culture was not, and to judge from *Singin' in the Rain* neither were white guilt and anxiety on that score. This is not surprising, given the economics of the entertainment business. If ever there were an arena in which profit was to be had, this is it. ("The moment that interests me in these narratives," Lott writes of early minstrelsy, "is the one in which black sounds fill the air and fascinated white men understand for the first time that there are fame and money to be made" ["LT," p. 38].) What is more surprising is the way *Singin' in the Rain* announces the source of its concern. Its story could easily have been told without dancing savages and *The Duelling Mammy* (and the Charleston), and the appeals to *The Jazz Singer* as the first sound film could have pointed to dimensions of that work other than the blackface number. I said earlier that it is the very gratuitousness of these references that demands our attention. Actually, they are not *gratuitous* at all, at least not in the root sense of that word (*gratis*, free). Rather, they are moral payoffs in an economy in which "there are fame and money to be made." They are the "memories" that surface in the process of "forgetting," as though, in a perverse bargain, they must be admitted *in order* to be overridden.[43]

But *Singin' in the Rain* goes the process of negation one better, for it not only footnotes its plagiarism but hitches the whole to a morality tale exactly *about* plagiarism: "people just don't *do* things like that!" In the world of the film musical—and it is important to remember here that *Singin' in the Rain* means to be not just the originary moment of the movie musical, but its key text—it is not enough merely to mention and silence, remember and forget, the source. An entire plot must be mobilized to accomplish the forgetting of "the efficient expropriation of the cultural commodity 'blackness'" in an arena, the film musical, that was not only high stakes, but the essence of American cultural vitality for the better part of three decades ("LT," p. 24).[44] Poor Lina carries a heavy burden. She is the scapegoat not only for all the actors, male and female alike, whose voices flunked the shift to sound, but for all the white performers who danced the art of unseen others—which is to say for the film musical itself. No wonder her exposure must be so brutal and her humiliation so complete; she is the repository of a guilt so much greater than her own.

In 1985, an aging Gene Kelly narrated the MGM-produced anthology of film dance called *That's Dancing!* "In 1983," he declares near the end, "film dancing entered a new era. Music videos began to play on television and in motion picture theaters, offering audiences a stylized and exhilarating form of dancing on the screen. The most innovative and certainly the most successful exponent of this new medium is a young and gifted composer, singer, dancer, and choreographer who obviously will be leading the way for some time to come: Michael Jackson!" With those words, Kelly introduces the final dance sequence of the *That's Dancing!* compilation: Jackson's "Beat It." "And that's dancing!" Kelly intones at the close of Jackson's routine, and the credits for *That's Dancing!* roll.[45] One wonders whether Kelly would have been so generous to Jackson eight years later, after the appearance of "Black or White," an eleven-minute music video said to have premiered simultaneously in twenty-seven countries to an audience of some 500 million viewers.[46] Because its infamous ending bears on the subject of this paper, I include a discussion of it here by way of a coda.

In fact, in 1983 when "Beat It" was released, and even in 1985 when *That's Dancing!* was made, Michael Jackson was one of very few black stars to have appeared on MTV. For some years after the advent of the new era and the "new medium," MTV—yet another venue in which money was to be made—had notoriously higher thresholds for African-American performers, though it regularly featured white artists singing "black" songs (for example, Teena Marie or George Michael, whose album *Faith* was resented and even boycotted in some black circles on grounds that it was trying to "pass" on the R&B charts) and/or white artists (for example, Peter Gabriel and Madonna) who, like Gene Kelly in *The Pirate*, surrounded themselves with an "aura" of black musicians and dancers.[47] In short, the new disposition of race on MTV in the 1980s looked remarkably like the old disposition of race in the movie musical of the 1930s and 1940s, with the brilliant but also token Jackson holding down a position not unlike that once occupied by Bojangles Robinson.[48]

"Black or White" opens with a young white boy (Macaulay Culkin) playing heavy metal music too loudly in his bedroom. His father orders him to turn it down, and in revenge the boy turns up the amp and blasts his father through the roof into outer space. The father lands in Africa amidst dancing tribesmen, who morph into dancing Balinese women, who in turn morph into dancing Native Americans, and so on through a series of ethnic dance performances, with Michael Jackson always at the center singing the title song "Black or White." Meanwhile, back in America, the Macaulay Culkin figure is now hanging out on the street with a group of hip-hoppers and miming a rapper as he lip-synchs an adult male voice. We move to a recording studio and, still over the title song 'Black or White," witness another morphing sequence, this time of faces (black, white, Asian, blond, dark, male, female, and so on) blending into one another. The recording session ends and people drift away, leaving only a black panther that, once outdoors, morphs into Michael Jackson. Alone on a dark, abandoned street, he begins the dance that met with so much public consternation that it was cut from nearly all subsequent broadcasts of the video.[49]

At the point that we move to the street, day gives way to night, vivid color to something like dark blue and white, fast cutting to longer takes, international flitting about to a single, focused location, cheer to gritty intensity, racial harmony to black panther,[50] and, most strikingly, music to silence, or rather to silence punctuated by the natural sounds of Jackson's movements (tapping, panting, hitting things) and a reiterated scream. No singin' here, just dancin', with no music at all, for nearly five minutes.

And on a back street.[51] The identity of that street emerges gradually. Early details (wind, leaves, newspapers, cat) recall Jackson's earlier video "Billie Jean," but when the camera pans and brings into view the telltale lamppost, and when we then see, in closeup, Jackson's feet stamping in puddles on a street that at first seemed dry, we recognize the terrain of the Kelly classic.[52] The connection is sealed when Jackson interrupts his own dance routine to tilt his hat forward, hoofer-mode, and indulge a quick Kelly-style tap sequence. But no sooner are we situated in *Singin' in the Rain* than the mode changes. The dance turns increasingly sexual, as Jackson grabs his crotch and thrusts his pelvis, and increasingly violent as he takes his "umbrella," a crowbar, and starts smashing first car and then store windows. To be sure, the windows all bear hate graffiti ("Hitler lives," swastikas, "nigger go home," "no more wetbacks," "KKK rules"), and the video ends with the rubric "Prejudice is ignorance," but networks were less impressed by the pieties than by the sheer violence of it all. When it comes right down to it, no message in the world is good enough to sustain the image of a black man atop a car battering it to smithereens.[53] The video ends with a snippet from *The Simpsons*.

Just what Jackson meant by putting his dance in the "Singin' in the Rain" frame is not clear. What *is* clear is that it is racially loaded. This is, after all, the final sequence of a video that is titled "Black or White" and that features a white kid imitating black hip-hoppers (indeed, lip-synching a rap song, in Michael Jackson's shadow), a white man landing in Africa amidst dancing natives (in a scene remarkably like the dancing cannibals scene in *Singin' in the Rain*), two racial morphing sequences, black and white babies sitting on top of the world, lyrics that insist "I'm not going to spend my life being a color," a black panther (out of and into which Jackson morphs) on an inner-city street, a sequence of racial graffiti, a moral about prejudice, and a dance number by a black man—the greatest show dancer of our time—in something awfully close to whiteface. Actually, as the censors clearly saw, the video falls into two distinct parts: the cheerful singing part and the angry dancing part. If the first seems committed to the erasure of racial difference ("I'm not going to spend my life being a color"), the second reinstates it with a vengeance as the black man, under the sign not of the police but of a black panther, does what, in the American imaginary, black men do on dark and now policeless inner-city streets: practice violence as an art form.

If this is an homage to the man who inducted Jackson into Hollywood's hall of dance fame, it could hardly be more perverse. I would propose that its eruption has all the force of a return of the repressed, and insofar as it has unequivocally to do with race, I would venture further to say that, intentionally or not, it works to "un-cover" or "de-blackface" *Singin' in the Rain*. It obliges us to ask whether Kelly came by that street corner honorably and to consider what talent sources might have been behind *his* "curtain" and, by extension, behind the "curtain" of the white dance musical in general. Some forty years after Cosmo faltered at the gap between *The Duelling Cavalier* and *The Dancing Cavalier*, Michael Jackson vehemently dances forth its numbers.

Notes

I owe a debt of my own to Michael Rogin, Kathleen Moran, Richard Hutson, Joshua Clover, and James Williams for help and productive argument along the way.

1 So says Rudy Behlmer, *America's Favorite Movies: Behind the Scenes* (New York, 1982), p. 256. See also Hugh Fordin, *The World of Entertainment! Hollywood's Greatest Musicals* (New York, 1975), p. 352; hereafter abbreviated *WE*. By visiting all the misvoicings onto Lina, *Singin' in the Rain*, like Hollywood film in general, makes the woman carry a double burden of "lack"; so argues Kaja Silverman, *The Acoustic Mirror: The Female Voice in Psychoanalysis and Cinema* (Bloomington, Ind., 1988), esp. pp. 45–57.

2 To Simpson's "People just don't *do* things like that," Lina retorts, "People! I ain't people! I'm a [quoting from a newspaper] 'shimmering, glowing star in the cinema feerm-a-*ment*!'"

3 According to Clive Hirschhorn, the resemblance is coincidental. "No one has managed to discover why. Gene prefers not to think about the similarity, while Betty Comden and Adolph Green advanced the theory that Freed wrote it without realizing he'd once produced a picture with so similar a song in it" (Clive Hirschhorn, *Gene Kelly: A Biography* [Chicago, 1975], p. 213; hereafter abbreviated *GK*). Similarly Behlmer: "No one has ever discovered whether this was an amazing coincidence, a private joke between songwriters, or an innocent and amusing pastiche. Everyone in the unit preferred, apparently, not to bring up the subject to Freed" (Behlmer, *America's Favorite Movies*, p. 262). "Only a man of Cole Porter's tact and distinction would have chosen to ignore the existence of that song," Fordin noted (*WE*, p. 359). For a fuller discussion of the phenomenon of recycled or cannibalized songs, see Jane Feuer, *The Hollywood Musical* (Bloomington, Ind., 1982), pp. 96–106; hereafter abbreviated *HM*.

4 The letter in toto reads:

> Dear Ralph [Wheelwright]: Just received the copy of the advertising billing for *Singin' in the Rain*, and I notice that you omitted the most important credit of the last ten years in not giving credit to those famous writers and composers of screen musicals, Nacio Herb Brown and Arthur Freed.
>
> I do not care how much you reduce my credit as the producer, but as an artist I rebel against not receiving proper credit as a lyricist. I know you will plead you have been so tied up with *Quo Vadis* and learning how to spell Mervyn LeRoy, and your new duties on the Executive Board of this great studio have made you a little ruthless in giving anybody else credit.
>
> However, remember the old days when you were just a fella like one of us— plugging along, and try to incorporate this credit, which, after all, is the only thing that can sell the picture.
>
> Thank you. [Quoted in *WE*, pp. 361–62]

5 See Behlmer, *America's Favorite Movies*, p. 267.

6 See ibid., pp. 267–68. See also Silverman's discussion of the sexual politics of *Singin' in the Rain*'s sound relocations in *The Acoustic Mirror*, esp. pp. 45–57.

7 Behlmer has Noyes (see Behlmer, *America's Favorite Movies*, p. 267); Fordin has Royce (see *WE*, p. 358). Although the confusion may reflect a real name change on Betty's part, I suspect from the rhyme that it is the result of faulty transmission, in which case the issue of credit is even more poignant.

8 Feuer, "The Self-Reflective Musical and the Myth of Entertainment," *Quarterly Review of Film Studies* 2 (Aug. 1977): 315; rpt. in *Genre: The Musical*, ed. Rick Altman (London, 1981), pp. 313–26.

9 The exception is the Don/Cosmo/Kathy trio "Good Morning," which is also an impromptu, tap-based number, though a rather run-of-the-mill one.

10 "Dancing is a man's business, altogether," Kelly said in an interview, "but women have taken it over" (quoted in Marshall and Jean Stearns, *Jazz Dance: The Story of American Vernacular Dance* [New York, 1968], p. 196; hereafter abbreviated *JD*). Note the Stearns: "Perhaps it is enough to add that the question of whether or not dancers were sissies *never arose in the native American tradition of vernacular dance*" (*JD*, p. 355).

11 Peter Wollen, *Singin' in the Rain* (London, 1992), p. 57; hereafter abbreviated *SR*. Wollen also writes of Kelly's tendency to "carry" his ballet training in his upper body: "In dance terms he was, so to speak, determined to be upwardly mobile, adding a ballet carriage and arm movements above the waist to tapping feet below" (*SR*, p. 14).

12 Arthur Freed (lyrics) and Nacio Herb Brown (music) originally wrote the song for the *Hollywood Music Box of* 1927. It was included in MGM's films *Hollywood Revue of* 1929, *Hi Beautiful*, and *Little Nellie Kelly*. See *GK*, pp. 206–21.

13 As Kelly tells it:

> "Then a couple of days later I was running through the lyrics of the song to see if they suggested anything other than the obvious when, at the end of the first chorus, I suddenly added the word 'dancing' to the lyric—so that it now ran 'I'm singin' and *dancin'* in the rain'. Instead of just singing the number, I'd dance it as well. Suddenly the mist began to clear, because a dance tagged onto a song suggested a positive and joyous emotion." [*GK*, p. 215]

For a full account of the dance itself and a summary of what has been said about it, see *SR*, esp. pp. 9–29.

14 Dance can in fact be faked more than one might imagine. The tap sounds (which in the thirties and forties were in themselves sufficiently popular to be broadcast on radio) can be dubbed (as Debbie Reynolds's were by Gene Kelly and Ginger Rogers's were by Hermes Pan), and the visible dancing can be fixed by segmenting and editing, "so that the feet do not belong to the dancer or the movements are so abbreviated that the dance is effectively created in the montage." But by a variety of means, including "the use of long takes and wide frames," Kelly made it clear that visible dance—his "own province"—was unfaked (*SR*, p. 57).

15 "American show dance *is* because it borrows; American show dance *is* because it is vulgar. . . . Show dance is a convention of body movement drawn from a variety of sources and applied to commercial entertainments for the purpose of artistic communication,

unabashed diversion, or both" (Richard Kislan, Hoofing on Broadway: A History of Show Dancing [New York, 1987], pp. xv, xiv).

16 Further:

> If and when your act appeared on the stage of the Lincoln, or even better, the Lafayette Theater in Harlem, your routine must be notably different. Once word got around that an act was booked at these theaters, other dancers lined up, and as soon as the doors opened, rushed down to the front rows. "They watched you like hawks," says Baby [Laurence], "and if you used any of their pet steps, they just stood right up in the theater and told everybody about it at the top of their voices." [JD, p. 338]

17 The source of O'Connor's backflips in "Make 'Em Laugh." For a specific discussion of the Nicholas Brothers' influence on Gene Kelly, see Jerome Delamater. Dance in the Hollywood Musical (Ann Arbor, Mich., 1978), pp. 81–82.

18 The athletes listed by Kelly in his television program Dancing: A Man's Game.

19 See Delamater, Dance in the Hollywood Musical, p. 162.

20 Delamater, Dance in the Hollywood Musical, p. 79. See also Rusty Frank, Tap! The Greatest Tap Dance Stars and Their Stories, 1900–1955 (New York, 1990), hereafter abbreviated T; and JD; and also note 29 below.

21 On the racial politics of the Charleston, see JD, esp. pp. 110–14.

22 Michael Rogin, "Making America Home: Racial Masquerade and Ethnic Assimilation in the Transition to Talking Pictures," Journal of American History 79 (Dec. 1992): 1065.

23 For a full discussion (with extensive bibliography) of the racial and gender politics of The Jazz Singer, see especially Rogin, "Blackface, White Noise: The Jewish Jazz Singer Finds His Voice," Critical Inquiry 18 (Spring 1992): 417–53. Although Feuer's book is not concerned with race, it broaches the subject in its repeated suggestion that the "flow of energy from performer to audience" on which the musical rests stems from the "blackface 'mammy-song' tradition" (HM, p. 1).

24 Needless to say, the presence of cannibals is especially fitting in a film as dependent on artistic cannibalizing as this one is.

25 The film makes yet another joke on the subject when Kathy throws a cake at Don but misses, hitting Lina instead and leaving her with a white face.

26 See Sigmund Freud. "Negation" (1925), The Standard Edition of the Complete Psychological Works of Sigmund Freud, trans. and ed. James Strachey, 24 vols. (London. 1953–74), 19:235–36, and Jean Laplanche and J.-B. Pontalis, The Language of Psycho-Analysis, trans. Donald Nicholson-Smith (New York, 1973), pp. 261–63.

27 For an extended discussion of what Wollen calls the "single most memorable dance number on film," see SR, pp. 9–29.

28 As Frank sums it up, "Dancing on street corners was an integral part of many a dancer's schooling, and it was not, by any means, casual. There a dancer had to demonstrate bona fide skill to 'survive.' If a dancer could not 'cut it,' there was just no staying on that particular corner. Corners were ranked, and a dancer's goal was to move up to the top corner" (T, p. 128).

29 The history on this point is abundant but frustratingly scattered. The single best source is JD. Delamater's Dance in the Hollywood Musical, which is overwhelmingly about white dancers, deals with African-American contributions in a couple of pages (indexed as "Black

dancers, influence of"). In that short entry, designed simultaneously to acknowledge the black contribution and to justify his own lack of attention to it. Delamater notes the crucial importance to the film musical of eccentric dance ("eccentric" dancers being those who developed their own nonstandard movements and sold themselves on their individual styles) and goes on to say that

> eccentric dancers in general have often been black, but with the prevailing fear in Hollywood that black performers might hurt a film's chances of success, few got the opportunity to establish themselves. Those who did, however, left a strong mark, for their performances not only displayed their own individual talents but also represented the enormous influence—direct and indirect—which black dancers had on all other contemporary popular dancers. Blacks had invented tap dancing as we know it, and they had, in turn, taught it to whites who, in their turn, became famous exploiting what they had learned. . . . Although it is unfortunate that more of the great black dancers of the first half of the twentieth century did not appear in film, it is a fact that dance in film has been almost exclusively a white dancer's field. [Delamater, *Dance in the Hollywood Musical*, pp. 78–79]

30 The Bojangles dance begins with a large black shape dominating stage center, roughly in the form of a head, with large white lips and a hat, surrounded by chorus dancers. The lips and hat disappear and we realize we're looking at two huge, overlapped shoe soles. The chorus girls pry apart the soles, which turn out to be attached to enormous legs, at the distant crotch of which we see a tiny Fred Astaire in blackface. The enormous legs are then rather startlingly detached from Astaire's body and carried off by the chorus girls. Fred steps down on his own (tiny) legs and embarks on a Bojangles-style tap dance in front of large shadows. For the case for homage, see Arlene Croce, *The Fred Astaire and Ginger Rogers Book* (1972; New York, 1987), p. 107.

31 Rogin, "Blackface, White Noise," pp. 450–51. On the NAACP-Hollywood agreement of 1942, see Thomas Cripps, *Slow Fade to Black: The Negro in American Film 1900–1942* (1977; New York, 1993), esp. pp. 3–7 and 349–89.

32 See George Lipsitz, "Against the Wind: Dialogic Aspects of Rock and Roll," *Time Passages: Collective Memory and American Popular Culture* (Minneapolis, 1990), pp. 99–132. The last few years have seen the cultivation of what might be called open racial covering. The film *The Commitments*, for example, in which a character figures the Irish as the blacks of Europe, purports to be pure homage to 1960s soul music, but the film soundtrack advertised at the end is by the Commitments. The issue of real profits and white denial of same emerged sharply in the contrast between two appearances of Wilson Pickett, one within and the other without the film. Actually, Pickett never appears in *The Commitments*, but the rumor that he might turn up to jam with the Commitments after his own Dublin concert looms over the film's third act and is an idea with all the force of the Kelly–O'Connor anecdotes about black validation. In what is for all practical purposes the film's final scene, the band's manager, alone on the streets after a last disastrous performance, encounters a limousine driven by a black chauffeur who addresses his invisible passenger as Mr. Pickett. The status of the black performer as the structuring absence could hardly be clearer. In a PBS interview about two weeks after *The Commitments*'s American release, Pickett really did appear, and he made it abundantly clear that for him the film had nothing to do with

homage and everything to do with royalty rip-off. Cases like Pickett's "Midnight Hour" were the subject of "Rhythm, Royalties. and the Blues: The Dirty Little Secret of the Music Business," *Nightline*, ABC News, 6 Mar. 1995. Nor, according to a *Newsweek* article on the subject (Rick Marin and Allison Samuels, "A Risky Business," *Newsweek*, 18 July 1994, pp. 56–57), have rappers done much better for themselves.

33 Rogin, " 'Democracy and Burnt Cork': The End of Blackface, the Beginning of Civil Rights," *Representations*, no. 40 (Spring 1994): 10. The Rogin essays referred to in this essay are forthcoming in a book to be published this year. |EDITOR'S NOTE: This is a reference to Rogin 1996.|

34 Which is very little, thinks Rogin: "The most obvious fact about *The Jazz Singer*, unmentioned in all the critical commentary, is that it contains no jazz" (Rogin, "Blackface, White Noise." p. 447).

35 That the idea still has force is suggested by Joni Mitchell's recent confession, "You know, in my entire adult life, my favorite compliment—and I think a true compliment should be inspiring, not just flattering—was received from a blind black piano player. And what he said was, 'Joni, thank you for your music—it's genderless and raceless' " (quoted in *San Francisco Chronicle*, 6 Dec. 1994. p. E12).

36 Both subscribe, in effect, to Norman Podhoretz's 1963 declaration:

> Yet just as in childhood I envied Negroes for what seemed to me their superior masculinity, so I envy them today for what seems to me their superior physical grace and beauty. I have come to value physical grace very highly, and I am now capable of aching with all my being when I watch a Negro couple on the dance floor, or a Negro playing baseball or basketball. They are on the kind of terms with their own bodies that I should like to be on with mine, and for that precious quality they seem blessed to me. |Norman Podhoretz, "My Negro Problem—and Ours," *Commentary* 35 (Feb. 1963): 99|

See also bell hooks's discussion of the passage in her "Reconstructing Black Masculinity," *Black Looks: Race and Representation* (Boston, 1992), p. 96.

37 One could argue that the musical numbers that feature a white man between and above a black man or men (for example, Gene Kelly and the Nicholas Brothers in *The Pirate*, Dan Dailey and the Berry Brothers in *You're My Everything*) flesh out exactly this white (male) fantasy.

38 The remark appears on the last page of his autobiography, and it is his sole comment on "the history and the philosophy of 'the dance.' " He writes that he revolted against ballet but is vague on just what he revolted *into*. His book closes as follows: "When you come to the evolution of the dance, its history and philosophy, I know as much about that as I do about how a television tube produces a picture—which is absolutely nothing. I don't know how it all started and I don't want to know. I have no desire to prove anything by it. I have never used it as an outlet or as a means of expressing myself. I just dance." A variety of sources attest to Astaire's involvement with black tappers. See *T* and Cripps, *Slow Fade to Black*, esp. p. 99: "Fred Astaire proudly boasted of appearing on the same vaudeville card with Bill Robinson."

39 As Rogin, on reading this essay in manuscript, summed it up, "the movie makes all the references to *The Jazz Singer* as an anxiety-of-influence false trail; it pretends it's about

talking pictures and *not* blackface (surely Maxie as a blackface Jew is perfectly conscious)" (Rogin, conversation with author).

40 I would suggest that the impassioned quality of Croce's defence of the Bojangles dance indicates that she too knows; see note 30 above.

41 Eric Lott, "Love and Theft: The Racial Unconscious of Blackface Minstrelsy," *Representations*, no. 39 (Summer 1992): 37; hereafter abbreviated "LT." See also his *Love and Theft: Blackface Minstrelsy and the American Working Class* (New York, 1993).

42 Writes Lott: "The primary purpose of early blackface performance was to display the 'black' male body, to fetishize it in a spectacle that worked against the forward motion of the show and froze 'the flow of action in moments of erotic contemplation,' as Laura Mulvey has written of women in cinema" ("LT," p. 28).

43 This is by no means the only thing *Singin' in the Rain* denies. Its focus on the failure of the female voice denies its origin in male concerns; its presentation of itself as folk art denies its money-making raison d'etre; and its exposure of sound technology belies its own sound practices. On the first, see note 2. On the second and third, see Feuer, *The Hollywood Musical*. Feuer is particularly struck by the way *Singin'* negates (that is, remembers in order to forget) sound technology: "It's as if we've been given a complete confession in order to conceal the real crime," she writes (*HM*, p. 47).

44 According to Fordin (*WE*, p. 362), *Singin'* cost $2,540,800 to make and grossed $7,655,000 (on its first run).

45 *That's Dancing!* prod. David Niven. Jr. and Jack Haley. Jr., dir. Haley, 105 min., MGM/UA, 1985, videocassette.

46 See Michael Jackson, *Dangerous: The Short Films*, prod. Ute Leonhardt, dir. David Lynch et al., 112 min., MJJ Productions, 1993, videocassette. The broadcast premiere of "Black or White" was on Fox. For a somewhat different take, see Lott, "The Aesthetic Ante: Pleasure, Pop Culture, and the Middle Passage," *Callaloo* 17 (Summer 1994): 545–55.

47 Performers in the latter category, conspicuously British ones like Gabriel, often took the righteous position that they were at least offering black backup performers work, even work that located their talent in their own bodies; but the income and fame differential remains.

48 Robinson's racial position has long been a sore point. See, for example, *JD*, esp. p. 151; Lynne Fauley Emery, *Black Dance from 1619 to Today* (1972; Princeton. N.J., 1988), pp. 231–33 and n. 61; and Donald Bogle, *Toms, Coons, Mulattoes, Mammies, and Bucks: An interpretive History of Blacks in American Films* (New York, 1973).

49 Whether the whole event was staged as a publicity stunt remains an open question. Certainly the commercial video used the uproar for all it was worth.

50 Reported Mary Hart of *Entertainment Tonight:* "He was only trying to interpret the animalistic instincts of the panther into a dance" (in Jackson, *Dangerous*).

51 I can't help noting that, as if in mute deference to the centrality of the tradition, *That's Dancing!*'s compilation of show dance, ballet, and modern dance stars and numbers is bookended by street-dance scenes: kids break-dancing to a boom box at the beginning and, at the end, the inner-city dance-war "Beat It."

52 Kelly would have us believe that he was inspired by "children . . . splashing about in rain puddles" and that he "decided to become a kid again during the number" (quoted in *SR*, p. 17), but there is a touch of vehemence in his splashing, and it does escalate—to be interrupted and contained only by the sudden appearance of the law. On "Black or White"'s

street, no policeman enters. The law that we imagine kept even back alleys in order in 1952, and is said to have stopped street dance, is nowhere to be seen in 1991.

53 This is not the first rewriting of "Singin' in the Rain" as an exercise in violence. In a no-less-infamous scene from A *Clockwork Orange* (1971) Alex sings and dances the song as he uses his "umbrella," a club, to beat a woman to death and her husband within an inch of his life ("I'm singin'"—bash—"and dancin'"—bash—"in the rain"—bash bash). Whether Jackson's "Black or White" video was also gesturing toward the Kubrick film is not clear. What is clear is that both reflexes seem to "know" something about the "Singin' in the Rain" number that the film *Singin' in the Rain* and the voluminous commentary about it both deny.

New Deal Blackface

MICHAEL ROGIN

13

Nostalgic longing for an imaginary southern past served contemporary political integration in depression and wartime America. "Let me sing of Dixie's charms, of cotton fields and mammy's arms" is how "the uncrowned king of minstrelsy" opens and closes the Al Jolson/Irving Berlin musical, *Mammy* (1930). (The number would become *The Jolson Story's* theme song. Compare the *Mammy* production number with the celebrating blacks at the end of *Judge Priest*). At *Mammy's* end the Jolson character, wrongly accused of attempted murder (his rival loaded the gun for the blackface stage routine), rides the rails home to his mother. Enveloping her in hugs, kisses, and tears, Jolson sings, "Whatever comes my way, I'm everything to my mammy." As he sings about mammy in the minstrel parade that ends the film, the camera isolates on a black mammy in the crowd.

Minstrelsy also appropriated Abe Lincoln. When Bing Crosby and Marjorie Reynolds celebrate Lincoln's birthday in blackface, in *Holiday Inn's* march through the national holidays, they are backed by two segregated bands. One is in whiteface, one in blackface. Mamie (Louise Beavers) and her pickaninny children join in for the chorus: "Who was it set the darkies free? Abraham." (Beavers had to force feed herself and put on a southern accent for her mammy roles,[1] rendering Kafkaesque her reassurance to her prospective employer at the beginning of *Imitation of Life*, "I don't eat like I look.") Judy Garland calls Mickey Rooney her "Abe Lincoln" in *Babes on Broadway* because the production he is putting on to send settlement house children to camp will free her from "slavery" to her job. Mickey and Judy lead the extended minstrel number that saves the show, ends the film, and mobilizes minstrelsy for the war effort, "Black Up for That Blackout on Broadway." *The Jolson Story* ends with a medley of plantation songs: "Waiting for the *Robert E. Lee*," "Rock-a-Bye My Baby with a Dixie Melody," "Old Black Joe," "My Mammy." Jolson sings again, to initiate the music in the sequel, "If it's true what they say about Dixie, . . . if it's true that's where I belong."

To hide minstrelsy's roots in northern, proslavery idealizations of the South, which it was repeating, Paramount moved Dan Emmett from New York to New Orleans for *Dixie*. Blackface female impersonation and homoerotic physical play, cleansed of their ribaldry, are fun for the whole family. In the vision of interracial harmony to which these nostalgic films return, the Civil War, not race relations, is the source of division in American life. Blackface heals that division in allowing whites playfully to expropriate black. Southern domestic repose supports northern acquisitive self-making, the southern parvenu and redneck replace the black beast, and Warm Springs, Georgia (location of the "Little White House" and home of the "Southern Negro . . . [who lifted FDR] into his bed" each night) joins with Tammany Hall to perpetuate the Democratic Party politics out of which blackface had originally sprung, namely, Martin Van Buren's alliance between the planters of the South and the "plain republicans" of the North.[2]

The innocent national childhood in *Dixie* and *Swanee River* was also—as in the *Babes in Arms* minstrel number performed by the children of retired vaudevillians—the point of origin for Hollywood. The line from minstrelsy to motion pictures not only rooted the present in the past; it also made the entertainment business the vehicle for national integration. The New World religion of *The Jazz Singer*, blackface makes America "God's country" in *Babes in Arms*. As method and signifier of American patriotism, the minstrel number has pride of place in the military musical narrated by and starring Ronald Reagan, *This Is the Army*. Promoting army minstrel shows during the war, the USO called minstrelsy "the one form of American entertainment which is purely our own." When the *New Yorker* placed *Dixie* alongside the war movie *Pilot Number 5*, the "Democracy and Burnt Cork" title of the review implied blackface's contribution to the war effort.[3]

Blackface also served the war effort in Jolson's comeback to entertain the troops and help the Jews in *Jolson Sings Again*'s version of World War II. Thanks to *The Jolson Story* and *Jolson Sings Again*, when Jolson performed for Korean War soldiers he was once again a national icon. Lt. Gen. Walton Walker regretfully declined viewing the show, he wrote Jolson, because "I have a show of my own." If war was theater, theater was mobilized for war. Named 1949 Personality of the Year by the Washington, D.C., Variety Club, Jolson received the award from the under secretary of defense. He visited the White House, where President Truman remembered seeing him in minstrel shows in his youth. Author of Warren Harding's 1920 presidential campaign song, Jolson was moving along with other Jews from the pre-New Deal GOP to the cold war Democracy. The performer "died in action," as Columbia Pictures' Harry Cohn put it, suffering a heart attack after his trip to Korea. Eulogized by Eddie Cantor as "a casualty of war just as much as any soldier who died on the battlefield," he received, posthumously, the Pentagon Order of Merit. Obituaries marked Jolson's ascent from "part of a mob scene in a Yiddish play" (Israel Zangwill's *Children of the Ghetto*), through blackface, to inauguration by the mass audience as "king," "the greatest single entertainer of our time."[4]

In defining Americanness as entertainment, however, blackface musicals slid from content to form, presenting American identity in terms of performance and self-making. Calling attention to their nostalgia, blackface musicals are self-reflexive at their core. They make themselves as performances, and not the world they represent, the basis for American patriotism. The blackface performative proleptically subverts the wish for subversion in its postmodern copy by the power of the cross-dressing original. Synecdochic for Hollywood, blackface gives America its meaning—self-making through role-playing—in films like *Holiday Inn*, *Swanee River*, and *Dixie*.

There is a primal scene in every blackface musical: it shows the performer blacking up. [. . .] The scene lets viewers in on the secret of the fetish: I know I'm not, but all the same. . . . The fetish condenses the unanalyzed magical significance assigned to blacks, functioning like the substitute phallus in Freud's analysis and like the commodity in Marx's. Signifying transvestite masquerade and the expropriation of black labor, burnt cork fetishized not only blackness but sexual difference and the commodity form as well. But although blackface is detachable and reattachable—like Freud's fetish—making visible the pleasure of putting on and taking off burnt cork may seem to violate the Marxian/Freudian rule that demystifying the fetish interferes with its work. If the fetish is a story masquerading as an object, then bringing the story into consciousness should deprive the fetish of its magic. What remain hidden, however, are the historical crimes embedded in the fetish's invidious distinction; here white over black parallels man over woman (if we revise Freud to make the phallus itself a fetish) and capitalist over worker. In a culture that mythicizes self-making, moreover, the blackface fetish acquires power by being shown to be put on; blackface joins white power over black to personal mobility and self-expression. But what looks like uncovering origins, exposing how the magic works, is the deepest mystification of all, for it attributes the ability to change identity to individual construction of the self.[5]

"Fifteen nights a year Cinderella steps into a coach and becomes queen of Holiday Inn," says Marjorie Reynolds as she applies burnt cork to her face. The cinders transform her into royalty. Although blackface was often justified as disguise, as in the *Holiday Inn* scene, that was itself a ruse, for the audience was always in on the secret. Dirt was the magical, transforming substance in blackface carnivalesque (particularly transgressive for the blackface Jew, since the term ham actor originated from the use of ham fat to wipe off burnt cork). On the one hand, the filthy mask ("Dirty hands, dirty face," sings young Jakie Rabinowitz) brought the performer down to the earthy substrate, the ape he aped; but on the other, the masquerade identified him not with the mammy but with the trickster. Orality in its performed form was less the sucking mouth of nurture and more the signifying mouth of changing identity.* Black mimicry, black performance, the black mask, the technique by which the subjugated group kept its distance from and mocked its oppressor, was itself expropriated and made into a blackface performance for whites.[6]

The mammy singer asks for unconditional love by pretending to be what he is not. Like mammifying, signifying evokes childhood, the protean playfulness of unfixed racial and sexual identity. Having starred in four domestic melodramas of parent–child devotion (as son in *The Jazz Singer* and *Mammy*, as father in *The Singing Fool* and *Say It with Songs* [1929]), Jolson reverted to playing Gus, the vaudeville trickster of his wildly successful Broadway shows—one of which, *Big Boy* (1930), he brought to the screen. The double and successor to *Mammy*, *Big Boy* displays Jolson in blackface not just for musical numbers but for the entire film, not as a minstrel who longs for his mother but as a jockey in love with his horse.

Blackface comedy sanctioned sexual aggression; the minstrel mouth has teeth, and, as Bernard Wolfe put it, underneath the "magnanimous caress" was "the malevolent blow."[7] After blacked-out mayhem in *Big Boy*, for example (the restaurant lights go off), Gus emerges holding a brassiere. *Swingtime*'s adult, phallic version, "Bojangles of Harlem," opens on a large hat and head with white lips that turn into shoe soles. A blackface Fred Astaire appears at the crotch of the giant black legs formed when chorus girls pry apart the shoes. Separated from Astaire and taken off by the chorus girls, the legs dance behind him as if they were his shadows. Blackface dresses up the trickster Astaire, whom we have seen black up and who remains under burnt cork in the cardsharp scene that follows the dance. An homage to the African American tap dancer Bojangles Robinson, the number also quotes *The Jazz Singer*, for Astaire's blacking up seduces both women (here financial backer and ingenue rather than mother and girl friend) between whom he is torn.[8]

---

* "Al Jolson made a million bucks looking like that," Richard Pryor says to Gene Wilder, convincing him to put shoe polish on his face and act the trickster. Pryor and a blacked-up Wilder together elude the law in *Silver Streak* (1976).

Since mammy nurtured whites, maternal longing brought white and black into intimate bodily contact. Sexual conquest, by contrast, insisted on the racial boundary. Minstrel nurture, sex, and trickster aggression nonetheless had in common their self-proclaimed black roots, and the blackface musical used two methods to separate the blackface performer from African Americans and justify white theft. One, adumbrated in *The King of Jazz*'s opening cartoon, juxtaposed the creative white in blackface to the primitive black. The other, the comedy technique of *Whoopee!*, wiped off the burnt cork to celebrate the virtuoso underneath the mask. The former rooted performance in organic nationalism; the latter trod a line between self-aggrandizement and self-exposure.

Show business biopics invoke black music as the raw material for the American national sound. Brief scenes in *Swanee River*, and *The Jolson Story*, featuring work songs, spirituals, or jazz, establish African Americans as the source of the music made by white men. (Lou Silver, the orchestra leader in *The Jazz Singer*, was musical director for the Foster biopic.) Foster hears a black work song at the beginning of *Swanee River*; it inspires "Oh! Susanna." His girl friend can finish the tune properly because she was "brought up on Negro music." Foster envies her, though at least he "had a colored nurse." "They have something all their own. It's music from the heart, the beat of a simple people, . . . and by jingo, it's the only real American contribution to music." Repaying his debt to African Americans, Foster composes "Old Black Joe" for his wife's faithful slave. African Americans sing "Swing Low, Sweet Chariot" on a Mississippi riverboat near the beginning of *Dixie*; Dan Emmett (Bing Crosby) joins in, reducing the black singers to a supporting chorus. When Jolson comes upon a New Orleans jazz band in *The Jolson Story*—"They call it jazz. . . . There are no words, but you could make words for it"—he breaks with the old-timey music of Dockstadter's minstrel show. "Why can't I pick my own [songs]?" he pleads with Dockstadter. "Well, not exactly my own. I mean, it's stuff I picked up. They just need to be polished up by somebody good in New York."*

For some listeners the gap between the briefly heard Afro-American music and the eviscerated tunes that dominate the films would not only fail to establish a genealogy but would also endanger the intended aesthetic hierarchy. (The breakthrough Jolson popular song attributed to the influence of jazz is "My Mammy.") The movies themselves, unconscious of that self-subversion, reveal their theft anxiety by displacing robbery from the hero to a blackface trickster who robs him. Mr. Bones steals Emmett's money and then becomes his collaborator; E. P. Christy steals Foster's song and then becomes *his* collaborator. In *Rhapsody in Blue*, the tricksters are Oscar Levant, who does blackvoice, and Jolson, who sings "Swanee" in blackface. [. . .] Emmett and Foster, rather than black Americans, are the victims of theft, and these innocents, forgiving their confidence men, legitimate their own blackface robbery. Juxtaposing the authentic, supportive black to the blackface trickster, the films sanitize the trickery that the form, blacking up itself, proclaims.

With the appearance of African Americans onscreen in talking pictures, a blackface Jolson sometimes performed among them. Such juxtapositions, as in *Life*'s placement of Bing Crosby

---

* *Rhapsody in Blue* (1945) inverts the pattern, showing a sophisticated Hazel Scott in Paris performing Gershwin's "I Got Rhythm." *The Story of Vernon and Irene Castle* (1937) takes the opposite tack. Although the couple (Fred Astaire and Ginger Rogers) audition for their first show to the music of "Down by the Levee," the film entirely eliminates James Reese Europe, whose band backed the Castle dance craze and laid the foundation for New York jazz. Europe returns split in two, in white as the Castle factotum (Walter Brennan) and in black as the servant of Irene's snooty rival. (See Thomas R. Cripps, *Slow Fade to Black: The Negro in American Film*, 1900–1942 [New York, 1977], 252.)

alongside Bojangles Robinson, by demonstrating how well white played black, answered back to the advertised claim of Bert Williams and George Walker that blacks in blackface were the real thing. The climax of blackface as virtuoso performance, of course, came when the players removed their masks. Necessary also to establish the difference between black and white, wiping off the burnt cork entailed its own dangers, however. Gus turns to the audience at the end of *Big Boy*, surprising it with his uncovered white face. The self-revelation reassured southern audiences that no black man was engaging in verbal and physical abuse of whites.[9] But Jolson goes further. Reverting to minstrel reminiscence, he breaks character again to discredit his nostalgia. The old black Joe grandfather he's been invoking was named Moishe Pippick. As for the old Kentucky home, with mammy cooking ham on the stove—"That's not my house," says the Jewish comedian.

Jolson turned black disavowal into immigrant Jewish self-assertion in other movies as well. As part of an elaborate blackface *Wonder Bar* (1934) production number, "Going to Heaven on a Mule," Jolson reads a Yiddish newspaper in blackface. When his radio sponsor proposes another mammy number in *Say It with Songs*, the Jolson character rejects "I'll smother my mother with kisses when I get back to Tennessee" in favor of "I'll smother my father with bedushkas when I get back to Odessa." In the family reunion at that film's end, Jolson orders "ham and eggs. No, I was wrong. Just the eggs."

Jolson's most elaborate deconstruction of his mammy persona appeared before his film career began, in "Maaaaaam-my! Maaaaam-my! The Famous Mammy-Singer Explores His Native(?) Sunny Southland," published in the magazine for urban sophisticates, *Vanity Fair*. No one, according to the editor's note, was "more identified with the sunny Southland, . . . more irrevocably linked with cotton fields," than Jolson. The Jazz Age magazine was presenting the performer's account of his first trip south. According to Jolson, "Having spent the greater part of my life singing about my mammy in the sunny Sout', I had begun to believe that such a person really existed. The fact that I was born in St. Petersburg, Russia (not Florida!) had long since slipped my mind." But instead of "the Dixie of my dreams," the mammy singer found "thousands of tumble down shacks"; instead of the banjo-strumming "southern darkey, . . . famous wherever minstrel shows have played," he encountered a "northern negro" who told him he came to Florida in the winter because "the northern tourists is such easy pickings." "You are probably as eager as I am to get back to your mammy and the scenes of your childhood," insisted the blackface performer. "Boss," responded the allegedly real African American, "you can't be from down yonder or you wouldn't feel that-a-way." "Don't you miss the darkies humming . . . your mammy's chicken frying in the pan?" "Boss, . . . it wasn't until I came north that I knew a chicken had anything but a neck." The only "southern drawl" Jolson hears at Palm Beach is from south Delancey Street, and belongs to Marcus Loew; it is as if he is warning readers that Hollywood's Jewish moguls would soon be capitalizing on the blackface persona that another Jewish immigrant, Jolson, had invented. In claiming that theater owner Sam Shubert let him go south only after his loss of voice was diagnosed as a "suppressed desire" to see his mammy, Jolson was proleptically ridiculing the plots of two of his movies, *The Singing Fool* and *The Singing Kid*, in which the broken and restored parent–child bond explains the loss and recovery of his voice.[10]

The mammy role threatened to infantilize Jolson, and the spoof made it clear he was not the needy innocent he was portraying. Jolson's disavowal of the mammy singer was designed to remasculinize the performer. When he and his bride, Ruby Keeler, returned from their honeymoon and Jolson began filming *Mammy*, he was asked if his new wife was his mammy.

"Don't call her mammy. She is my mama," said the forty-two-year-old blackface star about the dancer less than half his age. "It's a dark outlook that faces me in my mirror."[11] Jolson wanted audiences to be aware that he knew exactly what he was doing. In its *Vanity Fair* version, reclaiming the immigrant Jewish American self as the maker of blackface also made room, unusually, for black signifying. Comic Jewish self-assertion was more likely to create Jewish/black solidarity when it was also a reminder that the immigrant Jew could never really wipe himself clean.

Self-assertive, ethnic self-mockery played well to Jolson's immigrant Jewish and cosmopolitan urban audiences. Robert Benchley and Gilbert Seldes, far from distinguishing Jolson's sentimentality from his irony, praised the performer's "supernatural," "demonic" presence. According to Seldes, Jolson was "so great that he cannot be put in any company." "John the Baptist was the last man to possess such a power," wrote Benchley. "It is as if an electric current had been run along under the seats."[12] The biblical John the Baptist began the conversion of the Jews; ethnic shtick showed Americanizing Jewish audiences that the mass entertainment idol was still one of them. But Jewish jokes reduced the popularity of the movies Jolson made after *The Singing Fool*. Instead of progressing forward to the deracinated American identity promised in *The Jazz Singer* and realized in "Sonny Boy," the later movies reverted to Jewish vaudeville. Eddie Cantor, who had also moved from vaudeville to Hollywood, became one of Universal's top moneymakers while Jolson released flop after flop. Cantor sustained his popularity in the 1930s by no longer playing the Jew.[13]

Jolson's Jewish self-exposure went too far not because of its method but because of its particularistic content. Audiences were turning away from the focus on ethnic conflict, not from masquerade itself. With the end of mass Jewish immigration, the dramatization of Jews becoming American was losing its appeal. In *Babes in Arms*, on the eve of World War II, blackface still Americanized ethnics; but generational conflict between Old World and New, like Americanizing campaigns against ethnic disloyalty, more and more belonged to the past. Blackface no longer negotiated immigrant rites of passage; that function of the form would move, as we shall see, to the racial-problem film.

Losing ground as ethnic self-assertion in depression and wartime Hollywood, blackface incorporated Jewish nostalgia after the war. The ethnic-family situation comedy was also featured on radio and early TV. The nostalgically remembered ethnic family not only tied the generations together; ethnic solidarity also dressed up class hierarchy and placed it in the past.[14]

The Jewish family carried a special significance. Although the extermination of the Jews made barely a dent in American political consciousness during the war, it became a subject of lament once the war was over. Not only decimated in Europe, Old World Jews were also disappearing from America. They returned to the screen not as the powerful, menacing patriarchs of the generational-conflict movies (even if sympathetic, even if ultimately defeated) but as subjects of affection. Jolson's and Gershwin's film parents are quaint old-people dolls, cute, caricatured, and deprived of authority. Instead of marking generational conflict, as in *The Jazz Singer*, blackface in *The Jolson Story* incorporates Jews of all generations. Jolson's obituaries, following the lead of the biopics, made "the mammy singer" good for all the Jews.[15]

The Jazz Singer joined romantic to generational conflict; the Jolson and Gershwin biopics displace the latter with the former. The jazz singer's postcard home, giving the immigrant son a new identity, announced his name change from Rabinowitz to Robin; the *Jolson Story* postcard, linked to the change in the boy's voice, announces his sexual coming of age. (Larry Parks, who plays the grown Jolson, enters the film immediately after the postcard.) The first postcard split the family; the second elicits parental pride in filial success. Jolson's parents initially resist his desire to sing in vaudeville, but they are won over so quickly that for most of The Jolson Story they are as caught up in his career as he is. "For me it's not necessary," says the father when Al remembers to put on a yarmulke at the homecoming meal—and with that the religious issue exits the movie. Far from opposing intermarriage, Jolson's father acts as his go-between in Jolson Sings Again. Blackface killed the jazz singer's father. In the Jolson biopics, it not only has parental support, but it also turns out to be good for Old World Jews. Jolson gives up show business for his wife, not his father, in The Jolson Story; in Jolson Sings Again, his father reminds him of Nazi atrocities to convince him to perform for American troops.

Enlisted in the service of the family, motion picture blackface was repeating the movement of nineteenth-century minstrelsy into the American home. Originally an all-male transvestite form, blackface had continued to play with gender in The Singing Fool and Whoopee! Burnt cork's homoerotic, ribald origins leave their traces in Dixie's minstrel routines, where blackface men, some in drag, roll around the stage together. Emmett's marriage proposals, to two different women, ignite fires (as suggested by camera cuts from the proposals to actual conflagrations). But Emmett marries the genteel, crippled woman, not the innkeeper's show business daughter, and his blackface rendition of "Dixie" at the end of the film calms the audience so that a third conflagration can be extinguished. This World War II movie washes out sexual and political conflict to make the Civil War serve domestic unity.

The minstrel motion pictures of the 1930s and 1940s, however, far from abandoning mutability and public performance for a naturalized private space, turned blackface into domestic artifice. Grounding romance on impersonation, these films bring performance into the most intimate, familial settings. [. . .]

Notes

1 Donald Bogle, Toms, Coons, Mulattoes, Mammies, and Bucks: An Interpretive History of Blacks in American Films, 2nd ed. (New York, 1989), 63.

2 Doris Kearns Goodwin, No Ordinary Time—Franklin and Eleanor Roosevelt: The Home Front in World War II (New York, 1994), 15 (on Warm Springs); Alexander Saxton, The Rise and Fall of the White Republic: Class, Politics and Mass Culture in Nineteenth-Century America (New York, 1990), 165–82 (on Democratic Party minstrelsy).

3 Joseph Boskin, Sambo: The Rise and Fall of an American Jester (New York, 1986), 88 (USO quotation); David Lardner, "Democracy and Burnt Cork," New Yorker, July 3, 1943, 38.

4 Variety, No. 19, 1949, Sept. 17, 1950; Motion Picture Herald, Sept. 29, 1949; Los Angeles Times, Oct. 24, 25, 28, 1950; Hollywood Citizen News, Oct. 24, 1950; Los Angeles Examiner, Oct. 25, 1950; all in Jolson file, MPAAS [Margaret Herrick Library, Motion Picture Academy of Arts and Sciences].

5 Karl Marx, Capital (New York, 1906), 1:82–83; Sigmund Freud, "Fetishism," in Collected Papers, ed. and trans. James Strachey, Joan Riviere, and Alix Strachey (London, 1959), 5:199; Marjorie Garber, Vested Interests: Cross-Dressing and Cultural Anxiety (New York, 1992), 121, 209, 249–50; Ellen Willis, A Primer for Daily Life (New York, 1991), 124–25.

6 "Film Actors Learn the Origins of 'Ham,'" *Columbia Pictures News*, undated [1946] clipping, in *Jolson Story* file, MPAAS; Henry Louis Gates Jr., *Figures in Black: Words, Signs, and the 'Racial' Self* (New York, 1987), 235–46; Ralph Ellison, "Change the Joke and Slip the Yoke," in his *Shadow and Act* (New York, 1964), 45–59.

7 Bernard Wolfe, "Uncle Remus and the Malevolent Rabbit," *Commentary* 8 (July 1949): 32.

8 Jim Collins, "Towards Defining a Matrix of the Musical Comedy: The Place of the Spectator Within the Textual Mechanisms," in *Genre: The Musical*, ed. Rick Altman (London, 1981), 137–43; Carol J. Clover, "Dancin' in the Rain," *Critical Inquiry*, 21 (summer 1995): 739, note 47.

9 Unidentified clipping, Sept. 17, 1930, in *Big Boy* file, MPAAS.

10 Al Jolson, "Maaaaam-my! Maaaaamy! The Famous Mammy-Singer Explores His Native(?) Sunny Southland," *Vanity Fair*, Apr. 1925, in Jolson file, MPAAS. Cf. The discussion in Michael North, *The Dialectic of Modernism: Race, Language, and Twentieth-Century Literature* (New York, 1994), 7.

11 *American Weekly*, Dec. 9, 25, 1928, in Jolson file, MPAAS.

12 Robert Benchley, *Vanity Fair*, in Jolson file, MPAAS; Gilbert Seldes, "The Daemonic in the American Theater," in *The Seven Lively Arts* (New York [1924] 1957), 166, 175–83.

13 See Henry Jenkins, *What Made Pistachio Nuts? Early Sound Comedy and the Vaudeville Aesthetic* (New York, 1992), 153–84.

14 George Lipsitz, *Time Passages: Collective Memory and American Popular Culture* (Minneapolis, 1990), 39–76.

15 David Wyman, *The Abandonment of the Jews: America and the Holocaust* (New York, 1984); Al Jolson, "The Best Role I Ever Had," *Coronet*, Aug. 31, 1946, and "AL JOLSON DIES," *Los Angeles Times*, Oct. 24, 1950, in Jolson file, MPAAS. Forty years after Jolson's death, one New York Jew remembered a friend mourning the entertainer because "he was a good Jew." The reminiscer had also loved *The Jolson Story* as a child, but he preferred to celebrate Jolson not for "sectarian" reasons but because "he sang 'Mammy' like nobody's business" (quoted in Sara Beshtel and Alan Graubard, *Saving Remnants: Feeling Jewish in America* [New York, 1992], 41).

Beautiful White Bodies 14

LINDA MIZEJEWSKI

The lavish Busby Berkeley numbers in *Ziegfeld Girl* insist on the spectatorial pleasures of showgirls, which the narrative scrambles to explain. Like the ornate costuming itself, the spectacles weigh down the film with their rich, troubling implications about gender, sexuality, fantasy, and riches. Furthering this argument about the Ziegfeld ideological legacy, I now turn to examples of Berkeley's earlier work, his staging and choreography in *Footlight Parade* and *Gold Diggers of 1933*, to track the social connotations of the visual production styles. My starting point is a singular visual effect that carries implications not immediately obvious: café au lait coloring and its evocation of the dusky belle.

The Ziegfeld Girl as dusky belle makes a subtle appearance in *Ziegfeld Girl*, when Judy Garland as Susan performs the specialty number "Minnie from Trinidad." This is one of the film's tributes to original *Follies* numbers, in this case the song "Miss Ginger of Jamaica," from the *Follies*' 1907 premier. While the original song had emphasized the singer's racial exoticism, "doing things up brown," as the lyrics proclaim, the song Garland delivers about islander Minnie is a bleached, Disney-style ballad that justifies onstage donkeys, straw hats, and palm trees, one of which sprouts from Garland's head. "Minnie," after all, is a comic number; at one point, Garland sings to the donkey, who also wears a funny straw hat.

Garland's makeup is a light café au lait, perhaps approximating the color of people in Ziegfeldian Trinidad, but it also approximates Garland's makeup in another 1941 performance, the minstrel number "Waiting for the Robert E. Lee" in *Babes on Broadway*, directed and choreographed by Busby Berkeley. In this number, Garland's feminine blackface is several shades lighter than the grotesque version worn by her partner, Mickey Rooney. On one level, Garland's two high-yellow performances reference each other as reminders of her theatrical virtuosity; blackface was a staple of the theatrical tradition that is the theme of both films. But on another level, considering the function of blackface as masquerade and as acknowledgment of racial difference, these performances also reinforce Garland's own ambiguous star status as "different," not glamorous, not quite in sync with Hollywood's categories of attractive heterosexuality.[1] Garland's on-screen blackface premier had actually occurred in the 1939 *Babes in Arms*' minstrel number (also directed and choreographed by Berkeley) in which she and Rooney both wear traditional dark blackface with exaggerated white mouths. As Minnie and as the minstrel miss on Rooney's arm, Garland represents her own paradoxical marginality as an MGM star, a factor that aligns her with [. . .] camp readings of Ziegfeld [. . .].

In short, the Minnie performance and the similar café au lait performance in *Babes on Broadway* that same year foreground Garland's status as not-exactly-Ziegfeld Girl, significantly registered here in both racial and sexual terms. The "not-exactly-Ziegfeld" status is the gap between the overt sexuality of the original "Ginger from Jamaica" and its comic version as "Minnie." As opposed to the sexy, bad-girl, dusky belle performances occasionally taken on by Ziegfeld Girls, Ziegfeld's women coon shouters were comics: Fanny Brice, Sophie Tucker, Nora Bayes. Their variety acts punctuated the grand Girl displays; they were the defining, contrasting "bodies between" the displays of Glorified Girls, like the dancer in the other costume color witnessed by Edmund Wilson. The effect of a suntanned Judy Garland in "Minnie" is similar; the real Ziegfeld Girls, the Lana Turner and Hedy Lamarr characters, float or pose in the same number, in no way connected with the comedy of the donkeys and the plump, decidedly nonromantic Don Pedro to whom Garland sings.

During the Ziegfeld era, the dusky belle of white revues was both a reference to and a displacement of her black counterpart in the *Darktown Follies* and in the black musicals. Similarly, Garland's blackface in MGM musicals exemplifies the loss and absence of black female talent on-screen in those musical films after *Hallelujah* (1929).[2] The elaborate *Babes on Broadway* minstrel number, with its surprising reversals of white costumes and black faces, suggests a photographic negative, but the reversals actually go the other way: white bodies have replaced the black ones from the lively tradition of black musicals that would not have much of a cinematic life. Berkeley's choreography was infused with black–white patterning as visual design that, in the minstrel numbers in *Babes in Arms* and *Babes on Broadway*, cleverly enacts the black–white tensions of musical theater.[3] These moments relentlessly delineate color lines by invoking and representing what has been banished, just as the black chorus girl was both forbidden but vividly pantomimed on the Ziegfeld stage to specify the whiteness of the Glorified Girl.

A similar dynamic of substitution and racial definition can be glimpsed in the uses of Berkeley's chorus girls in *Footlight Parade* (1933). This film contains no blackface, but in its most telling moment of dislocation and disavowal, it reimagines African American children as white showgirls. Preoccupied about ideas for his new production number, the harried director character played by James Cagney looks off-camera, in a well-lit medium shot on a busy street, at the sound of water and voices. "Look at that!" he exclaims with the excited earnestness that is the backstage musical's code for inspiration. "That's what that prologue needs! A mountain waterfall splashing on beautiful white bodies!"

The eyeline match shot, however, is not a waterfall and "beautiful white bodies" but rather a grainy, dimly lit long shot of a black neighborhood; African American children play around a gushing fire hydrant, while in the background, blurred sidewalk figures of a black crowd look on. In the plotline. the ensuing stage production inspired by this scene is one of Busby Berkeley's most baroque numbers, "By a Waterfall," in which hundreds of Anglo female bodies swim, twirl, glide, and cavort supposedly as part of an elaborate theatrical prologue, though filmed and edited as a physically impossible fantasy.

The other physically impossible fantasy, an African American scene transformed into an upscale white production, involves a more basic but ideologically powerful visual trick. The Cagney character, Chester Kent, literally cannot see blackness except as a way of seeing whiteness.[4] The edited sequence offers the same "white" reading to the viewer: a medium shot of Cagney exclaiming about "beautiful white bodies" is followed by the eyeline match of what he sees, the grainy shot of the black children in the black neighborhood. The darkness and distance of the countershot ensure that the black faces are not clearly visible. Berkeley's "By a Waterfall" acts out the preferred, white, upscale alternative to darker bodies in another, less valuable scene.

In the following shot, Cagney excitedly asks an attending policeman, "Do you get it?" The policeman. caught up in the enthusiasm of Cagney's inspiration, suddenly becomes a show business entrepreneur himself. "I have ideas too, Mr. Kent!" he exclaims as he jumps into Cagney's car, which takes them both to the theater. The double prompting of the producer and the street cop implies an interplay of pleasure and policing—entertainment and constraint—that is rarely suggested so blatantly in Hollywood cinema. Racial visibility in 1930s cinema had been addressed by a ban on the representation of miscegenation in the Production Code, the film industry's self-censorship apparatus, which was adopted in 1930 and enforced rigorously after 1933. But interracial relationships in Hollywood studio films were also thoroughly prohibited on the level of narrative spectatorship and performance. A light-skinned black performer such as Nina Mae McKinney could perform within an all-black cast of Hallelujah, but a cinematic taboo hovered around the scenario of a sexually provocative black performance for a white audience—the dynamics of Harlem nightclubs or previous black musicals—if this spectator relationship alone suggested miscegenation.[5] Generally, this cinematic coding and taboo keep invisible the racial dimensions of sexual desire. The cop in Footlight Parade, as a representative of legal power and its supposedly comic complicity in this scene—"I have ideas too"—is particularly ominous in light of the fact that the resulting "By a Waterfall" sequence was, Mast tells us, "a great favorite of Adolf Hitler."[6]

The Cagney character, Chester Kent, was probably based on Chester Hale, musical prologue producer of New York's Capitol Theater (c. 1925–38), who, along with Ziegfeld, utilized the choreography of Ned Wayburn. Prologue choreographers were expected to create new shows weekly, which often toured large theaters that could accommodate fairly extravagant productions.[7] Kent, who is characterized as a quick-minded, endlessly energetic perfectionist in charge of hundreds of showgirls, also more than slightly resembles the public persona of Ziegfeld himself, the "manager of unfailing resource . . . a trim, athletic, fastidiously groomed young man" who "keeps his alertly inventive mind working like a machine gun." Ziegfeld had died just two years before this film was made, and Footlight Parade can easily be read as one of his posthumous Hollywood beatifications.

Like Ziegfeld watching his best stars go to Hollywood, Chester early in this film watches dejectedly as crowds throng the new talking-picture theater, abandoning the musical theater of Broadway. Chester resolves this problem through two highly inventive inspirations during the course of the plotline. The black street scene gives him the idea for a stunning novelty number. Earlier, he is inspired when he buys cheap, mass-produced aspirin and suddenly realizes that he can mass-produce musical prologues. The first inspiration takes place in a drugstore, the second on a city street, locations clearly outside the theaters where Chester works. But Chester repeatedly shows that for him there is no outside to this theater, as evidenced in his "seeing" the street scene as a musical revue. As theorists of the musical genre have pointed out, this approach to "the world as entertainment" is a common cue for a character's heroism or likability; in the backstage musical in particular, it reinforces the sense of the show business world as microcosm or more intense version of the world outside the theater.[8]

In Footlight Parade this theatrical "world" represents not just entertainment but a classed and racialized economy as well. As more recent film history has emphasized, the sumptuous movie palaces of the type portrayed in *Footlight Parade*—theaters large enough to stage musical productions—were showcases themselves, offering class-specific ideas about fashion, leisure, and decor: chandeliers, thick carpeting, velvet drapes. So the theater itself demarcated no clear boundary between the opulence of the stage productions and the opulence of the architecture or between desirable accoutrements inside the theater and those outside. In *Footlight Parade*, there is not even a clear demarcation between the glamour of the diegetic theater audience and the glamour onstage. The men in these audiences wear tuxedos, and the women wear fashionable gowns that match, in upscale fashion, the costuming they are seeing in the stage productions. This mirroring effect represses the status of the "work" onstage by suggesting a continuum of a privileged world of leisure and visual pleasure. The audience that has purchased this view and this fantasy sees itself idealized in a display in which working-class young women masquerade as elegantly attired showgirls. When the three grand revue numbers, including "By a Waterfall," erupt out of any logical narrative space, the dissolution of boundary is complete.[9]

This presents a dilemma, for commodity value cannot be established without hierarchical differences. In the "By a Waterfall" number, the effect of the identical white bodies performing for the identically white audience requires another location, an "outside," a site of lesser value. The space of the movie palace can be valuable only if some other site is not. The glimpse of the black neighborhood underscores what might otherwise be taken for granted: that the glamour of the movie palace depends on its racial whiteness. As Richard Dyer argues in a 1988 essay, whiteness as a "norm" needs to be constructed, paradoxically because whiteness is "everything and nothing," which is precisely "the source of its representational power." An effective strategy of construction, Dyer suggests, is "reference to that which is not white, as if only non-whiteness can give whiteness any substance."[10] The reference to the black children in the "Waterfall" performance operates as such a construction, handily doubling the sexual value of the showgirls as a conflated economic and racial desirability.

Racial difference signifies sexual desirability here, but desirability cannot even be divisible into racial, sexual, and economic registers in this film. The "beautiful white bodies" are powerful because they are not reducible to any one of these registers without the implication of the others. Within a narrative saturated with anxieties about business, money, and profits, certain showgirl bodies have economic value only within a particular theater, which in turn must occupy a hierarchical space. The shot of the black children in the street provides a glimpse of another theater, so to speak, a black neighborhood in which children play and curious spectators line the sidewalk. A number of devaluations occur with this shot. Most obvious, as a "depression musical," *Footlight Parade* relegates poverty—which affected blacks and whites alike—to blackness, literalized as the impoverished production values in this dim, fuzzy shot of the black neighborhood. When this scene is transformed, whitened, and reenacted as the "Waterfall" number within the movie palace, the desirability of the showgirls has been located within many other social desires. Within the movie palace, displays of the jewelry, satins, tuxedos, chandeliers, velvet curtains, and showgirls—that is, the visual displays on both sides of the stage—have value and meaning because of what has been glimpsed and excluded.

The anxious contention about entertainment value—a "real" Broadway as opposed to a black entertainment scene—has very discernible sources in New York City nightlife during this era, [. . .] When *Footlight Parade* was made in the early 1930s, the clubs of Harlem were still providing a thriving black musical scene that for white audiences was thrilling and transgressive. From 1925 to 1935, white customers flocked to these clubs looking for enact-ments of white fantasies about black sensuality and "primitive" black sexiness, especially as embodied in lighter-skinned black women. These Harlem performers, like the chorus girls in the African American revues, provided a racial/sexual alternative to the middle-class "niceness" of the Ziegfeld Girl. The denial made by Chester Kent on the street, seeing beautiful white bodies instead of black children, is very much a denial of the threatening uptown scene with its alluring black showgirls. The Ziegfeld history provides one of the frameworks by which this racial construction would have made cultural sense as a 1930s text: the Glorified American Girl performs at the New Amsterdam or Ziegfeld Theater, while darker women "glorifying the Creole beauty" dance in a less expensive musical on another street.

My argument here has been that Berkeley's women as mass-produced images materialize and complete the production of women as glorified and trademarked, "an actual process invented by Zieggy." One of my larger arguments in this book is that the Ziegfeld Girl's two most obvious trademark features, her whiteness and her heterosexuality, were contended sites of definition during the Ziegfeld era. Whereas *Footlight Parade* suggests the racial significance of the showgirl body, Mervyn LeRoy's *Gold Diggers of 1933*, also choreographed by Berkeley, foregrounds the importance and slippery marketability of her heterosexuality. Like the black street scene glimpsed in *Footlight Parade*, the two "other scenes" glimpsed and recuperated in *Gold Diggers* are prostitution and, less obviously, lesbianism. Prostitution is hardly a subtle subtext in a film about gold digging, but the film's cynicism about this issue—Ginger Rogers and the chorus girls wear giant gold coins in the opening production number—implies that for women, desire is no prerequisite for sexual relationships with men.

The relatively long cultural life of Avery Hopwood's 1919 play *Gold Diggers* attests to the popularity of this snappy, comic chorus girl story. *Gold Diggers* ran for two years on Broadway with former Ziegfeld Girl Ina Claire as its star and then went on tour. Warner Brothers produced a silent film version in 1923 and a musical version, *Gold Diggers of Broadway*, in 1929. The latter was so successful that the Warners remade the film in 1933, 1935, and 1936; the story resurfaced once more on Broadway Television Theater in 1952. In every version, a romantic plotline of mistaken identities and backstage shenanigans eventually matches chorus girls to wealthy men, a narrative no doubt made credible by real-life chorines who had made careers out of such associations—including Ziegfeld Girls Marion Davies and Peggy Hopkins Joyce.[11]

The 1933 film version of *Gold Diggers* foregrounds issues of money and employment by specifically citing the depression and its impact on theater, in the narrative itself and in its best-known production numbers, "In the Money" and "Remember My Forgotten Man," the latter a tribute to unemployed World War I veterans. The presence of a sympathetic prostitute in "Forgotten Man" is a clue about the film's theme, for the narrative and staging of *Gold Diggers of 1933* suggest straightforwardly that the only reliable work for women is sex—illegally, as prostitution, or legally, as marriage. Gold digging, conveniently enough, refers to both.

Berkeley's chorus girl numbers in this film amplify previous, accumulated meanings of the chorus girl's body as a product suitable for show. Campy and outright kinky at times, the chorines appear as sparkling currency or "canned goods" to be pried open for pleasure ("Pettin' in the Park"). Not surprisingly, the chorus girl body as prized commodity is given distinctively Ziegfeldian connotations through the costumes, sets, and choreography. The elaborate stagings involve staircases, creative lighting effects, and platforms; the costuming and choreography are matched to the elaborate sets, so that the floral pattern in the staging of "The Shadow Waltz" rhymes with petal-shaped skirts.[12] The Ziegfeldian lavishness is a strong marker of predepression plenitude, reinforcing what film historians call the utopian dimension of the musical. *Gold Diggers of 1933*, however, harshly contrasts these utopian theatrical numbers with the grim economic realities of theatrical workers, the chorines who do not get paid when the show closes down.

As most of the film's critics point out, women's work and the necessity of working for a living are foregrounded in this film. The chorus girls are represented as independent, often sassy, resourceful modern women. Yet the film is unable to represent any woman's paid work except on-stage. One hard-up chorus girl claims to be working in a drugstore, but she is never seen there, so the only work visualized for women is the chorus line. The most forward gold digger of them all, played by Ginger Rogers, is explicitly marked as sexually active; one of her colleagues cracks that the male show producer would not know her "with clothes on." The film goes to great pains to expose the contradictions in the women's economic predicaments and in men's foolishness in falling for superficial female images. The priggish, wealthy characters J. Lawrence and Peabody dismiss the vulgarity of theater women but are also drawn to them—and in the spirit of good, satirical romantic comedy, they eventually marry them, though this will also transform the chorines into respectable society wives. The dynamic is familiar from Ziegfeld advertising and hype: upscale setting and costume creates, for women, a direct visual relationship with an upper class and enables her class mobility. The access is possible because she has been choreographed into behavior that fits the visual package: the beaded evening gown and the elbow-length gloves are the wearing of a discipline. At their most Ziegfeldian, the chorus girls in this film form a giant neon violin, a reference to classical music and its milieu, to which they have access literally through their bodies as plastic, malleable elements in a larger design.

Gold Diggers of 1933 has attracted a great deal of critical attention, especially by feminist film theorists, because its excessive spectacles, outrageous production numbers, and female ensemble cast offer rich, multiple, often contradictory readings. The startling first musical number alone, in which commodified chorus girls are literalized as currency, doppled with gold coins from hair to crotch, has been described as camp comedy, depression-era cynicism, unabashed voyeurism, Foucauldian power paradigms, sexual and commodity fetishism, and spoofs of anti-prostitution reform discourse.[13] That is, the woman-as-currency visual metaphor immediately brings to bear both historical and psychoanalytic frameworks, as well as readings that tend to veer in extreme directions, from misogyny to feminist camp.

The Ziegfeld history, as an additional context for this film, sheds light on the ambiguities of the showgirl figure herself, given the Ziegfeldian agenda to elevate the chorus girl to a "pricey item" and downplay her connotations as prostitute and contemptible property—all of which are registered in the course of the 1933 *Gold Diggers*. Yet *Gold Diggers* also reveals how heterosexuality—the linchpin of the entire chorine economy—can be comprised of purchasing power and "work" rather than desire. The upscale showgirl, Berkeley's version of the Ziegfeld Girl as gold coin or violin in this film, is commodified and publicized as heterosexual because the economy supports it, not because there is an innate physical or psychological inclination, or even a pleasure, involved from her perspective. Pamela Robertson's reading of this film, emphasizing its appeal to female spectators, argues its stark social message about women's lack of choices in a depressed economy and in a visual/mass-media economy as well, so that prostitution or self-commodification becomes a necessity for survival.[14] I would add that heterosexuality itself is necessary for survival in *Gold Diggers*—or at least the appearance and maintenance of heterosexuality, which is the more important question pushed by the excessive Ziegfeldian performances of the "model" woman/commodity/mannequin/showcase Girl. This is the case because desire, even more than whiteness, is impossible to "see" and thus must be explicitly choreographed. Its choreography becomes more apparent, however, with slippages of difference, just as the whiteness of the Ziegfeld Girl is made more apparent by the inclusion of Minnie from Trinidad, Ginger of Jamaica, and café au lait.

By questioning the status and locations of female desire, prostitutes and lesbians have always been culturally linked as figures threatening the organization of heterosexuality. The chorus girl is part of this grouping because as a working girl she disengages or denaturalizes female dependence on men, reframing that dependence as a business exchange. *Gold Diggers of 1933* exemplifies these issues of female public visibility and self-commodification that had always hovered around the chorus girl figure. Frothy media representations of the chorus girl marked an underlying excitement and trepidation about a more serious, if displaced image: a line of women on the job, women who work in the public sphere. [. . .] The chorus girl as a figure of modernity was split between cutting-edge and retrograde discourses: on one hand, the new female independence in mixed-sex working and leisure worlds and, on the other hand, the connotations of the oldest profession in the world, a continuation of traditional negative connotations about actresses.[15] Just as more women entered and stayed in the workforce, slowly moving into professional fields, the chorus girl role suggested that women's continuing work is sex, an extension of the private realm, thus also reinforcing the notion that women's "real" work is making themselves presentable for show.

In *Gold Diggers of 1933*, the comic character Trixie (Aline MacMahon) provides a slippage of difference, unsettling some of the cultural assumptions about this sexual work. Trixie, the oldest and toughest of the three chorine heroines, is never neatly aligned into a coherent sex-gender visual sign and is the character who most blatantly discusses heterosexuality as a business. Within the codes of the film, the actress Aline MacMahon is the least conventionally attractive of the costars, her long features and large body a clear contrast to the standardized cuteness and smallness of Ruby Keeler, Joan Blondell, and Ginger Rogers. For Trixie, marriage is an alternative occupation not necessarily connected to love or romance: "When show business was slow, I used to live on my alimony. Now I can't collect a cent of it. Married three of them against a rainy day. Now it's pouring and they haven't an umbrella between them!"[16] Hard times and Trixie's scheming lead to yet a fourth marriage, to the elderly Peabody, another exchange of sex for financial security, with minimal sentimental touches.

The ambiguity of Trixie, the not-quite-glamorous version of the chorus girl, is also apparent in Hank in *Broadway Melody* and Susan in *Ziegfeld Girl*, recurring characters who resist the "safer" meanings of the chorus girl as pleasure for men/exhibitionist desire of women. As opposed to the romantic comedy enacted by the other chorus girls in this film, Trixie's comedy is bawdy and less feminine—the comedy of camp, as Robertson points out, and also the comedy of the "unruly woman," smart-mouthed and aggressive.[17]

Trixie's comedy also undercuts the more glamorous enactments of gold digging in the production numbers (the association with glittery costumes and gorgeous women) and in the plotline's romanticism (the "true" love of J. Lawrence and chorine Carol). In addition, her comedy undermines the heterosexuality of these couplings, in which female sexuality may only be a convenient arrangement. In the exchange of sexuality and gold, there is always an ambiguity about who has been cheated and who has been exploited, an ambiguity of the "value" of sexual pleasure and desire.[18] In the chorus girl–gold digger paradigm, female pleasure is usually associated with the jewelry, hats, and general financial security sought by the women characters. Two of the subplots code this transaction as romance, but the Trixie character employs a different code altogether.

Mellencamp notes that Trixie is "cross-dressed as a policewoman" in the kinky "Pettin' in the Park" number.[19] The oddness of this description (how can a woman be cross-dressed as a woman?) belies its accuracy. In this dance number, Trixie is shot three-quarter length in her uniform coat and cap, so the effect is definitely drag. Trixie's cop is a joke, with a number of male policemen/dancers reminding us that this is men's work and that women doing such work are transgressive. Cross-dressed, MacMahon as Trixie could easily be an inscription of the mannish and possibly lesbian career woman, the embodiment of the "unnatural" place of woman in the workforce. She reappears in this costume, strangely enough, in the penultimate scene revealing the three united couples, when she announces that she is a bride, and the incongruous effect underscores the humor of her character. Again, the effect is drag until the next shot reframes her and reveals that along with the cap and uniform top, she is actually wearing a skirt.

The comedy of this costume for Trixie slyly insists on its sexual twist. The comic cops in "Pettin' in the Park" are policing sexual activity, acting as bourgeois (and hence laughable) social constraints on natural activity, male–female coupling. So Trixie is doubly out of place, as an outsider to the heterosexuality on display and as a transgressive female body in the customary place of a man. There is nothing cutesy about Trixie in drag—this is not Ginger Rogers in a sailor suit but Aline MacMahon looking butch and confirming the nonalignment of Trixie's character with the romantic trappings that make gold digging acceptable. My emphasis here on the sexual instability of Trixie's character and plotline only continues what the film already posits as funny: that gold digging creates strange bedfellows. The Trixie–Peabody arrangement is especially incongruous in its mismatches of ages, classes, and personalities, but Trixie's semiotic mismatches scramble the sexual pairing here as well.

Just a year before the release of this film, a less cynical version of chorines rising to wealth appeared in *Blondie of the Follies* (1932), which starred two former Ziegfeld Girls, Marion Davies and Billie Dove. Its advertisements in Hearst newspapers made the biographical connection of Blondie and Marion Davies unmistakable: "Blondie's amazing career, from tenement obscurity to the dazzling heights of Broadway fame, is a story so interesting we can no longer keep it from you. Thrilling romance . . . popular acclaim . . . parties . . . penthouse apartment . . . all part of her soul-stirring struggle for success."[20] The plotline of this film, positing the big break for two chorus girls through their associations with wealthy men, indeed sketches out Davies's "amazing career." In the familiar wife-or-showgirl dichotomy, one showgirl chooses marriage, the other a show business career, in the comforting *Broadway Melody* tradition.

Marion Davies's rise from chorus girl to Ziegfeld Girl to film star provided a titillating, real-life narrative for this era. William Randolph Hearst was captivated by Davies's performance in a 1915 Broadway revue. By the time she was "glorified" by Ziegfeld in the *Follies* the next year, she was Hearst's mistress, shamelessly publicized in his newspapers as an outstanding showgirl. Her biographer, Fred Lawrence Guiles, claims the journalistic promotions suggested her role in the *Follies* was far greater than it actually was; even though she is frequently cited as "ex-Ziegfeld Girl," her career with Ziegfeld lasted no more than a year—a clue to the *Follies'* prestige. The caption over her full-page photo in a 1916 *American Weekly* read "Marion Davies, the Type of Chorus Girl Who Marries Captains of Industry and Coronets: For Every Man, There's

'One Dangerous Girl.'"[21] Hearst did not marry his "dangerous girl," but his publicity helped launch her from the Follies to other stage work and eventually to Hollywood, where she would star in Hearst's film company. While Blondie of the Follies has fairly disappeared from cultural memory, Davies's far more enduring cinematic presence is her metonymic appearance as the hysterical Susan Alexander in Citizen Kane, a representation that unfortunately elides Davies's considerable comic talent in her own film work.

Blondie and Susan Alexander suggest respectively the frothy fairy tale and the bitter melodramatic versions of the woman staged by an ambitious man. Likewise, the Cinderella version of the Ziegfeld Girl (Sally) competes with its darker rendition (Lana Turner in Ziegfeld Girl) in cinema because her meanings have always hovered between reversible cultural images of women: consumer/consumable, working girl/gold digger, chorus girl/call girl. Even the golden Gloria of Glorifying the American Girl suffers in her swift trajectory from department store to Follies display, learning only in the finale that she has exchanged womanhood for an iconic abstraction—icy mannequin perfection. Ziegfeld's favorite, stuffy, pretentious word for it was "pulchritude," with which the Ziegfeld Girl in film was both blessed and afflicted.

Notes

1 See Richard Dyer's extensive discussion of Garland's appeal to gay men, partially because of this status as not glamorous, in Heavenly Bodies: Film Stars and Society (New York: St Martin's, 1986), 141–94.
2 Julie Dash's 1982 independent film Illusions comments richly and ironically on this simultaneous black absence on-screen and the behind-the-scenes usage of black voices and music.
3 Gerald Mast traces this tension from Al Jolson's blackface in The Jazz Singer to the 1949 Jolson Sings Again in Can't Help Singin': The American Musical on Stage and Screen (Woodstock, N.Y.: Overlook, 1987), 89.
4 In the larger social scene, as bell hooks points out, "most white people do not have to 'see' black people (constantly appearing on billboards, television movies, in magazines, etc.)" so that "they can live as though black people are invisible." See "Representing Whiteness in the Black Imagination," in Cultural Studies, ed. Lawrence Grossberg et al. (New York: Routledge, 1992), 340.
5 This taboo illustrates how race inflects codes of cinematic spectatorship and how female sexual display operates within specific "looking structures" involving both gender and race. See Jane Gaines, "White Privilege and Looking Relations: Race and Gender in Feminist Film Theory," in Issues in Feminist Film Criticism, ed. Patricia Erens (Bloomington: Indiana University Press, 1990), 197–214. For a history of the black showgirl and the limitations of Hollywood representation, see Donald Bogle, Brown Sugar: Eighty Years of America's Black Female Superstars (New York: Harmony, 1980).
6 Mast, Can't Help Singin', 134.
7 These details come from Barbara Naomi Cohen, "The Dance Direction of Ned Wayburn: Selected Topics in Musical Staging, 1901–1923" (PhD dissertation, New York University, 1980), 161–62.
8 See Jane Feuer on "the myth of spontaneity" in "The Self-Reflective Musical and the Myth of Entertainment," Quarterly Review of Film Studies 2, 3 (1977): 313–26. In addition, Chester's

genius works in the tradition of depression musicals as described by Richard Hasbany: corporations are villainous and inhuman, but the individual genius entrepreneur is privileged and glamorized. See "The Musical Goes Ironic: The Evolution of Genres," *Journal of American Culture* I (1978): 128. On the capitalist ideology of depression era musicals, see Eric Smoodin, "Art/Work: Capitalism and Creativity in the Hollywood Musical," *New Orleans Review* 16, 1 (1989): 79–87.

9   See Siegfried Kracauer, "The Mass Ornament" (1927), trans. Barbara Correll and Jack Zipes, *New German Critique* (1975): 67, on the mirroring effect of spectacle and spectator. See also J. P. Telotte, "A *Gold Digger* Aesthetic: The Depression Musical and its Audience," *Postscript* 1, 1 (1981): 18–24. Telotte describes the boundary-breaking effect of the typical Berkeley production number, "an illusion of a practically limitless, even labyrinthine world" (19).

10   Richard Dyer, "White," *Screen* 29, 4 (1988): 45, 47.

11   See Jack F. Sharrar, *Avery Hopwood: His Life and Plays* (Jefferson, N.C.: McFarland, 1989), 114–19, for details of Hopwood's play and its circumstances. The wealthy marriages of Ziegfeld Girl Peggy Hopkins Joyce are described in David Grafton, "Peggy Hopkins Joyce, Inc.," *Forbes* 400, 23 Oct. 1989, 68–70.

12   See Martin Rubin's descriptions of these numbers in *Showstoppers: Busby Berkeley and the Tradition of Spectacle* (New York: Columbia University Press, 1993), 103–106. Patricia Mellencamp has cited the influence of the Tiller Girls in the precision dancing, but I would add that the concepts of these numbers clearly recall the style of Berkeley's mentor, Ziegfeld. See "The Sexual Economics of *Gold Diggers of 1933*," in *Close Viewings: An Anthology of New Film Criticism*, ed. Peter Lehman (Tallahassee: Florida State University Press, 1990), 191.

13   Pamela Robertson sums up the major interpretations of this film in *Guilty Pleasures: Feminist Camp from Mae West to Madonna* (Durham: Duke University Press, 1996), 65–71, as well as offering her own feminist-camp reading of the narrative and production numbers on pages 57–65 and 70–73. Robertson's historicization of the gold digger and prostitute references in this film are especially helpful; see 74–84.

14   Ibid., 82. Robertson also points out that the Berkeley numbers are readable as lesbian enactments and eroticizations; see page 69.

15   For a description of the relationship between prostitution and theater in early American history, see Claudia D. Johnson, *American Actress: Perspective on the Nineteenth Century* (Chicago: Nelson-Hall, 1984), 13–16, 30. The association of chorus girls with prostitution is also discussed in Derek Parker and Julia Parker, *The Natural History of the Chorus Girl* (Indianapolis: Bobbs-Merrill, 1975), 11–14.

16   James Seymour, David Boehm, and Ben Markson, screenplay of *Gold Diggers of 1933*, in *Gold Diggers of 1933*, ed. Arthur Hove (Madison: University of Wisconsin Press, 1980), 54.

17   See Kathleen Rowe's analysis of this comic female figure in *The Unruly Woman: Gender and the Genres of Laughter* (Austin: University of Texas Press, 1995), especially 25–49. Rowe lists androgyny as one of the signifiers of the unruly woman, but mixed gender signs can explicitly signify the lesbian as a more direct affront to heterosexuality.

18   William D. Routt and Richard J. Thompson claim the showgirl–money exchange is a "'mad' riddle of value-meaning," because it is impossible to ascertain which party has received something more or less valuable, sexual pleasure or money: "Women receive what is really (culturally) of value in exchange for what is not. . . . But perhaps the men are receiving what

is truly valuable and the women what is not." See "'Keep Young and Beautiful': Surplus and Subversion in *Roman Scandals*," *Journal of Film and Video* 42, 1 (1990): 27.

19 Mellencamp, "The Sexual Economics of *Gold Diggers of 1933*," 179.
20 *New York American*, 25 July 1932.
21 Quoted by Fred Lawrence Guiles, *Marion Davies* (New York: McGraw-Hill, 1972), 65.

Select Bibliography

Altman, Rick (ed) (1981) *Genre, the Musical: A Reader*, London: Routledge.

Altman, Rick (1987) *The American Film Musical*, Bloomington: Indiana University Press. Chapter reprinted in this reader.

Altman, Rick (1999) *Film/Genre*, London: BFI.

Arbuthnot, Lucie and Gail Seneca (1982) "Pre-text and Text in *Gentlemen Prefer Blondes*," *Film Reader* 5: 13–23. Excerpted in this reader.

Babington, Bruce and Peter Williams Evans (1985) *Blue Skies and Silver Linings: Aspects of the Hollywood Musical*, Manchester: Manchester University Press.

Babuscio, Jack (1984) "Camp and the Gay Sensibility," in *Gays and Film*, rev. edn, Richard Dyer (ed), New York: Zoetrope, 40–57.

Balio, Tino (1993) *Grand Design: Hollywood as a Modern Business Enterprise, 1930–1939*, Berkeley: University of California Press.

Barrios, Richard (1995) *A Song in the Dark: The Birth of the Musical Film*, New York: Oxford University Press.

Belton, John (1974) "The Backstage Musical," *Movie* 24: 36–43.

Clark, Danae (1995) *Negotiating Hollywood: The Cultural Politics of Actors' Labor*, Minneapolis: University of Minnesota Press. Chapter on *42nd Street*.

Clover, Carol J. (1995) "Dancin' in the Rain," *Critical Inquiry* 21: 722–47. Reprinted in this reader.

Clum, John M. (1999) *Something for the Boys: Musical Theater and Gay Culture*, New York: St. Martin's Press.

Cohan, Steven (1993) "'Feminizing' the Song-and-Dance Man: Fred Astaire and the Spectacle of Masculinity in the Hollywood Musical," in *Screening the Male: Exploring Masculinities in Hollywood Cinema*, Steven Cohan and Ina Rae Hark (eds), London: Routledge: 46–69. Excerpted in this reader.

Cohan, Steven (1999) "Queering the Deal: On the Road with Hope and Crosby," in *Out Takes: Film and Queer Theory*, Ellis Hanson (ed), Durham, N.C.: Duke University Press: 23–45.

Cohan, Steven (2000) "Case Study: Interpreting *Singin' in the Rain*," in *Reinventing Film Studies*, Christine Gledhill and Linda Williams (eds), London: Edward Arnold: 53–75.

Cohan, Steven (2001) "Judy on the Net: Judy Garland Fandom and the 'Gay Thing' Revisited," in *Key Frames: Popular Cinema and Cultural Studies*, Matthew Tinkcom and Amy Villarejo (eds), London: Routledge: 119–36.

Crafton, Donald (1997) *The Talkies: American Cinema's Transition to Sound 1926–1931*, Berkeley: University of California Press.

Croce, Arlene (1972) *The Fred Astaire and Ginger Rogers Book*, New York: Galahad Books.

Cuomo II, Peter N. (1996) "Dance, Flexibility, and the Renewal of Genre in *Singin' in the Rain*," *Cinema Journal* 36.1: 39–54.

Dalle-Vacche, Angela (1992) "A Painter in Hollywood: Vincente Minnelli's *An American in Paris*," *Cinema Journal* 32.1: 63–83.

Delamater, Jerome (1978) *Dance in the Hollywood Musical*, Ann Arbor: UMI Research Press. Includes interviews.

Doty, Alexander (2000) *Flaming Classics: Queering the Film Canon*, New York: Routledge. Chapters on *Wizard of Oz* and *Gentlemen Prefer Blondes*.

Dyer, Richard (1977) "Entertainment and Utopia" rpt. *Only Entertainment*, London: Routledge, 1992. Reprinted in this reader.

Dyer, Richard (1986) *Heavenly Bodies: Film Stars and Society*, New York: St. Martin's Press. Chapters on Marilyn Monroe, Paul Robeson, and Judy Garland. Chapter excerpted in this reader.

Dyer, Richard (1991) "*A Star is Born* and the Construction of Authenticity," in *Stardom: Industry of Desire*, Christine Gledhill (ed), London: Routledge: 132–40.

Dyer, Richard (2000) "The Colour of Entertainment," in *Musicals: Hollywood and Beyond*, Bill Marshall and Robyn Stilwell (eds), Exeter: Intellect Books: 23–30.

Eyman, Scott (1997) *The Speed of Sound: Hollywood and the Talkie Revolution, 1926–1930*, Baltimore: Johns Hopkins University Press.

Farmer, Brett (2000) *Spectacular Passions: Cinema, Fantasy, Gay Male Spectatorships*, Durham, N.C.: Duke University Press: 69–109. Chapter on the musical.

Fehr, Richard and Frederick G. Vogel (1993) *Lullabies of Hollywood: Movie Music and the Movie Musical*, 1915–1992, Jefferson, N.C.: Mcfarland.

Feuer, Jane (1977) "The Self-reflective Musical and the Myth of Entertainment," *Quarterly Review of Film Studies* 2: 313–26. Reprinted in this reader.

Feuer, Jane (1993) *The Hollywood Musical*, 2nd edn, Bloomington: Indiana University Press.

Fischer, Lucy (1989) *Shot/Countershot: Film Tradition and Women's Cinema*, Princeton, N.J.: Princeton University Press. Chapter on *Dames*.

Fordin, Hugh (1975) *The World of Entertainment: Hollywood's Greatest Musicals*, New York: Avon. Also reprinted in 1984 under the title The Movies' Greatest Musicals: *Produced in Hollywood USA by the Freed Unit*, New York: Frederick Ungar, and in 1996 under the title *M-G-M's Greatest Musicals: The Arthur Freed Unit*, New York: Da Capo Press.

Frank, Rusty E. (1990) *Tap! The Greatest Tap Dance Stars and Their Stories, 1900–1955*, rev. edn, New York: Da Capo Press. Interviews.

Fricke, John (1992) *Judy Garland: World's Greatest Entertainer*, New York: Henry Holt.

Gabbard, Krin (ed) (1995) *Representing Jazz*, Durham, N.C.: Duke University Press.

Gabbard, Krin (1996) *Jammin' at the Margins: Jazz and the American Cinema*, Chicago: University of Chicago Press.

Gomery, Douglas (1985) "The Coming of Sound: Technological Change in the American Film Industry," in *Film Sound: Theory and Practice*, Elisabeth Weiss and John Belton (eds), New York: Columbia University Press, 5–24.

Gomery, Douglas (1986) *The Hollywood Studio System*, New York: St. Martin's Press.

Harvey, Stephen (1989) *Directed by Vincente Minnelli*, New York: Harper and Row.

Haver, Ronald (1988) A Star is Born: The Making of the 1954 Movie and its 1983 Restoration, New York: Harper and Row.

Henderson, Amy and Dwight Blocker Bowers (1996) Red, Hot & Blue: A Smithsonian Salute to the American Musical, Washington: Smithsonian Institution Press.

Hirschhorn, Clive (1991) The Hollywood Musical, 2nd edn, New York: Portland House. Comprehensive year-by-year chronology with complete listings of numbers and performers for each film.

Hoberman, J. (1993) 42nd Street, London: BFI.

Jenkins, Henry (1990) "'Shall We Make it for New York or for Distribution?' Eddie Cantor, Whoopee, and Regional Resistance to the Talkies," Cinema Journal 29.3: 32–52.

Kaufman, Gerald (1995) Meet Me in St. Louis, London: BFI.

Knox, Donald (1973) The Magic Factory: How MGM Made An American in Paris, New York: Praeger. Oral history.

Landy, Marcia (2001) "Mario Lanza and the 'Fourth World'," in Key Frames: Popular Cinema and Cultural Studies, Matthew Tinkcom and Amy Villarejo (eds), London: Routledge: 242–58.

Lawson-Peebles, Robert (ed) (1996) Approaches to the American Musical, Exeter: University of Exeter Press.

Leff, Leonard J. (1999) "'Come on Home with Me': 42nd Street and the Gay Male World of the 1930s," Cinema Journal 39.1: 3–22.

Lippe, Richard (1986) "Gender and Destiny: George Cukor's A Star is Born," CineAction! (Winter): 46–57.

Marshall, Bill and Robyn Stillwell (eds) (2000) Musicals: Hollywood and Beyond, Exeter: Intellect Books.

Mast, Gerald (1987) Can't Help Singin': The American Musical On Stage and Screen, Woodstock, N.Y.: Overlook Press,.

McCullough, John (1989) "Imagining Mr. Average" CineAction! (Summer): 43–55.

McLean, Adrienne L. (1997) "The Thousand Ways There Are to Move: Camp and Oriental Dance in the Hollywood Musicals of Jack Cole," in Visions of the East: Orientalism in Film, Matthew Bernstein and Gaylyn Studlar (eds), New Brunswick, N.J.: Rutgers University Press.

Mellencamp, Patricia (1991) "Spectacle and Spectator: Looking Through the American Musical Comedy," in Explorations in Film Theory, Ron Burnett (ed), Bloomington: Indiana University Press: 3–14. On Singin' in the Rain.

Mellencamp, Patricia (1995) A Fine Romance: Five Ages of Film Feminism, Philadelphia: Temple University Press. Chapter on Gold Diggers of 1933 excerpted in this reader.

Mizejewski, Linda (1999) Ziegfeld Girl: Image and Icon in Culture and Cinema, Durham, N.C.: Duke University Press. Chapter excepted in this reader.

Mueller, John (1981) "The Filmed Dances of Fred Astaire," Quarterly Review of Film Studies 6.2: 135–54.

Mueller, John (1984) "Fred Astaire and the Integrated Musical," Cinema Journal 24.1: 28–40.

Mueller, John (1985) Astaire Dancing: The Musical Films, New York: Knopf.

Naremore, James (1993) The Films of Vincente Minnelli, New York: Cambridge University Press. Chapters on Cabin in the Sky and Meet Me in St Louis.

Neale, Steve (2000) Genre and Hollywood, London: Routledge,

Parish, James Robert and Michael R. Pitts (1992) The Great Hollywood Musical Films, Metuchen, N.J.: Scarecrow Press,

Polan, Dana (1986a) "'Above all else to make you see': Cinema and the Ideology of Spectacle," in *Postmodernism and Politics*, Jonathan Arac (ed), Minneapolis: University of Minnesota Press: 55–69.

Polan, Dana (1986b) *Power and Paranoia: History, Narrative, and the American Cinema 1940–1950*, New York: Columbia University Press.

Polan, Dana (1987–88) "Stock Responses: The Spectacle of the Symbolic in *Summer Stock*," *Discourse* 10.1: 117–34.

Prock, Stephan (2000) "Music, Gender and the Politics of Performance in *Singin' in the Rain*," *Colby Quarterly* 36: 295–318.

Renov, Michael (1982) "From Fetish to Subject: The Containment of Sexual Difference in Hollywood's Wartime Cinema," *Wide Angle* 5: 16–27.

Roberts, Shari (1993) "'The Lady in the Tutti-Frutti Hat': Carmen Miranda, a Spectacle of Ethnicity," *Cinema Journal* 32.3: 3–23. Excerpted in this reader.

Robertson, Pamela (1996) *Guilty Pleasures: Feminist Camp from Mae West to Madonna*, Durham, N.C.: Duke University Press. Chapter on *Gold Diggers of 1933* excerpted in this reader.

Robertson Wojcik, Pamela (1999) "A Star is Born Again or, How Streisand Recycles Garland," in *Falling for You: Essays in Cinema and Performance*, Lesley Stern and George Kouvaros (eds), Sydney: Power Institute, 177–207.

Roen, Paul (1994) *High Camp: A Gay Guide to Camp and Cult Films*, Vol. 1, San Francisco: Leyland Publications.

Rogin, Michael (1996) *Blackface, White Noise: Jewish Immigrants in the Hollywood Melting Pot*, Berkeley: University of California Press. Chapter excerpted in this reader.

Rubin, Martin (1993) *Showstoppers: Busby Berkeley and the Tradition of Spectacle*, New York: Columbia University Press. Chapter excerpted in this reader.

Rubin, Martin (1996) "The Crowd, the Collective, and the Chorus: Busby Berkeley and the New Deal," in *Movies and Mass Culture*, John Belton (ed), New Brunswick, N.J.: Rutgers University Press.

Savoy, Eric (1999) "'That's ain't *all* she ain't': Doris Day and Queer Performativity," in *Out Takes: Essays on Queer Theory and Film*, Ellis Hanson (ed), Durham, N.C.: Duke University Press: 151–82.

Schatz, Thomas (1981) *Hollywood Genres: Formulas, Filmmaking, and the Studio System*, New York: Random House.

Schatz, Thomas (1988) *The Genius of the System: Hollywood Filmmaking in the Studio Era*, New York: Pantheon.

Schatz, Thomas (1997) *Boom and Bust: American Cinema in the 1940s*, Berkeley: University of California Press.

Siefert, Marsha (1995) "Image/Music/Voice: Song Dubbing in Hollywood Musicals," *Journal of Communication* 45 (Spring): 44–64.

Smoodin, Eric (1989) "Art/Work: Capitalism and Creativity in the Hollywood Musical," *New Orleans Review* 16: 79–87.

Staiger, Janet (1992) *Interpreting Films: Studies in the Historical Reception of American Cinema*, Princeton, N.J: Princeton University Press. Chapter on *A Star is Born* (1954).

Stanfield, Peter (1997) "'An Octoroon in the Kindling': American Vernacular & Blackface Minstrelsy in 1930s Hollywood," *Journal of American Studies* 31: 407–428.

Telotte, J.P. (1984) "Ideology and the Kelly-Donen Musicals," *Film Criticism* 8.3: 36–46.

Tinkcom, Matthew (1996) "'Working Like a Homosexual': Camp Visual Codes and the Labor of Gay Subjects in the MGM Freed Unit," *Cinema Journal* 35, 2: 24–42. Excerpted in this reader.

Westbrook, Robert B. (1990) "'I Want a Girl, Just Like the Girl That Married Harry James': American Women and the Problem of Political Obligation in World War II," *American Quarterly* 42: 587–614.

Williams, Alan (1981) "The Musical Film and Recorded Popular Music," in *Genre: The Musical*, Rick Altman (ed), New York: Routledge: 147–58.

Wolfe, Charles (1990) "Vitaphone Shorts and *The Jazz Singer*," *Wide Angle* 12.3: 58–78.

Woll, Allen L. (1983) *The Hollywood Musical Goes to War*, Chicago: Nelson-Hall.

Wollen, Peter (1992) *Singin' in the Rain*, London: BFI.

Index